Environmental Policy and Household Behaviour

Sustainability and Everyday Life

Edited by Patrik Söderholm

Routledge
Taylor & Francis Group

LONDON AND NEW YORK

First published by Earthscan in the UK and USA in 2010

Published 2016 by Routledge
For a full list of publications please contact:
Earthscan
2 Park Square, Milton Park, Abingdon, Oxfordshire OX14 4RN
711 Third Avenue, New York, NY 10017

Routledge is an imprint of the Taylor and Francis Group, an informa business

First issued in paperback 2015

Copyright © Patrik Söderholm 2010. Published by Taylor & Francis.

ISBN: 978-1-84407-897-4 (hardback)

Typeset by MapSet Ltd, Gateshead, UK
Cover design by Susanne Harris

A catalogue record for this book is available from the British Library

Library of Congress Cataloging-in-Publication Data

Environmental policy and household behaviour : sustainability and everyday life /
edited by edited by Patrik Söderholm.
    p. cm.
  Includes bibliographical references and index.
  ISBN 978-1-84407-897-4 (hbk)
  ISBN 978-1-138-96887-5 (pbk)
  1. Environmental policy. 2. Environmental policy—Citizen participation. 3.
Sustainable living. 4. Household ecology. 5. Environmental policy—Sweden—Case
studies. 6. Environmental policy—Sweden—Citizen participation—Case studies. I.
Söderholm, Patrik.
  GE170.E576693 2010
  333.72—dc22
                                                                    2010000825

Contents

PART I: ENVIRONMENTAL POLICY AND THE HOUSEHOLD: CONCEPTUAL ISSUES

PART II: EMPIRICAL ANALYSES OF
THE SWEDISH CASE

PART III: CONCLUDING PART

List of Figures, Tables and Boxes

FIGURES

TABLES

List of Acronyms and Abbreviations

ABC   Attitude, Behaviour and Context
ACF   Advocacy Coalition Framework
Coop   Cooperative Retail Chain in Sweden
CPI   Consumer Price Index
DDT   dichlorodiphenyltrichloroethane (pesticide)
EPI   Environmental Policy Integration
EU   European Union
Formas   Swedish Research Council for Environment, Agricultural
            Sciences and Spatial Planning
GEC   Good Environmental Choice (Swedish eco-label)
HUT   Households' expense survey
ICA   Cooperative Retail Chain in Sweden
KF   Cooperative Retail Chain in Sweden
KRAV   Control Association for Alternative Cultivation
kWh   Kilowatt hour
NAT   Norm Activation Theory
NEP   New Ecological Paradigm
NGO   Non-governmental organization
NHTS   National Household Travel Survey
PBC   Perceived Behavioural Control
PCE   Perceived Consumer Effectiveness
Prop   Swedish Government Bill
SCB   Statistics Sweden
SDA   Swedish Dairy Association
SEPA   Swedish Environmental Protection Agency
SFS   Act (Swedish)
SHARP   Sustainable Households: Attitudes, Resources and Policy
            (A Swedish research programme on the role of environmental
            policy in the daily lives of households)
SIKA   Swedish Institute for Transport and Communications Analysis
SIS   Swedish Standards Institute
Skr   Swedish Government Communication
SOU   Swedish Government Official Reports

SSNC	Swedish Society for Nature Conservation
SVD	Svenska Dagbladet (Swedish nationwide newspaper)
TDM	Travel Demand Management
TPB	Theory of Planned Behaviour
TWh	Terawatt hour
UK	United Kingdom
UNCED	United Nations Conference on Environment and Development
US	United States
VAT	Value-added tax
VBN	Value-Belief-Norm
WC	Water Closet
WTP	Willingness-to-pay

1

Environmental policy and household behaviour: An introduction to the volume

Patrik Söderholm

BACKGROUND, OBJECTIVES AND SCOPE

It is increasingly recognized that environmental problems are not only the result of industrial activity in a few polluting facilities; they also stem from the millions of choices that people make in everyday life. The implementation of environmental policies therefore often requires ordinary people's active involvement, and many existing and new environmental requirements (e.g. Agenda 21) are expressed in terms of household-related activities like recycling and actively choosing eco-labelled products and services. Still, the successful implementation of such policies also poses significant challenges for policy-makers. *First*, it is often claimed that citizens in, for instance, Europe and North America, commonly hold strong environmental attitudes and values, and people generally say they are willing to undertake a number of household-related activities that promote a sustainable environment. Still, these attitudes do not always translate into daily behaviour. *Second*, various types of policy instruments (e.g. information campaigns, fees, regulations and infrastructural measures) are used to achieve household compliance with environmental policies and intentions. For such policy tools to be effective and legitimate, however, politicians and practitioners need an increased understanding of how policy interplays with household

1

values, attitudes and the constraints (in terms of time, money and knowledge) that they face in their daily lives.

Households who aim at integrating environmental concerns in their daily habits and decisions often face a so-called social dilemma situation, i.e. the individual interest is at odds with what is best for the collective. One of the main challenges for public policy is therefore to address and resolve this dilemma in ways that maintain – and strengthen – policy effectiveness and legitimacy. In the social science literature (not least in psychology research) it is suggested that the presence of norms – i.e. informal rules requiring that one should act in a given way in a given situation – may provide an important reason for a departure from a social dilemma outcome. Still, the study of households' pro-environmental behaviour is meaningful only if norms and attitudes and the relevant constraints, in terms of money, time and inconvenience facing households, are analysed in conjunction.

This book is a collection of jointly organized studies on the integration of household activities and values into the forming of an environmentally sustainable society in Sweden. The individual chapters all emanate from the multidisciplinary research programme *SHARP – Sustainable Households: Attitudes, Resources and Policy*. The programme has been carried out in joint cooperation between four Swedish universities, Luleå University of Technology, Linköping University, Umeå University and Karlstad University, over the time period 2003 to 2008. It has been supported financially by both the Swedish Research Council for Environment, Agricultural Sciences and Spatial Planning (Formas) and, in particular, the Swedish Environmental Protection Agency (SEPA). Since its inception, the overall objective of the SHARP programme has been to analyse the integration of household activities and attitudes into the forming of an environmentally sustainable society in Sweden. Specifically, the research programme as well as the contributions to this book aims at:

- investigating the role of households and household behaviour in achieving environmental policy objectives;
- analysing the constraints that households face when pursuing environmental activities, and how they organize and integrate these activities in daily life, given these constraints and in the presence of environmental attitudes and values;
- clarifying the circumstances under which environmental policy instruments will be effective and perceived by households as legitimate.

A few of the research studies presented in the book address theoretical aspects of the general design of environmental policy and how it impinges on households' daily activities, but much attention is also paid to empirical findings. Empirically the research presented focuses both on overall activity patterns in Swedish households, but it also presents in-depth studies on three partly interrelated types of household activities: (a) waste sorting and recycling behaviour; (b) overall consumption patterns and the active purchasing of eco-labelled products; and (c) mode of transportation behaviour.

The Swedish context is interesting for several reasons. Sweden often scores high in international rankings of environmental policy, and it is generally believed to be a forerunner in striving towards environmental and social sustainability. This is mirrored in, for instance, the country's low carbon emissions per capita and high household waste recycling rates. These and other policy progresses may thus offer important policy lessons for other countries. However, there are also clear signs of unsustainable behaviour (e.g. personal car use, high overall energy consumption per capita) – even in an international comparison. Environmental policy in Sweden therefore faces a number of important challenges, and some of these are related to the fact that public decision-making is highly decentralized in the country; policy instruments are typically designed at the municipal (local) level and there is a de facto territorial planning monopoly of Swedish municipalities. While the above may imply an opportunity to address specific geographic and cultural contexts in policy design and implementation, it also means that it can be difficult to implement national (and ultimately global) policies at the local level. Other policy objectives, such as regional economic growth, may easily dominate the local political debate and hence hamper policies and infrastructural projects that constrain, for instance, private car use and/or other specific consumption patterns.

The SHARP programme is multidisciplinary and the contributors to the volume represent a number of different academic disciplines and fields: environmental law, economics, political science, policy studies, psychology, history, as well as technology and social change. The respective chapters represent original studies and syntheses emanating from the six different research projects within the SHARP programme (see www.sharpprogram.se for details). For this reason our methodological approach differs from many earlier studies in that it combines analyses based on intensive structuring, involving deep interviews, time diaries and travel diaries with more extensive information about attitudes, behaviour and constraints gathered via surveys from a large number of households as well as through statistical analyses of large databases.

CONTENTS

The remainder of the book is divided into two main parts, each comprising four to five self-contained chapters, and finally a concluding part with a final chapter. The *first* part is general in scope and it provides a discussion of key concepts and analytical issues in the study of sustainable household behaviour and environmental policy, but it also presents broad empirical illustrations. The main contents of the four chapters that make up this first part of the book are summarized below.

Chapter 2, co-authored by Carina Lundmark, Simon Matti and Gabriel Michanek, discusses how contemporary environmental policies in Sweden and elsewhere tend to challenge our daily routines. For this reason these policies present a fundamental democratic challenge as freedom of choice and the pursuit of individual lifestyles are restricted. The authors explore the tension between environmental responsibilities and individual freedom of action as it is presented in Swedish environmental policy and legislation. An important finding is that an environmental norm manifests itself in the country's official policy documents, clearly stating that particular behaviours, and even lifestyles, are preferable from an environmental viewpoint. The analysis, however, also suggests that the potential conflict between environmental obligations on the one hand and the pursuit of individual life projects on the other largely is avoided as environmental responsibility primarily is placed on individuals in their roles as consumers in economic markets, rather than on democratic citizens. There is thus scope for taking the step in policy away from overall guidance and information towards more clearly encouraging the development of politically skilled citizens.

Karin Skill and Elin Wihlborg note in Chapter 3 that the environmental challenge implies that public policy enters the domestic sphere. Thus, assessing the prospects for environmental citizenship implies not least an understanding of the everyday context in which householders take decisions and perform different activities. The analysis in the chapter builds on 60 semi-structured interviews with Swedish householders, and it revolves around a number of themes concerning everyday responsibilities that emerged through these empirical studies. One theme concerns the complexity of the environmental challenge, namely how to know what the environmental effects of the individual activities are, whose descriptions to trust and by what rationality the effects and efficiency of different policies should be assessed. Often environmentally motivated activities concern detailed aspects of everyday life, and they are involved in the regular performance of activities. For this reason householders simplify life through routines and practices, and focus on a specific subset of environmental activities. Moreover, this also implies that householders often rationalize their behaviour, and one activity (e.g. household waste sorting) may act as an excuse for more demanding activities that are more difficult to integrate in daily life (e.g. leave the car and take the bus instead). Overall, daily life makes up a complex whole, and it is therefore difficult to identify 'sustainable lifestyles'; the ability to take personal responsibility as a citizen in the domestic sphere will depend critically on a set of enabling conditions.

The physical and geographical context of sustainable household behaviour will be important also in determining how people understand, receive and form their response towards the official environmental norm. In Chapter 4 Simon Matti notes that this is imperative since new institutions and policy instruments aiming at initiating and sustaining individual pro-environmental action need, for their long-term effectiveness, to be perceived as being *legitimate* in the sense that they build on or can be justified by reference to core values already established in society. The analysis presented in this chapter aims at evaluating the public legitimacy of Swedish environmental policy aspirations, by analysing their correspondence with core values and attitudes held by the Swedish citizenry; and discuss in what ways issues of policy legitimacy may influence households' willingness to integrate environmentally friendly activities in their daily lives. The analysis reveals a distinct discrepancy between the image of citizens that emerges in official policy and the design of policy instruments and the image reflected by citizens themselves. Firstly, while personal freedom and self-determination are certainly prized by Swedish citizens, environmental protection is also prioritized when people weigh one value against another. This suggests that future environmental policy has good prospects for implementing effective environmental protection measures while remaining legitimate in the eyes of the public. Secondly, the discrepancy becomes apparent in the question of people's motives for behaving in an environmentally friendly way when people explicitly assert that the morally based willingness to do the right thing has greater impact on motivation than financial rewards or punishments.

In order to empirically investigate, not least in quantitative terms, the main determinants of pro-environmental behaviour, the associated barriers and facilitators need to be categorized and operationalized. Chapter 5, co-authored by Annika Nordlund, Louise Eriksson and Jörgen Garvill, summarizes four types of causal variables influencing environmentally significant behaviour. These factors take into account the importance of both moral values as well as the constraints that face citizens in daily life. They include: (a) contextual factors such as the physical, economic and social context in which the individual acts; (b) personal capabilities such as the knowledge, time and money available to the individual; (c) attitudinal factors, which include the values, beliefs, attitudes and norms the individual holds; and finally (d) the habitual quality of many everyday behaviours. In relation to different environmentally significant behaviours, the importance of these four factors may vary, and there are several examples of how different factors interact in determining behaviour. The chapter reviews the importance of different factors for environmentally significant behaviours within the central areas of consumption, waste handling, and travel behaviour. In addition, the relations between these factors (e.g. how attitudinal and habitual factors interact) in predicting pro-environmental behaviour are summarized. Based on studies conducted within the SHARP programme and other relevant studies, the way in which these factors may function as facilitators or barriers for environmentally sustainable behaviour is discussed.

By providing a general theoretical framework for understanding pro-environmental behaviour, Chapter 6 sets the stage for the *second* part of the book, which contains conceptually coordinated case studies of different household activities – e.g. consumption behaviour and environmental labelling, waste sorting, mode of transportation choice, etc. – and the impact of different policies in each case. This part comprises five chapters, and all of these focus on some (or all) of the factors in the review above, and the empirical investigations build on both context-rich studies of individual households with more aggregate investigations based on, for instance, survey data.

In Chapter 6, Hilde Ibsen discusses how a so-called alternative movement blossomed in Sweden in the 1960s and 1970s, and the political–ideological debate expanded to increasingly include environmental issues. An essential component of this new movement was the vision of ecologically sustainable communities. This chapter presents the results from an empirical study of the experiences of the first eco-village in Sweden, which was initiated in the late

1970s and is still present. The research involves follow-up interviews of how the eco-villagers view their active choice of a sustainable lifestyle, and how their day-to-day lives in turn have been affected by this choice. The outgrowth of the eco-village was based extensively on the homogeneous ideological background and composition of the founding group. Most of them already knew one another, and were highly educated. Taken as a whole, the analysis shows that ambition, capacity and knowledge appear to be key characteristics for reshaping daily life and independently translating concern for the environment into habitual behaviours. The experiences also illustrate that environmental efforts are both an individual and a collective responsibility in that the build-up of the eco-village was strongly dependent on support from municipal politicians and civil servants.

Chapter 7, authored by Kristina Söderholm, also provides an historical perspective of household behaviour in the environmental field. Specifically, it employs data on household consumption expenses, collected by Statistics Sweden over the time period 1958 to 2005, and analyses important changes and driving forces in consumption patterns over time. The author then adopts a socio-technological system perspective to illustrate how the Swedish state has – directly and indirectly – intervened in household consumption behaviour since the 1950s. The analysis shows that overall state housing policies, a state-supported rationalization of the construction process, initiatives to encourage society's car adaptation and the rationalization of the retail distribution from the 1940s and onwards, have in combination formed socio-technological systems in turn influencing and embedding households' consumption patterns. In sum, the socio-technological context in which people live their daily lives has historically had a distinct impact on Swedes' household consumption patterns, something that reinforces the need for an environmental policy that examines and explains opportunities to influence this same context. In the case where specific consumption patterns (e.g. car use) are structural requirements, altering norms of behaviour will be difficult. Moreover, an effective public policy for sustainable development should also focus attention on how multiple policy areas (e.g. monetary policy, housing policy, social policy, etc.) influence household consumption patterns.

The purpose of Chapter 8, co-authored by Mats Bladh, Kristina Ek and Patrik Söderholm, is to analyse the role of eco-labelling in influencing consumer choices in Sweden. It reviews the development of the most important labelling schemes (e.g. the Nordic Swan, KRAV, etc.) in the country, and highlights some important crossroads in their formation over time. The chapter also discusses – and attempts at explaining – the outcome in terms of green market shares for selected product groups. Eco-labelling typically entails a strong individualization, while many environmental issues require the collective adoption of attitudes, and labelling policies have often been most effective when combined with campaigns against explicitly harmful products. An in-depth investigation of the case of eco-labelled electricity shows that peoples' willingness to take personal responsibility in the green market place appears to be influenced by their perceptions of others' contributions and the environmental impacts of their choice, but it is also heavily determined by the extra costs (price premium) of the eco-labelled products compared to the conventional products offered. Moreover, the chapter illustrates that peoples' willingness to support market goods with strong public good characteristics is likely to depend on whether participation builds on shared as opposed to individual responsibility. It may often be less complicated to build acceptance for mandatory systems (as long as everyone is expected to contribute) rather than to rely on individual, voluntary choice. Households largely accept that the environmental issue is a matter of collective choice, which to a certain extent constrains the individual latitude for free choice.

In Chapter 9 Christer Berglund, Olle Hage and Patrik Söderholm investigate why Swedish households generally are keen to participate in waste recycling schemes, and the role of different types of policy instruments in promoting and maintaining high overall recycling rates. The chapter also addresses the issue of why some households – in spite of their current sacrifices in terms of effort and time – may be reluctant to be relieved from current recycling responsibilities. Norm-based policy instruments play a key role in engendering household commitment to recycling. For these to be effective, however, it is very important to maintain household confidence that recycling generally leads to positive environmental outcomes, and that their personal contributions are meaningful in this context. Economic incentives – such as weight-based collection fees – and infrastructure measures that facilitate recycling in daily life (e.g. curbside recycling) also have positive impacts on outcomes. Overall, recycling is generally perceived as easy to integrate in daily life, while other measures (such as reduced car use) impose much greater demands for changes in the way households have chosen to organize their lives. The chapter presents an empirical analysis of the determinants of inter-household preferences towards a policy change implying that households are relieved from their responsibility for transporting the waste to assigned drop-off stations. Some evidence of the existence of a mixed blessing of responsibility relief is identified; on the one hand people are relieved from responsibilities that take time away from leisure activities but they also tend experience a loss in self-image as the new policy removes from the individual the possibility to provide a public good that she feels pleased to provide on her own. An important policy implication of these findings is that there may exist a 'motivational inertia' making it difficult (or at least costly) for policy-makers to activate new norms for environmental activities in replacement of existing ones.

In many Western countries, the car is still the dominant travel mode for everyday travel. However, since traffic causes both local and large-scale environmental problems it is necessary to reduce the negative environmental effects of car use. Chapter 10, co-authored by Louise Eriksson, Annika Nordlund and Jörgen Garvill, discusses factors important for a change in households' travel behaviour. Based on studies conducted within the SHARP programme, both the acceptability and the behavioural effects of transport policy measures are reviewed. Even though a change in travel behaviour is essential from an environmental perspective, several difficulties are associated with this change, for example, external barriers (e.g. the possibilities to use an alternative travel mode) as well as internal barriers (e.g. the moral motivation to reduce car use). In order to facilitate a change in travel behaviour, different transport policy measures may need to be implemented. Push measures, such as raised tax on fossil fuel, attempt to make car use less attractive and pull measures, such as reduced ticket price for public transport, intend to improve the attractiveness of alternative travel options. If measures are going to be implemented successfully the public's acceptability is important. In addition, the behavioural effects of measures are important to consider for the selection of appropriate measures. Different measures as well as packages combining measures may be needed in order to achieve an acceptable and effective transport strategy. The chapter addresses both the effectiveness and the acceptance of different types of policies and policy combinations in the transport field, and the results are based on both mass survey data as well as on field studies of single households.

Finally, the third part of the book provides a concluding chapter, which addresses the most important implications for research on household behavioural change and not least lessons for policy instrument design and implementation aimed at addressing environmental concern at the household level.

ACKNOWLEDGEMENTS AND AUDIENCE

A lion's share of the empirical studies focused on conditions in four Swedish municipalities: Göteborg, Huddinge, Piteå and Växjö. The SHARP programme was monitored to ensure the academic and practical relevance of the research by an expert panel made up of representatives of SEPA, the four partner municipalities and academic researchers from a number of different universities in Sweden, Denmark and England. The following people were part of the SHARP programme expert panel for part or the duration of the programme:

- Erika Budh, PhD Economics, Environmental Economics Unit, Swedish Environmental Protection Agency, Stockholm, Sweden.
- Jonas Christensen, PhD Environmental Law, Ekolagen, Uppsala, Sweden.
- Andrew Dobson, Professor of Political Science, Keele University, England.
- Lars Drake, Associate Professor of Environmental Economics, Environmental Economics Unit, Swedish Environmental Protection Agency, Stockholm, Sweden (presently with the Swedish Chemicals Agency, Stockholm).
- Cecilia Mattsson, PhD Engineering, Implementation and Enforcement Department, Swedish Environmental Protection Agency, Stockholm, Sweden.
- Johanna Pettersson, Agenda 21 Coordinator, Municipality of Huddinge, Sweden.
- Helena Shanahan, Professor Emerita, Department of Food, Health, and Environment, Gothenburg University, Sweden.

- Henriette Söderberg, Associate Professor, City Office, City of Gothenburg, Sweden.
- John Thogersen, Professor of Economic Psychology, Aarhus School of Business, Denmark.
- Lars Wennerstål, Environmental and Public Health Manager, Municipality of Växjö, Sweden.
- Erik Westin, Implementation and Enforcement Department, Swedish Environmental Protection Agency, Stockholm.
- Åsa Wikman, Environmental Inspector, Municipality of Piteå, Sweden.

This group of researchers and policy practitioners has greatly contributed to the progress of the programme and thus to this volume. Their help and comments are therefore gratefully acknowledged. The contents of the book have also benefited from constructive comments from four anonymous reviewers. Moreover, financial support from the Swedish Environmental Protection Agency (SEPA) and the Swedish Research Council for Environment, Agricultural Sciences and Spatial Planning (Formas) is gratefully acknowledged. The opinions expressed in the book as well as any remaining errors, however, remain solely with the authors.

Finally, the book is intended to appeal to academic researchers, public servants at both the local and national level and to members of non-governmental organizations (NGOs) involved in promoting action towards reduced environmental impacts of household consumption and habits. There is an explicit focus on policy impacts and implications, and the level of analytical difficulty is accessible to senior college students and graduate students, and there should be no barriers with respect to scientific jargon or methodological specialization. The worldwide attention presently given to efforts of actively encouraging sustainable household behaviour provides a broad political context for the major themes and results of the book.

Part I

Environmental Policy and the Household: Conceptual Issues

2

The Swedish environmental norm: Balancing environmental obligations and the pursuit of individual lifestyles

Carina Lundmark, Simon Matti and Gabriel Michanek

INTRODUCTION

Public policy-making in general, and environmental policy-making in particular, is essentially a process concerned with values – choice in addressing collective problems, choosing between an abundance of alternatives (cf. Hall and Jenkins, 1995). This equally concerns the identification of desirable goals; the design of institutions within which these goals should be reached; and the selection of tools for moving development in the desirable direction. However, allowing one specific value to act as a guiding principle also implies that one or more values are sacrificed throughout the steps of the policy process. The overarching goals of security might, for instance, be chosen at the expense of privacy; top-down governmental control at the expense of decentralized public deliberation; and regulation at the expense of voluntariness. Public policy-makers, thereby, face the continuous challenge of balancing, sacrificing or trading-off conflicting values, thereby determining not only which route to take in addressing public problems (or, for that matter, which issues are identified as problems in the first place), but also how policy decisions and their implementation subsequently influence and are received by the public in their daily practices. In highly complex policy areas, such as the environmental policy area, where a large number of values and interests intersect, this challenge increases.

In this chapter, we explore the tension between environmental responsibilities and individual freedom of action. Although this conflict between basic values, including the strategies devised for addressing it, is relevant to examine in a range of policy areas, we believe it to be particularly salient in the environmental field. The all-encompassing nature of the environmental issue places the very fundamentals of current lifestyles, institutional structures and, thus, value-priorities underpinning developed economies centre stage. The individualization of environmental responsibilities, with calls for a new catalogue of civic duties, transformed consciousness and legal reform in its support, anchors this conflict between freedom and environment firmly within the private sphere of the household. In this chapter, we discuss, mainly from a theoretical perspective, the potential value-related conflicts that arise in environmental policy-making, specifically when directed towards the issue of household sustainability. Furthermore, drawing on empirical analyses of the case of Sweden, it considers how these conflicts are presented as well as handled in public policy and legislation. As such, the discussion in this chapter also serves as an introduction to the in-depth empirical case studies presented in the second part of the book, where examples on how value conflicts in policy, and the subsequent strategies employed for handling them, are experienced by household members in their daily life.

VALUE CONFLICTS IN ENVIRONMENTAL PUBLIC POLICY

Using a commonly applied definition, values are those basic *conceptions of the desirable* that underpin each individual's formation of personal ideals and preferences. Being of a broad and trans-situational nature, values function as a guide to both evaluation and attitude formation in all aspects of the individual's life. In particular, however, the significance of values for political preferences and choice has received significant attention, and values hold a key role in several well-known conceptions of politics, such as Easton's (1953) 'authoritative allocation of values', or Lasswell's (1936) struggle over 'who gets what, when and how'. At the macro level we can trace the basic principles for designing our fundamental political institutions to the desire for emphasizing, promoting or upholding a set of core values, for example freedom, democracy, equality or security. Modern institutional theory, as an example, views established value systems as constituting the frameworks within which policy-making takes place (cf. March and Olsen, 1984). At the micro level, these core political values are adapted to particular areas of governmental action and guide the formation and design of public policy as well as the choice of policy tools for implementing them. Within the policy process, values determine goal formation by guiding the actors' perception of what is important or desirable. In a general sense therefore, values are seen as the ultimate end of public policy. They permeate policy goals and theories about how to reach them, either explicitly where the goals themselves express a set of prioritized values or implicitly where policy goals function as instruments for reaching more fundamental values (cf. Amara, 1972; Thatcher and Rein, 2004). According to Jenkins-Smith and Sabatier (1993; and see notes therein for examples of empirical studies), the connection between the values held by policy actors and how they subsequently position themselves in policy decisions have been verified in a range of studies. For example, consider the proposition posed by Tetlock et al, (1996:27):

> Underlying all political belief systems are core or terminal values [...] that specify what the ultimate goal of public policy should be (e.g., economic efficiency, social equality, individual freedom, crime control, national security, racial purity and so on). Values are the backstops of belief systems. When we press people to justify their political preferences, all inquiry ultimately terminates in values that people find it ridiculous to justify any further.

Certainly, most policy domains are more often than not characterized by incorporating a range of incompatible values and interests. Indeed, according to Weible (2006), there is a growing recognition that the major conflicts surrounding contemporary public policy processes can be attributed to actors entering the policy process holding diverging values and, thus, political goals. As different policies typically generate different outcomes, an important aspect of the policy-making process is concerned with the selection and priority of those basic values towards which the outlined political strategies should aim. Pertaining to the settlement on goals this calls for the need to negotiate, make trade-offs or in other ways deal with value conflict throughout the processes. As an example of a fundamental, goal-oriented value conflict that must be handled within a public policy domain, Birkland (2005:162–168) points towards the inherent incompatibility between the basic values of liberty and security (see also Rokeach, 1973). As many political thinkers have recognized, any increase in the latter (through, for example, the very creation of a state, granted a monopoly on coercive power) unavoidably brings with it a trade-off of the former. This incompatibility has spawned many fundamental ideological debates on the size, role and authority of political government.

Within the environmental policy domain, these types of basic value-conflicts are particularly salient, which leads Rydin (1999, 2005) to conclude that environmental policy analysis has much to gain by incorporating an exploration of the values, beliefs, arguments and motivations that underpin governmental programmes and constitute the environmental discourse. The environmental domain covers multiple dimensions of individual and societal life and therefore gives rise to myriad potential conflicts, ultimately dependent on how priorities among basic competing values are struck, for example concerning welfare priorities across the in-group/out-group divide (Hajer, 1995; Baker et al, 1997; Dryzek, 2005). In particular, a classical value conflict pertaining to the environmental policy domain concerns the value of freedom: the balancing of rights and responsibilities and the subsequent importance (or interpretation of) granted personal autonomy and self-direction. This concerns specifically household-oriented environmental policy, as this explicitly requires behavioural change (or participation) on the level of single individuals; where the impact of the single individual's activities are either negligible or difficult to discern; and means that the government expresses a desire to influence behavioural choices in the private sphere. From this perspective, a significant challenge for policy-makers is therefore to handle the conflict between environmental protection and individual autonomy, which can be expressed as a value conflict between, on the one hand, the necessity of behavioural change and individual responsibility taking in order to protect the environment and, on the other, the principles of autonomy and self-direction, rule of law and the protection of personal integrity.

If public policy itself is the embodiment of value-determined political goals, policy instruments is the means through which policy seeks to change public patterns of behaviour in order to reach these goals. Counter to rational models of the policy process, however, the choice of policy tools does not follow causally from an agreement on desirable ends. Rather, values also constitute the backdrop for designing policy tools. Thus, even in those instances where an agreement on desirable ends exists, how best to reach these ends might still be disputed and amount to conflict over means or strategies (Hall and McGinty, 1997; Birkland, 2005). Within the environmental policy domain, the many different political strategies suggested and implemented with the common aim of preventing ecological destruction clearly signify these differences in preference of means to an end. An arsenal of policy tools is currently in use to make actors behave according to environmental policies and intentions, and although governments commonly apply several different tools simultaneously, the balance between them nevertheless reveals how priorities between different basic values are struck in the endeavour of realizing political sustainability aspirations. For example, how personal freedom of action is valued or interpreted by political government can be deduced from the extent to which informative, economic and regulative policy tools respectively are applied, signalling the balance between, on the one hand, voluntariness and, on the other, compulsory participation. Similar conclusions can also be inferred from considering the design of specific types of instruments. Are, for instance, informative tools designed as objective information with the purpose of allowing for citizens to make well-informed personal choices, or as education on the proper conduct for reaching a predetermined goal? Are economic tools designed as incentives, making certain lifestyle choices more attractive than others and thus pulling people towards more preferred directions, or, as monetary punishments, pushing people away from making certain choices in their day-to-day life? Lastly, are legal rules accompanied by an apparatus of monitoring and enforcement with the purpose of punishing rule violation, or does legislation directed towards individuals' patterns of behaviour rather take the form of norm-building behavioural recommendations?

AIM OF CHAPTER

Our aim in this chapter is to consider more closely how this value conflict between environmental responsibilities and individual freedom of action is manifested in Swedish household-related environmental policy and legislation, as well as to explore the strategies applied to solve or remedy it. First we discuss how the concept of freedom has been constructed in politics. To nuance our discussion of this environmentally related value conflict, we have divided it into three distinct parts: personal integrity, autonomy and self-direction, and rule of law. Each part discusses, first, the theoretical conflict facing policy-makers in the process of designing policy and selecting policy tools. Thereafter, we consider more closely how Swedish environmental public policy addresses the balance between these opposing values.

For the empirical parts of the chapter, a significant part of our conclusions on how the balance between environmental obligations and the pursuit of individual lifestyles are handled builds on qualitative analyses of official Swedish environmental policy documents during the 12-year period between the years 1994 to 2006 (e.g. Matti, 2006, 2009). In this respect, our study represents a distinct period in the development of contemporary Swedish environmental policy and will therefore also provide a chronological context to the analysis, ranging from the initial implementation of the United Nations Conference on Environment and Development (UNCED's) Agenda 21, which initiated a new direction for national environmental policy, to the present day. Although more relevant when explicitly concerned with tracing policy change or learning (e.g. Sabatier, 1988), the fact that the exploration of policy belief systems covers a period of 12 years means that this part of the analysis allows for comparison and contrasting over time. This, in turn, is anticipated to provide a thorough exploration of the reasoning and argumentation within the policy discourse.

PERSONAL INTEGRITY

The very rationale for the research programme on which this book builds is that implementation of environmental policies commonly requires people's active involvement, not only or even primarily as citizens, but as household members, recycling their household waste and purchasing products with low environmental impact, just to give a few examples. These ideas not only present challenges to peoples' daily life, they also challenge established theoretical conceptions on what constitutes the proper distinction between public and private spheres. Are issues of personal integrity at all handled when directing policy towards activities in the private sphere – and, initially, is the private sphere seen as a legitimate arena of action for political government?

The sphere of citizenship – the private/public divide

The notion of a public/private divide demarcating the sphere in which the acts of involvement are presumed to be taking place, was evident already with the classics of political philosophy, most notable in the civic-republican tradition building on Aristotle's assertion of man as a 'political animal' where participation in the public life of society was considered the only route to the good life (cf. Heywood, 2004:55–64). Following this tradition, the public sphere is a place for citizens to work collectively for the common good, that is, the difference made by Rousseau (e.g. 1994) between 'the will of all' and 'the general will'. Thus, following the civic-republican tradition, the public sphere is connected with duties or obligations for the citizens to contribute to the common good (cf. Prokhovnik, 1998).

This stands in sharp contrast to the liberal tradition, where the public/private divide is an important concept for avoiding the state authority's arbitrary involvement in individuals' private lives, thereby being a prerequisite for individual autonomy. Here, the focus consequently is on liberty – on rights rather than duties – manifested in the individual citizen's rights to participate in democratic decision-making, primarily by exercising the right to vote. According to Turner (1990:197–8) as early as the protestant revolutions in renaissance Europe and their uprisings towards papal authoritarianism a notion of the existence of a public/private divide of citizenship was suggested. Here, a private sphere closed for state authority was created, in which the 'moral authority of the individual was to be achieved' without involvement from the contemporary authorities (Turner, 1990:198). This, in turn, strongly inspired early liberal theorists to further propose a restriction of the state's power, not allowing any state intervention in questions on the individual's faith, moral, opinion or consciousness (Mill, 1998; Locke, 2002). Also following more contemporary notions, the liberal citizen primarily uses the public sphere of politics and market for pursuing predominately personal interests (Turner, 1990; Rawls, 1993).

Despite their differing understandings of, and reasons for, making this private/public divide (see more on autonomy and self-direction below), both proponents of the liberal and the civic-republican traditions unite in their focus on citizen participation *in process*. They both place citizenship activities exclusively in the public sphere and within the relations between state and individual; and thus denote participating in decision-making processes or in other ways giving service to, or engaging in, the life of the community, whether it be in the form of voting, voluntary association or through a broader kind of public service (cf. Prokhovnik, 1998; Dobson, 2003). Thus, traditional concepts of citizenship focus on participation and accountability, either in 'politics proper' (Curry, 2000:1062) or in the broader life of the community, denoting either a right to participate or a duty to do so.

A greening of the citizenship concept in line with contemporary environmentalism offers a whole new theoretical framework, and a simultaneous movement from focusing process-oriented participation towards participation *in action* as the embodiment of civic rights and obligations. Emanating from the notion of environmental problems as essentially being an issue of the unequal use of ecological space in all aspects of an individual's life, ecological citizenship follows the attempt made within feminist theory to reconceptualize the private/public divide (Dobson, 2003). As each person's occupation of ecological space can not intellectually nor practically be confined to traditional public life of society, it is recognized here that also activities in the private sphere (within the family, household or community) are to be thought of as being of citizenly character, thereby indicating that a governmental policy for promoting citizenly environmental activities also can include suggestions for a more far-reaching transformation of actions in the traditionally defined private sphere of individuals' lives. Thus, civic obligations can also take place outside the narrow political arena (i.e. outside the public, political institutions) and activities within the household, for example waste handling or private consumption, should be thought of as political and therefore also subject to the, state enforced, rules of society (Prokhovnik, 1998). Whether these rules themselves suggest a smaller or larger state intervention is, then, a different question altogether. The conception of the public/private divide interconnects with the types of values expressed as motivational factors for participation and recognized as civic virtues. Whereas traditional civic-republican citizenship draws on values supporting civil service and protection of the community (e.g. courage, strength and obedience), ecological citizenship also recognizes motivational values that draws on the relations between citizens themselves, as these are what essentially defines the concept, place and obligations of ecological citizenship (e.g. social justice, personal responsibility, care and compassion, cf. Dobson, 2003:136–7).

The sphere of citizenship in environmental politics

The past decades have seen a re-evaluation of the responsibility for both causes and solutions to the environmental problem, which places the activities of the individual at the centre of attention (Maniates, 2001; Micheletti, 2003; Skill, 2008; Micheletti and McFarland, 2009). This focus on individual environmental responsibility is intimately connected to the way in which the sources of the present environmental situation have been reinterpreted. Today, environmental problems are no longer believed to be the sole result of industrial activities in a few polluting facilities, a belief that either implicitly or explicitly places the responsibility for amendment on political government as well as on business and industry, and promotes end-of-pipe regulations and technology standards as the overarching solution. Rather, the contemporary conceptualization suggests that the sources of environmental problems are to be found also in the millions of choices people make every day, in their diverse roles as citizens, consumers and household members. The amendment of these problems therefore requires that every individual takes responsibility also for the global and intergenerational consequences his/her actions produce (cf. UNCED, 1992; Hobson, 2002, 2004). This, however, is not to say that amending the environmental situation is a task to be bestowed on the single citizen or the household exclusively, thus allowing for governments and multinational corporations to avoid their responsibility. Within established environmental discourses, there is an expressed need for involving citizens in the day-to-day work towards sustainability *alongside* the more comprehensive efforts made and measures taken by politicians and within the global business community. This understanding of the single individual's impact on the environment, which today is found within the international political leadership and scholars of political ecology alike, is commonly illustrated by the ecological footprint (Wackernagel and Rees, 1996); an idea adapted early on by environmental movements and greens directing attention also towards lifestyle issues in mainly the industrialized part of the world. According to Dobson (2007:281):

> *The ecological footprint is the environmental space we occupy as we go about our daily lives – and because we go about our daily lives in very different ways, our ecological footprints are of different sizes. The planet on which we live is of finite size; therefore, there is a limited amount of environmental space to share out. Fairness demands that we all have roughly the same amount of space, but ecological footprint analysis suggests that some of us have too much.*

The ecological footprint and related concepts are prominently used as an illustrative indicator of the negative and asymmetrical effects the daily activities in each individual's lifestyle have, both directly on the ecosystem and indirectly on other individuals' possibilities to meet their basic needs. As such, the idea of an ecological footprint, and in particular acknowledgement of the fact that individuals in certain parts of the world let their activities expand way beyond what would be possible had the resources been evenly distributed, also constitutes an important foundation for one of the core notions within the green movement: the principle of social justice. A major obstacle in the way of sustainability is, thus, that the size of (almost) every individual's ecological footprint is considerably larger in the industrialized, high consumption parts of the world, than in the less developed world (Global Footprint Network, 2008). This, consequently, effectively prevents both present generations living in developing countries, as well as future generations in general, to ever be able to meet their needs (cf. Dobson, 1998; Carter, 2001).

In line with the ever-increasing attention to deliberative practices within contemporary democratic theory (cf. Torgerson, 1999), public participation in the policy-making processes also is viewed as necessary for aiding politicians in making more environmentally sound decisions by taking into account local ecological knowledge; for initiating comprehensive learning processes integrating ecological considerations in the public consciousness; as well as for strengthening the legitimacy, acceptability and transparency of political measures and policy instruments. There is a strong deliberative undertone embedded in the Rio agreements, which refers to 'broad public participation in decision-making' as a prerequisite for sustainable development (UNCED, 1992:23.2). The recommendations outlined in Agenda 21 have therefore, on the national level, been interpreted as suggesting a bottom-up process focusing on the local levels of action and denoting the role of municipalities; non-governmental organizations; people's movements, households and single individuals (SOU, 1997:105). Thus, to solve or mediate the problems with environmental degradation, the contemporary environmental political discourse pictures active public participation to be imperative, both as procedural involvement and, in particular, as actual contributions to ecological sustainability in day-to-day activities. An important role for the state in realizing ecological sustainability is thereby to encourage and motivate its citizens to participate both in public and private spheres, and to provide local initiatives with the means necessary for involvement to be possible in practice. A question we ask in this chapter is how citizen participation is expressed through Swedish environmental policy, where are the prescribed activities presumed to be taking place, exclusively in the public sphere or in both the public and the private spheres, respectively? And, conversely, what motivational values or civic virtues are thereby put forward through the policy documents?

The public/private divides in Swedish environmental policy

In Swedish environmental policy, the need for citizen participation in environmental work draws on the deliberative connotation embedded in the Rio agreements mentioned above, anchoring decisions on sustainable development among the citizenry. As an example, it is established that:

> *Open decision-making and planning processes where all citizens feel a sense of participation and have the will and the capacity to take responsibility for their actions constitutes an important foundation for the practical work with sustainable development. Important prerequisites are therefore possibilities for public control, dialogue and influence in the planning.* (Skr, 2001/02:50, 41)

The Swedish signing and subsequent implementation of the *Aarhus Convention* (Prop, 2004/05:65; Rskr, 2004/05:193) emanating from the 'Environment for Europe' ministerial conference held in the Danish town of Aarhus in 1998, indicate a step forward in this process. According to the convention, the public (single individuals as well as non-governmental organizations (NGOs)) shall be granted the right of access to information in environmental issues, participation in decision-making and access to justice (Prop, 2004/05:65). Lundqvist (2004) also notes that the Swedish government rhetorically both suggests and opens up for involving citizens in deciding on environmentally protective measures, in particular at the municipal level through the Local Agenda 21, which was to be characterized by a broad citizen partaking. Swedish environmental policy thereby places citizenship activities in the public sphere, where participation is narrowly defined as being equal to political action, either by the citizen directly or through membership in interest organizations working for the benefit of the environment. Also, the Swedish policy's focus on NGOs and people's movements as highly important actors in the environmental work (e.g. Skr, 1994/95:120; Prop, 2004/05:65) suggests that the delineation of the public sphere of citizenship in this respect follows the definition of what Turner (1990:209) describes as 'American liberalism', that is, as citizens' involvement in local voluntary organizations. Additionally, in particular the wordings of the Government Bill (Prop, 2004/05:65) on implementing the Aarhus Convention place great importance on the defence of the individual's environmental rights as a motivating factor for introducing, in particular, the access-to-justice principle, thereby signalling liberal interpretations of citizenship.

This policy focus on citizens' participation in making decisions on environmental issues is, however, overshadowed by another expression of participation for reaching sustainable development that suggests a comprehensive rethinking and 'adaptation of lifestyles' (Skr, 1996/97:50, 4). We also recall that these aspects of the Swedish policy rhetoric are entirely in line with the international environmental discourse's movement away from problem descriptions focusing on industry as the sole environmental villain and towards conceptualizing environmental degradation as a lifestyle problem, thereby turning the spotlight of attention towards single individuals or households as principal actors in the work towards environmental sustainability. For instance, the Swedish Environmental Protection Agency (e.g. SEPA, 1999:5007) identifies the present environmental problems as ultimately caused by people's ecologically unsustainable habits and practices, suggesting that 'if we change patterns of consumption, travel habits and other behaviour – in short, our lifestyle – we can improve the environment'.

Official policy documents both emphasize the need for broad participation among the public in general terms, and with regards to specific policy areas such as waste management (cf. Skr, 2001/02:68), climate policy (Skr, 2001/02:172) and in the choice of means of personal transportation (Skr, 2001/02:172). However, and similar to the results of previously conducted studies of how the individual–environment relationship is framed (e.g. Micheletti, 2003; Hobson, 2004; Seyfang, 2005), the main problem relates to unsustainable patterns of consumption on the level of individuals, which, by inference, leads to equally unsustainable patterns of production, waste and resource use (Skr, 1996/97:50; Skr, 2001/02:172). Indeed, individuals' consumption behaviour is by far the most commonly included example of an area of society where individuals can and should take on an increased individual responsibility. In turn, this indicates a central role for the individual, or rather the single consumer, also in amending the problem outlined in policy. By emphasizing the impact of activities conducted within the household, responsibility clearly stretches beyond a passive rights-claiming and public role for the citizen. Instead, the role for the Swedish citizen is framed in terms of active contributions, and points towards the need to take responsibility for building the good society, also in activities within the private sphere.

Although patterns of consumption are explicitly mentioned as being the problem, it is evident throughout the studied policy documents that the individual's activities in the market are seen as an integral part, or as an expression, of current unsustainable lifestyles in a broader perspective. Changing patterns of consumption, therefore, requires a comprehensive rethink of values, attitudes and behaviour (Skr, 1994/95:120; Skr, 2003/04:129, 29). By focusing on the necessity to change individuals' lifestyles and consciousness, the policy discourse makes a clear connection between activities within the private sphere of the household (and even the individual's mindset) and their global, or at least national, consequences. The notion of individual participation, then, comprises all-encompassing changes in both the way we live and think about the world. For instance, citizens are encouraged to both 'live and act environmentally friendly' (Skr, 2001/02:68, 10), and to internalize the new environmental norms (cf. Skr, 1997/98:13, 23; Skr, 2002/03:31, 23). Thereby, the individual is believed to have the ability to make a difference, by amending their lifestyle patterns in a more sustainable direction and by actively pressing for change through their daily actions and choices.

The inclusion of actions in the private sphere as being of citizenly character becomes even more apparent when considering that the procedural changes and policy instruments proposed in policy also involve the creation of a deeper personal engagement towards the environment; a transformation of values and attitudes regarding first and foremost the social and environmental components of the three-dimensional sustainability concept. It is close at hand to here make the connection between the environmental engagement expressed in policy and the above-mentioned values of personal responsibility and social justice central in ecological citizenship (Dobson, 2003). Moreover, participation in the public activities prescribed by environmental policies will, policy-makers seem to argue, generate a general environmental commitment among the citizenry. This will, in turn, be the driving force behind further development towards sustainability in society as a whole (Skr, 1994/95:120; Skr, 2001/02:50).

But it is not only the values preferences of political government itself that determine how the balance between obligation and personal autonomy is struck in public policy-making. Another value-based factor influencing both policy design and, more explicitly, the selection of policy tools are decision-makers' beliefs about the motivations held by those towards which the policy is directed. For example, the image of the citizen and their values determines if the political sustainability aspirations are seen as achievable through the use of instruments predominately drawing on voluntary participation (e.g. information and economic incentives), or if programmes for individual environmental responsibility taking requires the employment of legal or economic sanctions. Therefore, in the next section we ask also which image of the Swedish citizen that is manifested in official Swedish environmental policy as ready to voluntarily take on more extensive environmental obligations and take part in the collective processes for deciding which values and lifestyles policy should support, or as unable and unwilling to make these autonomous choices without guidance, and indeed steering, from the state?

AUTONOMY AND SELF-DIRECTION

As briefly mentioned when discussing the sphere of citizenship above, the role of state authority in theorizing on traditional citizenship ranges from being neutral and partial to facilitating and enlightening the individual. Liberal interpretations of state–individual relations suggest a vision of a rather passive and limited governmental structure, either in line with Nozick's (e.g. 1974) night-watchman state or in the form of the state not necessarily being physically limited, but when exercising its authority being 'political, not metaphysical' (Rawls, 1993:10). Thus whether focusing on classical liberal theory or more contemporary liberalism, limited and neutral government is seen as a prerequisite for citizens to enjoy freedom and personal autonomy, and for each and everyone to pursue a subjective understanding of the good life. In line with the conception of citizenship as 'passive and private' (Kymlicka and Norman, 1994:354), wherein individual rights and voluntarily participation in the public life constitute the main principles, the role of the state itself is also passive in the sense that its duties are limited to upholding either the citizenry's inviolable rights and liberties (as in classical conceptions of liberalism) or to provide fair procedures, equal opportunities and the autonomy of all citizens in realizing their independently chosen lifestyles (e.g. Dworkin, 1978; Rawls, 1999). In order to do this, and not by itself violating the rights of its citizens, the state has to be fundamentally neutral in metaphysical questions regarding for example values, beliefs or the good life. The state should with necessity prohibit the exercise of certain freedoms as they are violating the liberties of others, but is not allowed to prescribe certain lifestyles or behavioural patterns as being more preferable than others based merely on a preference for specified morals, values or beliefs. In practice, however, the neutrality and limitation of a contemporary liberal state can be expected to be less comprehensive than so far is being prescribed by the liberal tradition. At least two implications circumscribing the strict neutrality of the liberal need therefore to be acknowledged.

First, liberalism is by no means virtue free (cf. Dobson, 2003). Certain specific virtues are described necessary for acting as the good, responsible citizen also within the liberal democratic state. Thus, liberal government can also promote civic virtue among its citizens without violating the neutrality principle (Kymlicka and Norman, 1994:365; Dagger, 1997). Nevertheless, an important distinction must be made between virtues referring to the fulfilment of a *common good*, in the civic-republican tradition, and virtues necessary for upholding *fair procedures* (for example law-abiding and open-mindedness) by which citizens, based on individual preference, can lead their subjective good life. The latter, following for example Kymlicka and Norman (1994:366), includes such virtues as engagement in public discourse and participation through elections, and builds on the idea of democracy where decisions made by the government should be open for a free discussion. Thereby, it is possible to, by the strength of one's argument, persuade others without resorting to coercion, thus preserving democracy as a political system. This is, Kymlicka and

Norman (1994) assert, further connected to the liberal virtue of *public reason-ableness*: the duty of the liberal citizen to build his or her political claims on reasons that are political rather than private, and thereby able to create an 'overlapping consensus' (Rawls, 1993:134) among the many reasonable, but privately held, doctrines by which people unavoidably will choose to live in a free society.

Second, there are also limitations that might be placed on individual freedom as such, which again have consequences for the interpretation of the duties for the state within a liberal conception of citizenship. Extending the liberal rights discourse towards also incorporating environmental rights can very well be interpreted as an update of an 18th century ideal, thus not presenting any insurmountable challenges to liberal democracy per se. This has been suggested by, among others, Eckersley (1996:220), who in her attempt to revisit the liberal rights discourse suggests, while pointing towards the UNCHR, environmental rights to be considered 'the fourth generation of human rights'. Similar connections between liberal rights and environmental protection have been made in a range of variants, all giving an inkling of what Dobson (2003) refers to as the rights-based *environmental* citizenship (as opposed to ecological citizenship where justice instead is the core principle). For instance, relating to environmentally sensitive interpretations of liberalism, the Lockean Proviso to leave 'as good and as large' (Nozick, 1974:174–182; Locke, 2002:16) for others to enjoy as well his statement that 'nothing was made by God for man to spoil or destroy' (Locke, 2002:15) have been interpreted as carrying further opportunities for the state to limit also environmentally degrading activities without hindrance by the principle of individual liberty. So has the Rawlsian 'just savings principle' (Rawls, 1999:276–284) and even Nozick's (1974) conception of the negative rights principle been interpreted as denoting that also freedom from harm caused by environmental problems can been emphasized as a kind of liberty that the state has a duty to protect (cf. Eckersley, 1992; Attfield and Belsey, 1994; Wissenburg 1998)? The possibilities for a state to, in political practice and within the framework of liberal citizenship, prescribe environmental protection policies are certainly more generous than is declared through the traditional interpretation of the liberal state. The overarching duties for the state to protect individual liberties and to ensure individuals' opportunities to independently decide upon the roadmap to the good life are, though, still the core principle of this reasoning, where individual autonomy and equality of opportunity should work as trumps in all policy considerations (cf. Dworkin, 1978).

The civic-republican tradition presents a considerably different interpretation of liberty, and thus of the role of the state. As true freedom can only come about *through*, unlike the liberal interpretation as freedom *from*, the state, the state itself holds a duty to represent the common good, thereby protecting the citizens from corruption or an endless pursuit of narrow self-interests (cf. Curry, 2000; see also Rousseau, 1994; Machiavelli, 2003). The duty for all citizens is therefore to work towards the promotion of this good, by engagement in the public life of society through acts of civil service and political deliberation (cf.

Held, 1996; Delanty, 2000). However, as Kymlicka and Norman (1994:353) assert, to accomplish the collective action prescribed by civic-republicans as the basis for a good life, it is also necessary for individuals to be 'good' citizens who 'desire to participate in the political process in order to promote a public good', and for this certain civic virtues are needed. Consequently, the state is in turn ascribed duties to actively engage in the creation of good citizens by promoting certain lifestyles or virtues as more preferable, or 'right', than others; actively steering its citizens towards the common good through, for example, civic education. The state thus plays an important role as an instigator of the participation of citizens in whichever activities it deems necessary for fulfilling the policy's goals. In the case of environmental protection, the civic-republican state has an obligation to embrace *the* conception of sustainability and to enlighten its citizens about its content as well as on how to best reach it. Participation is, in line with what has been elaborated on before, not voluntarily, but conceived as a civic duty and mandated in a top-down fashion by governmental authorities.

Political ecology has, for obvious reasons, been rather sceptical towards the liberal principle of neutrality in questions on the good life and more inclined to draw on the interpretations of collectiveness and the morality of civic duty in the civic-republican tradition (Doherty and de Geus, 1996; Bell, 2001). It is, for example, precisely unrestricted individual freedom, absence of collectively enforced rules of conduct, and self-interested rational behaviour that lay behind the gloomy outcomes in Hardin's (1968) 'The tragedy of the Commons'. At the same time, being a political goal, the desired end state of ecological sustainability stands in stark contrast to the means-oriented politics of liberal democracy, and the capability for the contemporary (liberal) democratic state to effectively remedy the social dilemma of environmental protection has therefore been strongly questioned from mainly a green theoretical perspective. In his conception of ecological citizenship, Dobson (2003:205) instead draws on the duties and obligations of civic-republicanism, and opens up also for a state that, through civic education and policy-making, actively advances the normative foundations of ecological citizenship, by promoting the virtue of justice and 'pointing out that justice demands that individuals act in a way that are not always in their best interest'.

Based on these different interpretations of autonomy versus self-direction, the questions to direct to Swedish environmental policy documents are, therefore, is the state is thought of as primarily having a neutral role, facilitating the citizens to independently choose what to do and what kind of life to lead, or as having a responsibility in directing the citizens towards a definitive version of the good way of life? Are the prescribed policy instruments viewed as a means for *facilitating* voluntarily engagement by choice, or are they used as instruments for *enlightening* the citizenry and actively directing it towards *the* good way of life?

Autonomy and self-direction in Swedish environmental policy

The role of the state is rather ambiguously framed in Swedish environmental policy documents. On the one hand, the need for governmental authorities to create favourable opportunities for its citizens to make independent, but informed, choices as well as choosing to act in an environmentally sensitive way in their day-to-day practices is emphasized. The focus here is first and foremost on what governmental and municipal authorities can do to facilitate and assist more environmentally benevolent choices among the citizenry, which can be interpreted as expressing views in line with those on the passive state and, thus, the self-directing citizen. Regarding all household-related activities (for example consumption and transportation), the citizens will be provided with 'guidelines', 'knowledge', 'support', 'stimuli', 'possibilities' and 'easily accessible information' (cf. Skr, 2001/02:172, 5; Skr, 2001/02:68, 5; Skr, 2002/03:31, 28), but they are encouraged to evaluate it and select their actions independently without being steered in a specific direction by the state. Any particular actions and insights are, apart from sorting and recycling of household waste, not openly outlined as being particularly preferable in large sections of the documents. Rather, the state supports and aims to facilitate the voluntary transition towards sustainable living, by making available the possibilities, the choices and the knowledge needed for the general public to independently evaluate the environmental situation and engage in voluntarily action. Therefore, a range of policy measures are suggested that put pressure on municipalities and governmental authorities to provide the means necessary for citizens to make more sustainable choices in their day-to-day life. Strong focus is on knowledge mediation to increase consumer information, influence producers, authorities and organizations as well as facilitatating the single consumer to act in an environmentally positive way (Skr, 2003/04:129, 114).

Tying in with what has been said on the degree, character and sphere of citizen participation above, this apparently liberal account is at times contrasted with normative statements that go beyond state passivity and bottom-up deliberation. Despite the, at least rhetorically, great weight placed initially on individuals' participation also in the decision-making processes, the policy here leans towards a more active role for the state in educating its citizens on the changes necessary as well as actively engaging them in carrying these specific changes through. For instance, as the environmental aim of Swedish consumer policy is framed as 'such patterns of consumption and production *shall* be developed that reduces the strain on the environment and contributes to a long-term sustainable development' (Skr, 2001/02:68, 5, italics added), the necessity of the state also directing its citizens towards making these changes should therefore be evident. Conceiving citizens in this manner as 'instructible', even unaware of what their true interests are, not to mention how to reach them, brings with it a paternalistic role for the state, where the task is to 'prevent citizens acting against their own ("objective") interests' (Feichtinger and Pregering, 2005:236; see also Lundqvist, 2004:166–7). These types of reasoning that depict an active state, enlightening its citizens on how to behave, bear a close resemblance to the role of the state expressed within the civic-republican tradition, where citizens are not always aware of their own good and thus must be instructed on what is expected of them as good citizens.

The contrast between the state as either facilitating citizens' independent choices or as actively enlightening in a rather paternalistic manner, is explicitly put into focus when considering that, in particular, later dated policy documents contain an implicit understanding that earlier informational measures to some extent have failed. A conclusion founded in the observed fact that Swedish individuals, having been provided with environmental information, still do not act according to what is described as the policy goals; for example people's consumption continues to increase and a majority still drive their cars into work on a daily basis (cf. Skr, 2002/03:31, 5). Therefore, policy-makers conclude, additional and more easily accessible information is called for (and, as demonstrated above, also needs to be complemented by more effective policy instruments for steering behavioural change) (e.g. Skr, 2003/04:129). It thus seems reasonable to make the interpretation that the state's role in Swedish environmental policy is not solely to facilitate an informed and independent choice by citizens ready to take matters into their own hands, but rather to enlighten and steer the citizenry towards a certain perception of what constitutes good life projects. Following this line of reasoning, as long as the particular preferred perception is not observed in the minds and daily practices of all individuals, the information has not been sufficient or adequately interpretable and the state's efforts to demonstrate the 'good life' for its citizens must be continued.

Are Swedish citizens encouraged to exercise self-direction when making choices in their daily life, or is the government drawing up a strict boundary that separates the right from the wrong choices? Through the general formulations in policy documents from the national level, the outer boundaries for the 'environmental citizen's' lifestyle is certainly drawn up through indicating the need for, for example, a transformed transport behaviour or altered patterns of consumption. With respect to different policy areas (e.g. transportation, consumption or waste management), the citizens shall consume, choose and act in a manner to achieve the governmental policy goals, and the task of governmental authorities is to see to it that this 'responsible behaviour' is realized, if not on a voluntary basis, then through the introduction of more steering instruments (e.g. Skr, 1996/97:50; Skr, 2003/04:129). Here, the role of citizens in the work towards sustainability is thus strictly limited to a change of behavioural patterns in a predetermined direction, rather than deliberating on which behavioural patterns are in fact preferable. More detailed specifics for what a sustainable lifestyle would include is not provided from the policy rhetoric, though it is also clear that the construction of such details are both desirable and even in progress. The aim to further develop and clarify components of a sustainable lifestyle signals that there is indeed one lifestyle or, at least, pattern of private consumption more preferable than others and that the task for the government is to educate the citizenry on what this comprises. Thus, the possible interpretation that the lack of a specified lifestyle within the policy documents would suggest a role for the state as merely enabling the individual's freedom to independently choose their own, as long as it is not harming anyone else, is thereby not given any additional support.

Two further factors contradict the interpretation that a lack of specified lifestyle alternatives throughout the documents is preserving autonomy and freedom of choice. *First*, without exception, Swedish environmental policy defines one further important function for the state as an environmental actor: to be a good example for its citizens. The state, including all governmental authorities, shall front the work towards the sustainable society – indeed nationally, within the borders of Sweden, but also internationally as a leading country or pioneer and thus a model for others to follow (e.g. Skr, 1996/97:50, 3; Skr, 1997/98:13, 6; Skr, 2000/01:38, 5; Skr, 2001/02:172, 6). Being an example also brings with it a need for reform, which the Swedish government clearly picks up on, in particular when acknowledging also that the state has important contributions to make in the work towards ecological sustainability. One aspect of this is of course the ascription of responsibility, which not only is placed on citizens, either individually or as a collective, but also on state authorities, governmental agencies and local governments. 'To create an ecologically sustainable society', the Swedish government therefore establishes, 'all individuals and public bodies must share responsibility for the environment' (Skr, 2000/01:38, 27). This, however, puts focus on yet another relevant question regarding the state as passive or active, namely whether environmental issues are to be regarded as an *overarching* goal for *all* relevant policy areas? One interpretation of the government taking on environmental issues as the superior goal for all sectors in society is that it will emanate in an infringement of the autonomy of citizens, and a greater role for the state as actively steering towards one, preferred end state. With this in mind, it should also be pointed out that the long-standing strategy for sustainability in Sweden does include the aspiration to make environmental issues a core part of the policy-making processes in all areas of government (e.g. Skr, 2000/01:38, 5).

These aspirations pointing towards the environmental issues' incorporation in 'all politics', in daily life, in governmental and community work (SOU, 2000:52, 25), stem from the international processes of Environmental Policy Integration (EPI), which was initiated with the Bruntland Report's understanding that environmental issues cannot be managed as a separate policy area, but must be incorporated as a key principle in all aspects of political and societal decision-making. The importance of EPI (or sector integration) was picked up by the UNCED during the 1992 Rio conference, which included as one central part in the Agenda 21 the integration of environment and development in sectoral (i.e. non-environmental policy areas) decision-making (Persson, 2004:3). EPI in Sweden has followed, and in some respects even preceded international developments, and has thereby had a long-standing place on the national environmental policy agenda (cf. Lundqvist, 2004; Persson, 2004). For instance, the Government Communication 1996/97:50 comes to the conclusion that ecological sustainability shall be included as a goal in several sector policies, such as economy, communications, agriculture, fisheries, consumer issues, defence and foreign policy. All activities in these sectors shall emanate, as the Swedish government writes, 'from what nature and the environment can carry' (Skr, 1996/97:50, 34). In a similar fashion do the 16 Swedish National Environmental Quality Objectives aspire to be 'guiding or developing society as a whole and to be integrated in goal for other [than environmental] policy areas' (SEPA, 1999:5007:17–18; see also Prop, 1997/98:145; Prop, 2004/05:150).

The most explicit connection to the EU's EPI processes is, however, made through the formalization of sector responsibility for Swedish governmental authorities, which indicates that 'enterprises and authorities must integrate environmental concerns in their activities' (Skr, 2000/01:38, 6–7). It is within this framework that the Swedish government finds its role to be, for example, to assist a change in the market by directing public procurement towards environmentally friendly products (cf. Skr, 2001/02:172). Thereby, environmental issues are clearly understood as expressing a *normative* goal in Swedish policy.

Second, it must be remembered that Swedish environmental policy at the national level does not comprise any detailed suggestion as to how the widespread environmental participation should be accomplished other than through the use of 'a wide arsenal of tools and policy instruments, everything from legislation and taxes to "soft" tools such as information and voluntary commitments' (Skr, 2001/02:172). Instead, due both to the strong principle of local self-government in Sweden in general, as well as the apparent local focus of the Agenda 21, much of the responsibilities for promoting the transforma- tion to the sustainable society is transferred down from the national level to the Swedish municipalities, where '[e]ach municipal government must find the work methods and solutions best suited for the own municipality' (Skr, 1994/95:120, 9), thus leaving local government with the freedom to decide on adequate measures (UNCED, 1992:461; SOU, 1997:105; Skr, 2003/04:129). Regarding, for instance, waste management, each municipality is, through the Environmental Code (e.g. SFS, 1998:808, Chapter 15), legally responsible for collecting and facilitating the sorting and disposal of household waste not covered by the producer responsibility. The national government, thus, leaves much freedom for each municipality to decide by themselves how to best organize this work, but is both setting the frames, deciding on guidelines and providing financial incentives for the municipalities for falling in line with the national policy aspirations. This, naturally, works both to enhance the degree of autonomy granted by the state, in that the political practice of environmental issues is decided on locally, and to diminish self-direction in that the desired end result (determined nationally) is both clearly pointed out as well as supported by financial incentives (cf. Skr, 2001/02:68). This also goes for the inclusion of environmental perspectives in higher education, where the national government has no legal mandate to control in detail the content and structure of the courses given. The autonomy of the Swedish municipalities is regulated both through the Swedish constitution and other laws, and is therefore not easily overridden (Halvarsson, 1995). A similar, but not as strong, autonomy is granted the Swedish universities and colleges through the Higher Education Act of 1992, which obviously makes detailed governmental control more or less inadequate in both of these two cases. These might constitute reasons for the policies being unambiguous in their ambition to ensure lower levels the autonomy to independently decide on the specifics of citizen participation.

What stands clear, however, is the governmental aspiration to direct both municipalities and universities towards, in some way, approaching the specific issue of creating environmentally sensitive citizens and promoting those environmental duties ordained by the government throughout their respective area of responsibility. The freedom for lower authorities lies merely in the details, whereas the policy frames are determined on a national level in terms of directions and goals. For example, in the most recent Official Report on environmental education in Swedish schools, *To Learn for Sustainable Development* (SOU, 2004:104, 123), it is suggested that 'the pedagogical work shall be characterized by an ecological approach'. Thus despite the lack of specifications for what the sustainable lifestyle might encompass, the interpretation of the role of government as actively prescribing one direction of its citizens' lifestyles and a desire to educate the citizenry on this idea remains without contradiction. Although it might be considered a rather typical ambivalence of political rhetoric, the absence of an explicit definition of what should be counted as an 'ecological lifestyle' is in part explained by the constitutional freedom granted local government, and in part compensated by the governmental embracing of ecological concerns as a normative goal of all public decision-making and activities.

In sum, we conclude from this exploration of the policy's balancing of environmental obligations and individual autonomy that the overarching image provided of the citizen draws predominately on the inability of the citizen to either discover or, by him/herself, reach his/her true interests. Political authority therefore assumes the role of (in addition to facilitating behavioural change) *first* enlightening the citizenry on what constitutes the common good, and *second* directing them towards this overarching societal goal. Thus the Swedish government, albeit highlighting the pressing need to first facilitate a behavioural change by both structural and economic means, assumes a, following Feichtinger and Pregering (2005), paternalistic role in actively steering the citizens towards *the* politically sanctioned lifestyle. As such the expectance of an active citizenry is not as pronounced with regards to deliberating on the goals of Swedish environmental policy. Rather, the citizenry is in this respect viewed as in need of enlightenment by the benevolent state and therefore as positioned on the receiving end in a one-way communication (rather than as a part in a dialogue). Voluntarily deliberation is, thus, substituted for state control and influence, and freedom of action and thought for obedience and conformity. In sum, therefore, the self-determination and self-regulation of the individuals is not placed high on the environmental policy agenda and the 'from-above' perspective (cf. Eckersley, 1992; Lundqvist, 2004; Feichtinger and Pregering, 2005) is thus prevailing. Rather, what is framed as responsible choices is only perceived as adequate or acceptable to the extent that they match up to an objectively defined target. If this is not accomplished, more steering, more targeted education and less a freedom of choice is necessary.

In the final section of this chapter, we turn towards exploring how the obligation/autonomy conflict is manifested and handled as public policy translates into political practice in the form of legislation. In particular, we focus here on the requirement of rule of law in upholding the principle of individual freedom, and the challenges to this principle presented by environmental legislation directed towards individual patterns of behaviour.

THE ROLE AND THE RULE OF LAW

The role of law is generally twofold. One function is to solve conflicts between individuals; contract law is a clear example but also classic environmental 'neighbour law', where a polluting or otherwise disturbing activity negatively affects the surrounding area possessed by another landowner, tenant, etc. The other function (often overlapping the first) is to promote social interests, both by setting up legal barriers against unacceptable activities, in terms of, for instance, prohibitions and criminal sanctions, and also by more generally directing human behaviour so that political goals, such as sustainability, are obtained. The first role is basically rooted in private law, the second in public law. Although neighbour law still is important, the complex and large-scale character of today's environmental problems puts environmental law first of all within public law. Environmental law provides a great variety of instruments for public control of different sectors, such as industrial and energy production, forestry and agriculture and, to some extent, different household activities.

Typically for public law is the relation between the state (the government and institutions on different levels, included the municipal) and the individual. As the state often is seen as the stronger party,[1] with access to an array of coercion instruments, the individual is to some extent protected by legal principles related to the interest of individual freedom and the rule of law. The principle of legal certainty, emanating from liberalism, indicates that legal provisions and legal decisions should be foreseeable for the addressed individual (including households) so that s/he can know in advance and anticipate possible consequences, including to fully understand what constitutes a criminal act or omission (see Swedish Supreme Court in NJA case 2006:310). Issuing strict and foreseeable legal requirements is of course also desirable from an environmental point of view, but in practice it is often impossible due to the complexity and uncertainty that typically are connected to environmental impacts. The principle of legal certainty in connection with environmental law therefore is disputed (e.g. Basse, 1994; Westerlund, 1997; Nilsson, 2002; Michanek, 2008).

Not only legal certainty (foreseeability) is important for the individual. We are reluctant to issue strict rules or decisions that significantly limit the freedom of choice. The freedom for household members to choose how to structure everyday life, for instance choosing between transport means or different chemicals (paints, detergents etc.) is seen as important although certain forms of transport and certain chemical products are deemed to be more environmentally harmful than others. This issue is also related to the interest of a free market, legally protected, for instance by EC law (Michanek, 2008).

Furthermore, although legal requirements to take precautions apply and, as such, are regarded as legitimate, what is acceptable as means for compliance control? Inspections, injunctions and prosecutions are clearly interfering with interests of privacy and integrity for individuals. We may accept a legal requirement to avoid harmful detergents if there are functioning alternatives available, but how would we react if the local environmental inspector looks through the kitchen window? Many Swedes recognize the environmental norm to separate waste, but presumably fewer prefer to have 'waste detectives' with cameras hidden around waste recycling stations (Lundmark and Ödberg, 2007).

Environmental law approaches households

Environmental law has, in connection with the development of environmental policy, gained new targets for its environmental requirements, including members of households. To a certain extent, legal development thus reflects the understanding that reality has become increasingly complex and a great many sources of various magnitude and nature affect environmental status, even if households were not entirely absolved from responsibility in earlier law. For instance, central environmental control in the 1969 Swedish Environmental Protection Act was aimed primarily at industrial operations, but the law imposed environmental standards for all uses of land and water at risk of pollution and similar disruptions, thus including household uses. The same can be said about the chemicals laws enacted in 1973 and 1985: control focused on manufacturers and importers, but environmental standards were also directed at other handling, such as household use of chemicals. However, the Environmental Code of 1999 further expanded Swedish household-oriented environmental law, with clear connections to the principles expressed in Agenda 21. In order to promote the Code's sustainable development objectives, control should not focus only on monitoring and control of pollution, chemicals, waste, interference with the natural environment etc., but also on resource flows. In order to achieve an ecocyclical society, the Code imposes requirements for recycling and reuse and on conservation of materials, raw materials and energy. These requirements cross virtually all sectors of society and are thus also applicable to household activities.

What kinds of legal environmental standards can households encounter? Historically, households have been affected by environmental regulations primarily when a particular behaviour has been deemed a risk to human health and the environment in the *individual* case. This is still the case. Waste management can serve as an illustrative example. To prevent littering and pollution, the main rule requires households to sort out different substances from household waste and deliver them into assigned systems for waste disposal. The handling of chemical products is another example. Certain chemicals (such as DDT) are banned entirely, while others may only be handled by professionals or under special conditions. A third example is the construction and modification of buildings and civil works, as well as other interference that entails a significant modification to land or a water body.

It is easy to understand that households are affected by environmental requirements when, as in the foregoing examples, one can identify a relatively tangible risk in the individual case. But what about when there is no such risk and it is mainly households as a *collective* that cause the risks, for instance in connection with the normal use of dishwashing and laundry detergents? In these situations, informative and economic policy instruments play a key role in transforming household activity patterns in a more sustainable direction, which in some cases are based on legislation. In principle, however, mandatory legal instruments are also applicable in these situations, primarily through the 'general rules of consideration' set out in the Environmental Code. These rules include requirements to take protective measures and other precautions, acquire knowledge about environmental risks, avoid chemical products (including dishwashing and laundry detergents, for instance) when there are less dangerous alternatives, conserve natural resources and energy, and recycle and reuse. Exemptions from these requirements are provided only when someone takes an isolated 'measure' (as opposed to an 'activity' that is continual or recurring, such as commuting by car to and from work), while the connection to the Code's sustainability objectives is so vague that the measure is deemed 'of negligible significance in individual cases'. Examples of such cases are the choice of housing and vacation/holiday pursuits (Michanek and Zetterberg, 2008:114–117).

Although the fundamental premise of the Environmental Code is that the standards must apply to everyone, closer analysis of the rules shows that there are probably very few cases in which intervention would be actualized when the environmental risk is due only to the behaviour of households as a collective. The reason for this is that the requirements of the Environmental Code may not be unreasonable, which in essence means that the environmental benefit of a requirement must primarily be weighed against the cost of compliance. In addition, the drafting history of the Code (preparatory works)[2] shows that other circumstances must also be ascribed importance with regard to how a behaviour is judged, such as that it is 'generally acceptable', and 'personal privacy and freedom of choice' must be taken into account (Michanek and Zetterberg, 2008:133). Against this backdrop one can presume, even though the legal boundary is vague, that supervisory authorities do not prioritize requirements aimed at households if there is no relatively tangible risk to human health or the environment in individual cases.

The legal requirement to avoid a chemical product (e.g. a washing detergent) when there is a less harmful alternative available – the product choice requirement – is especially disputed as it applies to 'all' and therefore interferes with the everyday life of households. The norm is backed up by a criminal

34

sanction that applies not only in cases of intent, but also if a person is 'gravely careless'. As far as we know, this criminal sanction has never been applied in an individual case. Still, the mere existence of the criminal provision is clearly conflicting with the principle of legal certainty as it is difficult to foresee the border between what is legal and illegal. In order to determine if a certain chemical product is less harmful than another, one has to investigate the specific characters of the different products and also the features of the recipient to which the chemical may be exposed. Furthermore, the requirement does not apply if it is considered to be 'unreasonable' in the individual case, but what is 'unreasonable'?

Alongside the requirements that environmental law imposes directly on household activities, households are often affected *indirectly*, when legal obligations are imposed on others. The municipality is one important example of such a target, as municipal planning decisions on construction and other land use, affect the distance between neighbourhoods and workplaces and access to public transport. Likewise, municipal decisions on waste management plans (as required by the Environmental Code) affect households' options for waste recycling. Another example in which households are affected indirectly is the regulation of chemical products handling, where environmental requirements are directed primarily at manufacturers and importers. If the manufacturer of a particular product is banned by law, it affects households' freedom of choice, just as requirements for disclosure of the environmental risks of chemicals make it easier for households to make environmentally conscious choices. The relatively new requirements on petrol stations to supply alternative fuels is a similar example in which household activities are affected indirectly by environmental law.

In summary, legislation has an impact on households' green behaviour in various ways. The law often is the basis of economic and informative policy instruments. Mandatory legal requirements aimed at municipalities and other addressees shape social structures and other frameworks for household choices and behaviours. On the other hand, it can be presumed that a mandatory legal requirement aimed directly at households is meaningful primarily when there is a tangible risk to human health or the environment in the individual case, and not when risks should be ascribed to the collective behaviour of households. The modest application of the law to the lifestyle choices of private households may be seen as an indication that policy-makers prefer to use other types of instruments, rather than legal coercions, which is ascribed to the belief that individuals are relatively concerned about the environment and willing to voluntarily comply with policy directives, as well as rational respondents to economic instruments. In addition, the reluctance to control directly via legislation may indicate a belief among policy-makers that measures that clearly step away from voluntary compliance lack legitimacy among the public.

CONCLUSIONS

Following the international environmental discourse, as well as the Swedish official policy documents under scrutiny here, the aggregated activities of individuals, conducted within the privacy of their own home, amounts to a major problem that needs to be addressed, and changing lifestyles is therefore a key stone when building the ecologically sustainable society. The individual, according to Swedish environmental policy, therefore holds a responsibility (even a duty, although not enforced in law), equally shared by all individuals in Sweden, to amend their activities and contribute to the common good. As the main environmental impact of individuals' activities is expected to be related to their market behaviour, the individual's consumer role primarily is targeted when designing strategies for change. This is reflected both in the preference for market-based policy instruments as well as in the fact that motivations for change emphasize reciprocity rather than acknowledging the moral good of taking on a larger responsibility for the situation.

The role of the state in making as well as promoting environmental policy is, at least initially, somewhat unclear. An interpretation along the lines of the passive, neutral state is supported by the fact that much attention is given to the state's responsibility in creating possibilities for citizens to make informed choices, that is, traditional liberal concerns. Adding to this, the lack of any one specified lifestyle or specific environmental actions throughout the documents suggests that the state might keep the door open for independent interpretations of the good also in environmental terms, in line with an environmentally sensitive liberalism. Therefore, each citizen should be granted the opportunity to independently choose among numerous sustainable lifestyles. Contradicting this interpretation is the fact that use of the phrases 'informed' or 'responsible choices' seems to denote only the choice to follow the governmental recommendation laid down in policy.

While the general policy rhetoric presumes that citizens possess a certain measure of awareness and readiness to assume responsibility for the environmental consequences of their daily actions, it also presumes they are in need of a friendly push in the right direction, in order to clearly see their own best interests and come to understand how this can be achieved in practice. Thus, in the same way as the individual is expected to react rationally to monetary incentives, s/he also is expected to passively adhere to governmental instructions for change. Information and education, where the state enlightens the individual on the change required are therefore presented as an important complement to market-based policy tools. The attendant picture of citizens as passive consumers of products and information entails tremendous responsibility for national and local authorities to indirectly guide citizens through information about how this environmental concern should be expressed: guidance as to which values should be defended and how priorities should be set, rather than opening the door to widespread, public deliberations about these matters. Education and information with normative undertones are thus described as key instruments for increasing household contributions to sustainable development. Therefore, it is reasonable to assume that the traditional (liberal) function of the private sphere of citizenship, as the area wherein individuals independently and freely developed their opinions, their values and their consciousness, without being subjected to formal regulation, or even influence, by the state has been exchanged for a view on private aspects of citizens' lives as being open for the normative influence of the state. In practice therefore, the policy signals the existence of one set of environmental values that all citizens should share in order to reach the policy goal, and the possible choices for individuals are thereby not as abundant. Adding to this line of interpretation, a view on active engagement of the individuals in the actual process of deciding upon the values guiding environmental policy stands back in favour of the view of the citizen as controlled through the use informational instruments. Voluntary deliberation is, thus, substituted for state control and influence, and freedom of action and thought for obedience and conformity.

The (at least theoretically highly significant) conflict between state control, whether direct or indirect, and personal freedom is, however, scarcely mentioned in the policy documents covered by the analysis in this chapter. As part of avoiding this potential conflict and to align with the picture of the citizen as a consumer first and foremost, Swedish policy documents instead consistently wrap the effects of environmental protection in financial terms, in the hope that this will strike a positive tone among the public. Thus, analysis of the more specific policy arguments related to household motivations shows that policy-makers consider both positive and negative economic incentives the primary methods for bringing about behaviour modifications while maintaining the legitimacy of environmental policy.

The difficulty of handling the conflict between expanded environmental obligations for the individual, with maintained personal autonomy and self-direction, is evident also when turning towards legislation as a tool for forwarding public policy's sustainability aspirations. In particular, the legislature is incapable of regulating all environmental issues in detail; the reality is simply too complex and uncertain. A large number of known and as yet unknown situations in which environmental impact may be anticipated can be covered through generalized requirements. The general rules of consideration in the Environmental Code are the most important example of such rules, which thus fill a key 'coverage' function. However, vague requirements will inevitably come into conflict with the principle of legal certainty, since individuals cannot clearly see the boundaries of the disallowed and thus cannot either predict when they may be subject to sanctions or official intervention. This conflict of interest is also found when the rules are applied to commercial activities, but is probably stronger when households are concerned, because households typically have fewer financial resources. There are thus important arguments against the widespread use of mandatory legal requirements aimed at households. One may presume that such requirements, as today, could become meaningful primarily when there is a relatively tangible risk to human health or the environment in the individual case. However, legislation should be able to fill an important function by facilitating households' choices in favour of green behaviours and products. Towards that end, mandatory legal requirements could be imposed on municipalities, manufacturers, importers and other actors upstream from households.

There is a general need for legal development to manage this complexity, of which households are one component. Among others, the substantive controls in the Planning and Building Act could be tightened with a view to building physical structures that prioritize accessibility for households (such as access to public transport or recycling facilities) and thus promote green behaviour. Environmental quality norms set the limits for what the environment can tolerate, limits that apply to everyone, not least the impact originating with households. However, Swedish law lacks effective instruments for implementing these norms vis-à-vis various actors. The action programmes especially, which cover all actors whose activities have environmental impact as a collective, need to be clearer and more effective.

As the environmental impacts of household-related activities increasingly are acknowledged and addressed by policy-makers, attention is called to the political tightrope walk between effective environmental protection and the respect for individual autonomy in the private sphere of the household. In particular, the way in which the balance between core democratic values and environmental responsibilities is being struck, both in political discourse and throughout the law-making process, has proven of considerable relevance. The next chapter will address how these policy aspirations are received by the households themselves. Which value trade-offs are made when politics for sustainable development meets the complex structures of everyday life?

NOTES

1 This is not true for all situations: economically strong industrial companies possess more resources (e.g. technical and legal expertise) than, for instance, a municipal environmental authority, which clearly is the underdog in connection with, e.g. licensing.
2 Compared to most other states, probably Swedish preparatory works (e.g. Commission reports and Governmental Bills) still play a relatively important role when legal rules are interpreted in legal decision-making, although the importance of these documents was reduced after the membership in EU.

REFERENCES

Amara, R. C. (1972) 'Toward a Framework for National Goals and Policy Research', *Policy Sciences*, vol 3, pp59–69

Attfield, R. and A. Belsey (eds) (1994) *Philosophy and the Natural Environment*, Cambridge University Press, Cambridge

Baker, S., M. Kousis, D. Richardson and Y. Stephen (1997) 'Introduction', in S. Baker, M. Kousis, D. Richardson and Y. Stephen (eds) *The Politics of Sustainable Development*, Routledge, London

Basse, E. M. (1994) 'Retssikkerhed i miljøretten – hvilke begreber kan anvendes?' in E. M. Basse (ed) *Miljørettens grundspørgsmål, Bidrag til en nordisk forskeruddannelse*, Gadsforlag, København

Bell, D. (2001) 'How can Political Liberals be Environmentalists?' *Political Studies*, vol 50, pp703–724

Birkland, T. A. (2005) *An Introduction to the Policy Process: Theories, Concepts, and Models of Public Policy-making*, M.E. Sharpe, Armonk, NY

Carter, N. (2001) *The Politics of the Environment. Ideas, Activism, Policy*, Cambridge University Press, Cambridge

Curry, P. (2000) 'Redefining Community: Towards an ecological republicanism', *Biodiversity and Conservation*, vol 9, pp1059–1071

Dagger, R. (1997) *Civic Virtues: Rights, Citizenship, and Republican Liberalism*, Oxford University Press, Oxford

Delanty, G. (2000) *Citizenship in a Global Age: Society, Culture, Politics*, Open University Press, Buckingham

Dobson, A. (1998) *Justice and the Environment. Conceptions of Environmental Sustainability and Dimensions of Social Justice*, Oxford University Press, Oxford

Dobson, A. (2003) *Citizenship and the Environment*, Oxford University Press, Oxford

Dobson, A. (2007) 'Environmental Citizenship: Towards sustainable development', *Sustainable Development*, vol 15, no 5, pp276–285

Doherty, B. and M. de Geus (1996) 'Introduction', in B. Doherty and M. de Geus (eds) *Democracy and Green Political Thought. Sustainability, Rights and Citizenship*, Routledge, London

Dryzek, J. S. (2005) *The Politics of the Earth* (2nd edition), Oxford University Press, Oxford

Dworkin, R. (1978) *Taking Rights Seriously*, Harvard University Press, Cambridge, MA.

Easton, D. (1953) *The Political System*, Knopf, New York

Eckersley, R. (1992) *Environmentalism and Political Theory: Towards an Ecocentric Approach*, UCL Press, London

Eckersley, R. (1996) 'Greening Liberal Democracy: The rights discourse revisited', in B. Doherty and M. de Geus (eds), *Democracy and Green Political Thought. Sustainability, Rights and Citizenship*, Routledge, London

Feichtinger, J. and M. Pregering (2005) 'Imagined Citizens and Participation: Local Agenda 21 in Two Communities in Sweden and Austria', *Local Environment*, vol 10, no 3, pp229–242

Global Footprint Network (2008) *Ecological Footprint and Biocapacity, 2008 edition*, URL: http://www.footprintnetwork.com/download.php?id=509, accessed 4 May 2009

Hajer, M.A. (1995) *The Politics of Environmental Discourse: Ecological Modernisation and the Policy Process*, Oxford University Press, Oxford

Hall, C.M. and J. M. Jenkins (1995) *Tourism Policy: A Public Policy Approach*, Routledge, London

Hall, P. M. and P. J. W. McGinty (1997) 'Policy as the Transformation of Intentions: Producing program from statute', *Sociological Quarterly*, vol 38, no 3, pp439–467

Halvarsson, A. (1995) *Sveriges statsskick: fakta och perspektiv* (10th edition), Almqvist & Wiksell, Stockholm

Hardin, G. (1968) 'The Tragedy of the Commons', *Science*, 162:1243–1248

Held, D. (1996) *Models of Democracy*, Polity Press, Cambridge

Heywood, A. (2004) *Political Theory: An Introduction* (3rd edition), Palgrave
   Macmillan, New York
Hobson, K. (2002) 'Competing Discourses of Sustainable Consumption: Does the
   "rationalisation of lifestyles" make sense?', *Environmental Politics*, vol 11, no 2,
   pp95–120
Hobson, K. (2004) 'Sustainable Consumption in the United Kingdom: The "responsi-
   ble" consumer at "arm's length"', *Journal of Environment & Development*, vol 13, no
   2, pp121–139
Jenkins-Smith, H. and P. Sabatier (1993) 'Methodological Appendix: Measuring longi-
   tudinal change in elite beliefs using content analysis of public documents', in P.
   Sabatier and H. C. Jenkins-Smith (eds) *Policy Change and Learning: An Advocacy
   Coalition Approach*, Westview Press, Boulder, CO
Kymlicka, W. and W. Norman (1994) 'Return of the Citizen', *Ethics*, vol 104,
   pp352–381
Lasswell, H. D. (1936) *Politics: Who Gets What, When, How*, McGraw-Hill, New York
Locke, J. (2002) 'The Second Treatise of Government and a Letter Concerning
   Toleration', Dover Publications, New York
Lundmark, C. and C. Ödberg (2007) 'Lagen som normbildare? En studie av nedskräpn-
   ingsproblemet vid landets återvinningsstationer', *Förvaltningsrättslig tidskrift*,
   vol 69, no 3, pp215–244
Lundqvist, L. J. (2004) *Sweden and Ecological Governance: Straddling the Fence*,
   Manchester University Press, Manchester and New York
Machiavelli, N. (2003) *The Discourses*, Penguin Classics, London
Maniates, M. F. (2001) 'Individualization: Plant a tree, buy a bike, save the world',
   Global Environmental Politics, vol 1, no 3, pp31–52
March, J. G. and J. P. Olsen (1984) 'The New Institutionalism: Organizational factors
   in political life', *American Political Science Review*, vol 78, pp734–749
Matti, S. (2006) *The Imagined Environmental Citizen. Exploring the State–Individual
   Relationship in Swedish Environmental Policy*, Licentiate Thesis, Division of Political
   Science, Luleå University of Technology
Matti, S. (2009) *Exploring Public Policy Legitimacy: A Study of Belief-System
   Correspondence in Swedish Environmental Policy*, Doctoral Thesis, Division of
   Political Science, Luleå University of Technology
Michanek, G. (2008) 'Miljörätten och de uthålliga hushållen', in E. Olsen and T. Anker
   (eds) *Festskrift till Ellen Margrethe Basse*, Jurist- og Økonomforbundets Forlag,
   Köpenhamn
Michanek, G. and C. Zetterberg (2008) *Den svenska miljörätten*. Uppsala: Iustus
Micheletti, M. (2003) *Political Virtue and Shopping: Individuals, Consumerism, and
   Collective Action*, Palgrave Macmillan, New York
Micheletti, M. and A. McFarland (eds) (2009, in press) *Creative Participation:
   Responsibility-taking in the Political World*, Paradigm Publishers, Boulder, CO
Mill, J. S. (1998) *On Liberty*, Oxford University Press, Oxford
Nilsson, A. (2002) *Rättsäkerhet och miljöhänsyn, En diskussion belyst av JO:s praxis i
   miljöärenden*, Nerenius & Santerus, Stockholm
Nozick, R. (1974) *Anarchy, State and Utopia*, Blackwell Publishing, Oxford
Persson, Å. (2004) *Environmental Policy Integration: An Introduction*. PINTS – Policy
   Integration for Sustainability Background Paper, Stockholm Environment Institute,
   Stockholm

Prokhovnik, R. (1998) 'Public and Private Citizenship. From gender invisibility to feminist inclusiveness', *Feminist Review*, vol 60, pp84–104

Prop (1997/98:145) *Svenska miljömål. Miljöpolitik för ett hållbart Sverige [Swedish environmental objectives. Environmental politics for a sustainable Sweden]*, Government Bill, Swedish Parliamentary Record, Stockholm

Prop (2004/05:65) *Århuskonventionen [The Aarhus Convention]*, Government Bill, Swedish Parliamentary Record, Stockholm

Prop (2004/05:150) *Svenska miljömål – ett gemensamt uppdrag [Swedish environmental objectives – a joint task]*, Government Bill, Swedish Parliamentary Record, Stockholm

Rawls, J. (1993) *Political Liberalism*, Columbia University Press, New York

Rawls, J. (1999) *A Theory of Justice* (revised edition) Belknap, Cambridge, MA

Rokeach, M. (1973) *The Nature of Human Values*, Free Press, New York

Rousseau, J.-J. (1994) *Om Samhällsfördraget eller Statsrättens grunder*, Natur och Kultur, Stockholm

Rskr (2004/05:193) *Approval of 2004/05:MJU11 (Prop, 2004/05:65: Århuskonventionen)*, Parliamentary Decision, Swedish Parliamentary Record, Stockholm

Rydin, Y. (1999) 'Can We Talk Ourselves Into Sustainability? The role of discourse in the environmental policy process', *Environmental Values*, vol 8, pp467–484

Rydin, Y. (2005) 'Geographical Knowledge and Policy: The positive contribution of discourse studies', *Area*, vol 37, no 1, pp73–78

Sabatier, P. A. (1988) An Advocacy Coalition Framework of Policy Change and the Role of Policy-oriented Learning Therein, *Policy Sciences*, vol 21, pp129–168

SEPA (1999:5007) *Når vi miljömålen?*, Swedish Environmental Protection Agency, Stockholm

Seyfang, G. (2005) 'Shopping for Sustainability: Can sustainable consumption promote ecological citizenship?', *Environmental Politics*, vol 14, no 2, pp290–306

SFS (1998:808) *Miljöbalk [Environmental Code]*, Swedish Parliamentary Record, Stockholm

Skill, K. (2008) *(Re)Creating Ecological Action Space: Householders' Activities for Sustainable Development in Sweden*, Doctoral Thesis, Department of Technology and Social Change, Linköping University Press, Linköping

Skr. (1994/95:120) *Miljön – vårt gemensamma ansvar [The environment – our common responsibility]*, Government Communication, Swedish Parliamentary Record, Stockholm

Skr. (1996/97:50) *På väg mot ett hållbart ekologiskt samhälle [On the road towards a sustainable ecological society]*, Government Communication, Swedish Parliamentary Record, Stockholm

Skr. (1997/98:13) *Ekologisk hållbarhet [Ecological sustainability]*, Government Communication, Swedish Parliamentary Record, Stockholm

Skr. (2000/01:38) *Hållbara Sverige - uppföljning av åtgärder för en ekologiskt hållbar utveckling [Sustainable Sweden – evaluation of measures to support an ecologically sustainable development]*, Government Communication, Swedish Parliamentary Record, Stockholm

Skr. (2001/02:50) *Hållbara Sverige – uppföljning av åtgärder för en ekologiskt hållbar utveckling [Sustainable Sweden – evaluation of measures to support an ecologically sustainable development]*, Government Communication, Swedish Parliamentary Record, Stockholm

Skr. (2001/02:68) *Konsumenterna och miljön [The consumers and the environment]*, Government Communication, Swedish Parliamentary Record, Stockholm

Skr. (2001/02:172) *Nationell strategi för hållbar utveckling* [*A national strategy for sustainable development*], Government Communication, Swedish Parliamentary Record, Stockholm

Skr. (2002/03:31) *Utvärdering av miljömålet i konsumentpolitiken* [*Evaluation of the environmental goal in consumer policy*], Government Communication, Swedish Parliamentary Record, Stockholm

Skr. (2003/04:129) *En svensk strategi för hållbar utveckling* [*A Swedish strategy for sustainable development*], Government Communication, Swedish Parliamentary Record, Stockholm

SOU (1997:105) *Agenda 21 i Sverige: Fem år efter Rio – Resultat och Framtid* [*Agenda 21 in Sweden: Five Yeas After Rio – Results and Future*], Statens Offentliga Utredningar, Miljödepartementet, Stockholm

SOU (2000:52) *Framtidens miljö – allas vårt ansvar. Betänkande från miljömålskommittén* [*The Future's Environment – Our Common Responsibility*], Statens Offentliga Utredningar, Miljö- och Samhällsbyggnadsdepartementet, Stockholm

SOU (2004:104) *Att lära för hållbar utveckling* [*To Learn for Sustainable Development*], Statens Offentliga Utredningar, Utbildnings- och kulturdepartementet, Kommittén för utbildning för hållbar utveckling, Stockholm

Tetlock, P. E., R. S. Peterson and J. S. Lerner (1996) 'Revising the Value Pluralism Model: Incorporating social content and context postulates', in C. Seligman, J. M. Olson and M. P. Zanna (eds) *The Ontario Symposium of Values*, vol 8, pp25–47, Lawrence Erlbaum Associates Inc, New Jersey

Thatcher, D. and M. Rein (2004) 'Managing Value Conflict in Public Policy', *Governance: An International Journal of Policy, Administration, and Institutions*, vol 17, no 4, pp457–486

Torgerson, D. (1999) *The Promise of Green Politics: Environmentalism and the Public Sphere*, Duke University Press, Durham, NC

Turner, B. S. (1990) 'Outline of a Theory of Citizenship', *Sociology*, vol 24, no 2, pp189–217

UNCED (1992) Agenda 21 – Dokument från FN: s konferens om miljö och utveckling, Nordstedts (Agenda 21 – Document from the United Nation's Conference on Environment and Development), Stockholm

Wackernagel, M. and W. E. Rees (1996) *Our Ecological Footprint: Reducing Human Impact on the Earth*, New Society Publishers, Philadelphia, PA

Weible, C. M. (2006) 'An Advocacy Coalition Framework Approach to Stakeholder Analysis: Understanding the political context of California Marine Protected Area policy', *Journal of Public Administration Research and Theory*, vol 17, pp95–117

Westerlund, S. (1997) *En hållbar rättsordning – rättsvetenskapliga paradigm och tankevändor*, Iustus förlag, Uppsala

Wissenburg, M. (1998) *Green Liberalism. The Free and the Green Society*, UCL Press, London

3

Dealing with Environmental Responsibilities: Living Everyday Life as Political Participation

Karin Skill and Elin Wihlborg

INTRODUCTION

There has been a historical shift in the solutions to environmental problems, which has come to focus on individual responsibility to prevent problems. This is partly a response to a changed character of the environmental problems that oftentimes have global reach, and partly a response to the view of who is responsible for dealing with the problems. Everyday decisions like how to manage household waste, what to purchase for dinner or how to get to work are now considered to have consequences for the environment and others. By acting environmentally friendly and by taking a personal responsibility for the environment householders as citizens are expected to change the state of the world to a more sustainable place through increased political participation (UNCED, 1993; Aarhus Convention, 1998). Sustainable development connects local and global processes on practical and symbolic levels. What is made – or not made – in daily lives locally have global implications. Citizens can participate in a multitude of ways, and political participation can mean many different things (Skill, 2008). They can also understand their environmental responsibilities in different ways and act thereafter. In distinction to the previous chapter by Lundmark et al. that deals with the tension between environmental responsibilities and individual freedom of action in official Swedish environmental policies, this chapter focuses on householders' interpretations and day-to-day experiences of environmental responsibilities.

In the introduction to the book *Environmental Citizenship* (2006), the editors Andrew Dobson and Derek Bell ask how and where environmental citizenship can be *done* and this issue is the focus of this chapter. This is an important question since environmental citizenship transverses the so-called public–private divide, which challenges the Aristotelian tradition stipulating that being a citizen concerns activities mainly in the public domain (see the previous chapter of this volume for an extended discussion of the relationship between the private–public divide and different citizenship models). In the same book Sherilyn MacGregor criticizes how environmental citizenship tends to neglect the ways responsibilities are shared, and who it is that are performing both the 'labor- and time-intensive green lifestyle changes [and] the increased active participation in the public sphere' (MacGregor, 2006, p. 102). Paraphrasing Szerszynski (2006) it is important not to absent citizens from the 'quotidian business of the reproduction of daily life' (Dobson and Bell, 2006, p. 10). We have to ask what conditions are necessary to make citizenship practice possible. An important resource then is time, and MacGregor argues:

> *Citizenship, understood as being about active participation in the public sphere, is by definition a practice that depends on 'free time'; it is thus not designed for people with multiple roles and heavy loads of responsibility for productive and reproductive work.* (MacGregor, 2006, p. 108)

MacGregor brings the attention to the need to focus on what is going on within what is commonly treated as a black box – the domestic sphere, or the household (Shanahan, 2003). By looking into the quotidian practices of the households it becomes possible to discuss how democracy is done. It is not only important to investigate environmental attitudes, but also in what ways people behave. The ideal of the environmental citizen makes sustainable development an individual responsibility, what we call individualization. The individualization is lived through the complex everyday life and in this chapter we will show how householders use strategies of compensation and simplification to deal with their environmental responsibilities. The objective of this chapter is to focus on the everyday practices of households and how environmental activities are integrated in their day-to-day lives, and then analyse how these practices are connected to rights and responsibilities of environmental citizenship.

We argue that without a comprehensive understanding of the everyday context where different activities are performed by householders, it is not possible to understand the obstacles and opportunities for the promotion of environmental citizenship and sustainable development. In this chapter we will describe and analyse three different themes that concern how sustainable practices are intertwined through everyday life. The themes emerged through the examination of in-depth studies of daily life in Swedish households (see Skill, 2008). The main argument of the chapter is based on these characteristics of the everyday life, which will be used to illustrate and discuss why everyday life is important to take into account when investigating environmental citizenship. Householders are making many different decisions with an aggregated influence on society and environment, and everyday decisions have to be contextualized in relation to other activities and overall goals with life. Thus, the aim is to analyse how the householders discuss and approach their responsibility for the environment, and how they are motivated. The presentation here revolves around three themes concerning everyday environmental responsibilities that emerged through our analyses:

- The *complexity* of everyday life, which makes it difficult to know how to measure one environmental activity in relation to another.
- How householders in our study *compensate* some activities they know they could or should do, with others.
- Householders cannot reflect on the environmental impact of each and every activity, and therefore they have to *simplify it* through routines and practices, and focus on a specific set of so called environmentally friendly activities.

The chapter is developed through these three thematic discussions relating to the overall argument on the need to investigate the everyday practices of citizenship, and to contextualize single household activities. Taking responsibility by performing individual environmental activities must be understood in relation to the ongoing process of living everyday life.

In the chapter a Swedish case study is used in order to analyse the relationship between knowledge and perceptions of environmental problems among householders, and how it influences their activities as responsible actors. The present account is based on material from 60 semi-structured interviews with Swedish householders performed during 2004–2006 with a total of 64 individuals. Householders of different ages and sexes were recruited to the study, as well as households with varying numbers, and usually all members of the households participated in the interview. The aim was not specifically to recruit environmental activists. It is a qualitative ethnographic study that interprets how this group of Swedes argue about their practices. We will describe the householders' interpretations of environmental problems and what they expressed that they could do about them. The methodological approach was to ask the householders about the environmental problems they thought existed; then to follow up by asking whether they believed there was anything they could do in their households to counteract these problems. By using this approach the householders shared information on possibilities and constraints to act environmentally friendly, i.e. how concerns about the environment was related to their everyday practices.

The chapter proceeds as follows: first we will discuss theoretical contributions that we build our argument on concerning citizenship, households and structuration theory. We will discuss the relations between private–public, and structure–actor. After these sections we give a brief description of the main observations concerning the household practices. Then we move on to give a brief description of the three themes, which are illustrated by empirical findings from the material. Finally, we will sum up the discussion and point at some potential policy implications.

EVERYDAY LIFE IN THE HOUSEHOLD

As Dorothy Smith writes: '[t]he telling of this world is a potentially endless detailing of particulars' (1987, p. 6), which has posed a challenge for social studies of everyday life. Since sustainable development has a potentially all-embracing character an everyday approach is fruitful for analysing sustainable activities. When discussing everyday life in general terms, scholars have pointed out that we dream of escaping the boredom of everyday life and the oppressive routines, at the same time as the very idea of 'wasted time' can be horrifying (Gardiner, 2000; Highmore, 2002). In the search for meaningful time people who are economically well off engage in consumer society, which is driven by the desire for constantly new experiences. To a large extent these same characters of contemporary society is what might provoke the environmental crisis, and unsustainable practices (Oslo Declaration, 2005). Furthermore, some of the more severe criticism that the theory of ecological citizenship has faced concern the lack of attention to the everyday life aspect. For example, John Barry argues that the requirements and responsibilities of environmental citizenship make up a part-time work, and thereby seem too demanding (Barry, 2006; c.f. MacGregor, 2006). These extensive requirements have been related to an individualization of responsibility for the environment, which in turn has prompted discussions of what could actually be defined as political participation (Skill, 2008). Political participation is a rather vague concept having a multitude of connotations depending on one's theoretical perspective, and concerning *when* and *how* citizens can and should participate. Everyday activities can indeed be political and about participation in democracy and societal relations in general.

Many scholars have a desire to be able to *explain* everyday life (Highmore, 2002) and to find the 'motive' behind observed behaviour (Smith, 1987). Everyday life theorizing has thereby not merely sought to describe lived experience, but to transform it and govern it (Gardiner, 2000; Highmore, 2002). However, 'human life exhibits many non-rational tendencies, embodied desires and poetical qualities that cannot be captured in the reductive explanatory models favoured by positivist social science' – which simultaneously implies that it is difficult to govern it (cited in Gardiner, 2000, p. 8) both from individual, household and structural perspectives. This is important to take into consideration when investigating how environmental activities are incorporated or neglected in householders' everyday life, or how policies for changed everyday practices are met and implemented at the household level. Through the text we will focus on the householders' reasoning about their practices and routines, which is done with the three themes mentioned above.

'If everyday life ... goes by unnoticed ... then the first task for attending to it will be to make it noticeable ... in all its complexity and contradictions' (Highmore, 2002, p. 23). Several methodological suggestions for how to grasp what is continually produced have been put forth. While some have suggested surrealist inspired techniques of montage, and juxtaposition of totally unrelated images to 'defamiliarize' the everyday (Gardiner, 2000, p. 20, pp34–37), others have suggested time diaries to grasp and visualize activity patterns (Ellegård and Wihlborg, 2001). Through these methods we *do not discover* everyday life, but try to grasp what is *already known* (Gardiner, 2000, p. 23) and systematize the knowledge. In the analysis of the interviews we have found how the householders understand their environmental responsibilities, which we have categorized into three areas. Before moving on to the discussions about environmental responsibility in citizenship theory, it is important to talk about what a household is, and how a household relates to an individual since we discuss the individualization of responsibility.

The meaning of household – a private or a political sphere?

Traditionally the household has been considered to belong to a private sphere and thereby opposite to that of a public political sphere. However, ecological citizenship is a prime example of what Segerberg has called the politicization of everyday doings, and the individualization of responsibility for the environment (Segerberg, 2005). In this section our aim is to discuss: How can the concept of household be understood? What is a household activity? What household activities are political, and in what situations do householders act as citizens and perform citizenship – we need this in order to move on to our analysis of how the householders deal with their responsibility and the perceived sacrifices they have to make when living their everyday lives in a more environmentally friendly manner.

Since many environmental theories start out from a broad understanding of the political sphere, it is relevant to focus on the demarcation between the private and the public. This distinction has historical roots. Traditionally, the distinction has separated formal institutional contexts, such as paid work and school, from informal contexts that were not financed and/or controlled by the state and thereby beyond the political reach (Yuval-Davis, 1997). Feminists challenged this demarcation in the 1960s and 1970s and demanded, for example, that spousal and child abuse in the home were political matters that needed to be regulated (Wendt Höjer and Åse, 2001). By stating that the personal is political, feminism provoked a transformation of politics itself (Highmore, 2002). This challenge has now been extended to other matters, such as sorting household waste and choice of mode of transportation, which blurs the difference between the public and private spheres in politics. When the household is included in the political sphere it is not considered solely a private domain. It is along a similar line of reasoning about the interrelationship of the private and political spheres that ecological citizenship has been called for (Dobson, 2003). Depending on how we define the political sphere, the role of political participation will be different, such as the role of the citizen and her rights and responsibilities, as well as legitimate policy instruments. Segerberg has emphasized that the political can be defined according to *when* an activity is carried out (the 'doing' itself), and not always in spatial terms (*where*) (2005, p. 164). A related political aspect of environmentally friendly household activities is *who* conducts them, not at least from a gender perspective (Wihlborg and Skill, 2004).

Households as contexts

In households reproduction, decision-making and negotiation about resources and consumption take place, with consequences for sustainable development, the environment, and others living in the 'global household' (c.f. Linnér, 1998). To economize resources is one of the most central definitions of a household both from an analytical perspective and in practice. Taking the households as the unit of study can be different compared to focusing on individuals. We will delve into the question of the household as a place (the home connected to material socio-technological structures), and as a context (for example when being in the supermarket where grocery shopping is considered a household activity), or as a family when several people live together and have reciprocal relationships. The private household is often placed in contradistinction to the public sphere of industry and business in environmental studies, where production has received most attention. Despite their small individual size, households collectively account for half of the environmental destruction in Sweden (Shanahan et al, 2002), and much environmental pollution is causally linked to modern household technology (Mies and Shiva, 1993; Shove, 2003). This calculation is based on the distinction between the private and public spheres, a debatable distinction, since it is equally possible to argue that without households, no one would produce industrial goods or consume industrial output. We argue that householders are involved in not only consumption, but also production and reproduction. Through everyday life people usually have the option to produce something themselves, or purchase it from others, like making your own lunch box or buying it from a restaurant, or repairing the car oneself or taking it to the car mechanics and paying for the service. How much unpaid work can government expect the households to do in order to implement environmental policies, and who is it within the household who takes on the responsibility? This later question concerns gendered aspects of household work (Wihlborg and Skill, 2004). Cultural expectations and obligations affect the division of labour, certain values being considered male and others female. Household work can acquire a symbolic meaning and predict or confirm gender identity (Fenstermaker Berk, 1985), and certain household tasks are more gendered than others (Ahrne and Roman, 1997). In distinction to several researchers who focus on the intentionality of households and their activities (Hook and Paolucci, 1970; Åberg, 2004), we acknowledge that different house-holders may have different goals (Ahrne, 1994). This is why it is important to use the term *householder* or household member rather than to refer only to 'household'. Various epithets can further be given to an individual, and the context influences when they are applied and stressed such as householder, citizen, user or consumer.

A household can be connected to the physical building (i.e. the house) and the material and energy-related resources used in it, such as electricity, water, and fuel. When more and more people tend to live on their own, it implies increasing numbers of households and dwellings (Noorman and Schoot Uiterkamp, 1998). The house is a context in which people, depending on the type of housing arrangement (e.g. small house or apartment, subletting or ownership), can have an impact on and create conditions for acting in environ-mentally friendly ways. The design and location of the dwelling and its physical surroundings is essential for the householders' action space in relation to sustain-able development. Today's society is constructed on a multitude of integrated systems for electricity, telecommunication, transportation on roads, in the air, and on the seas, etc., which taken together form the conditions within which humans act. Householders are similarly integrated in social structures by which they are both 'created' and which they recreate, and we consider social and material structures to be intertwined. The household is also a place for recre-ation and many activities that can be considered as unpaid work take place here. These unpaid activities run a risk of becoming hidden from the public produc-tive paid work and are consequently not viewed as political or public. This has been criticized by feminist scholars for being a male-centred view of politics that makes unpaid life-sustaining work invisible, a view that even green political theory falls in (MacGregor, 2006). However, these unpaid activities are essen-tial for the expression of environmental responsibilities, since changes of daily activities are the main requirements of sustainable development.

The ideas of family and household have varied historically, and have sometimes even been used interchangeably (Yanagisako, 1979; Sontag and Bubolz, 1996). There is often a normative conservative imperative related to the meaning of the family as maintenance of values and norms. In recent decades, attention has been paid to internal household processes (Wilk, 1989; Ahrne and Roman, 1997), with a focus on negotiations about and division of resources and activities. Humans who live together do not necessarily share resources and/or experiences. Household members may, however, have moral understandings of reciprocity towards each other as family members that affect decisions and individual choices. Today almost half of Swedish households have only one member (Bladh, 2005). This does not, however, mean that they are isolated. The problematic aspects of defining 'household' are the customary emphasis on negotiations, division of labour, and organization, which are diffi-cult to apply to people living on their own. But individual activities are influenced by many others not present in time and space (Giddens, 1989). A household's internal structures and workings both create and are recreated by larger-scale cultural, economic and political processes (Moore, 1994). The interaction between the economic system and individuals takes place through taxation, welfare policies/programmes, pension funds, etc., and through cultural factors such as gender, consumer culture and political structures bound in a 'system of redistribution' (Moore, 1994, pp101–106; cf. Pennarz and Niehof, 1999, p. 5). With this concept of system of redistribution, households with one member are included. The above means that the boundaries of the household are fluid rather than solid (Cohen, 1999; Pennarz and Niehof, 1999).

The time spent on unpaid household activities is central when discussing how and why more environmental household activities are performed. Activities that are seen as more environmental friendly, like sorting household waste, and keeping up to date on the environmental consequences of activities and products, can be related to ecological citizenship. Unpaid household work when measured in hours, takes as much time as paid work (Forssell, 2002). It is somewhat difficult to measure and limit what constitutes 'household activities', which is a discussion in itself. Based on our earlier research (Wihlborg and Skill, 2004) we argue that it is as much a question on how activities are conducted as which activities are conducted that matters from an environmental point of view. It is not only important if we travel but how we travel, for example.

Living ecological citizenship – a theoretical approach

There are several green citizenship models. While ecological citizenship has been called for by Andrew Dobson (2003), others have asked for sustainable citizenship. In normative citizenship theories, people who are environmentally friendly are expected to be knowledgeable of and to take responsibility for the environmental consequences of their everyday activities more or less wherever and whenever they arise (Dobson, 2003). Decisions and responsibility are thus closely related. This requires continuous reflection, which to a certain extent counteracts routines, if these are assumed to be unreflected. In normative citizenship theories citizens are further expected to act for reasons beyond concern for personal interest and economic or material benefits, and to make sacrifices for the environment; however, these expectations will be problematized here. In this chapter we argue that this has to be understood in relation to ideas about the current Western society, which Niklas Luhmann for example has characterized as 'hypercomplex' (Luhmann, 1998). This concept helps the discussions about the context where individuals should take decisions and be knowledgeable. Similarly Ulrich Beck when talking about the current society as a risk society, has emphasized that not taking a decision is also a decision, which implies that individuals cannot 'escape' their responsibility (1996).

Here we will show what rights and responsibilities ecological citizenship distributes to citizens, and we will further relate this to traditional discussions about citizenship and what similarities and differences are possible to detect. The section ends with an outline of what an everyday life approach can contribute to an understanding of what environmental citizenship means in practice. In line with Lister (2003), we argue that the emphasis should be on the places and spaces where lived citizenship is practiced.

Environmental[1] or ecological citizenship has to do with the relationship between individuals and the common good (Dobson and Bell, 2006, p. 4). Here we will not be preoccupied so much with the role of the state, as with the interpretations by householders, even if the fact that many environmental problems are transboundary and international in nature and challenge the state as a 'container' of citizenship (Dobson and Bell, 2006). Environmental citizenship has historical roots and is not a completely new phenomenon, relying on feminist discussions. The principles that ecological citizenship builds on have consequences for the definition of political participation, since the ecological challenge demands 'constant' participation and not just in formal elections. It takes time, and demands extensive personal contribution. The environmental consequences of private activities cannot be governed with the same means as public activities, by permissions and controls and it is necessary to rely on voluntarism, or what is called virtue.

Since T. H. Marshall published his famous essay 'Citizenship and Social Class', in the 1950s, which proposes that the ability to perform one's duty as a citizen often depends on a set of enabling conditions, many political theorists have come to add social citizenship to the civil and the political citizenship (MacGregor, 2006). Here we consider that the social citizenship emphasizes the structures and contexts that individuals act within, and to discuss the relationship between actors and structures we use the structuration theory as proposed by Anthony Giddens. This will be discussed in the following section.

Structures and actors

This chapter is activity focused, and investigates the practices and motivations of the studied Swedish householders concerning their relationship with the environment. A central point of departure for our study and analysis is that institutional structures both govern and facilitate individual action, so research should focus on the relationship between structures and agency (Giddens, 1991). With the *theory of structuration* (Giddens, 1989), the aim is to analyse the opportunities and constraints householders perceive in their everyday activities in relation to sustainable development. We will focus on the everyday *doings* that are closely connected to *thinking* about the environment, making the two difficult to separate. Giddens (1989) emphasizes praxis, which is at the intersection between saying and doing as knowledgeable actors. The theory can be productively applied in analysing the householders' knowledge of and reflections on their behaviour and to the analysis of how they justify their activities. The focus on everyday praxis implies that Giddens does not only focus on people's abstract knowledge, but also on how they are able to act and respond to social circumstances in practice. In daily interaction people are aware of social rules. These are central notions for the analysis of sustainable development in the studied households.

At the centre of the structuration theory is the social interaction between actors and structures, systems and institutions, and the extent to which individual actors have 'agency'. Agency refers to doing and the remaking of what is already there (Giddens, 1989). The notion about the relationship between information and behaviour is central in environmental studies, and the idea that when people find out about how certain activities have detrimental environmental effects they will attempt to change these same practices. The central factors from the structuration theory that we want to rely on here concern individual intended activities that may not have the intended (collective) outcomes, and unreflected actions may recreate structures or influence the environment. This is central when trying to steer and govern society in a certain direction – for example towards sustainable development.

Thoughtless action and awareness of environmental consequences

Environmental behaviour is one example of an area where there has been a tendency to politicize 'thoughtless action' (Segerberg, 2005). This has challenged the definition of political participation as encompassing the *intention* behind activities, and related it to the *effects* or consequences of actions (Skill, 2008). The encounter between and mutual construction of actors and structures, in which intended attempts can have unintended consequences, may counteract sustainable development. Structures are normalizing and of various kinds, being material as well as immaterial. Through the way individual actors live everyday life they exercise an influence on the political structures, and similarly are influenced by these very same structures.

It goes without saying that the rationale for performing environmental activities is that they can be motivated by being environmentally friendly. This implies that there is a reason to perform them. Environmental activities thereby have a specific character in relation to other everyday activities that are carried out routinely, or with other motives. We argue here that this has to be understood in relation to the focus on discourse and reflexivity, and the need to motivate behaviour and activities in the current society where Beck (1996) has argued that not taking a decision is a decision as well. However, through the quotidian activities citizenship can be involved in unreflected practices that recreate structures.

When attempting to understand why people act the way they do, we acknowledge that people act out of many different reasons like to feel good about themselves, because they consider the cost or economic value, because they have desires, because they are forced to, because they believe they are expected to, or because they have observed how others do and act in the same way. Through everyday life all these are possible. However, as we will show here, many people relate their actions to the norm of being able to 'rationalize' motivate or explain why they do what they do. In this context the field study showed that the norm of altruism – that people should care about the environment for no other reason than that they are concerned about nature – is present in the ways that the householders argue. This norm motivates questions about the 'true reason' for environmental actions, like when questioning if a certain activity is not *really* performed because it is more economical and not because it is environmentally friendly for example.

When connecting the said and done with the concept praxis like Giddens does, to be 'thinking about the environment' is an activity in itself. This phenomenon can only be understood from the perspective that humans are expected to be able to *motivate their activities*, be knowledgeable about their influences etc. and to be consistent rather than contradictory (Barry, 2006). Barry for example asks whether a person can work at a nuclear power plant and recycle household waste without it being considered to be contradictory. We argue that the householders' practices have to be understood in relation to this ideal of being consistent, and that they are actively comparing different every-day activities against each other. Modern humans are expected to be rational and consistent. However, this aspect has to be understood in relation to the fact that it would be practically impossible to reflect on *all* alternatives, or on the environmental consequences of all activities. If a person did that she/he would probably be paralysed (Giddens, 1996). This has to be taken into account when demanding that citizens should take responsibility for the environmental consequences of their everyday activities.

Summing up our theoretical discussion before moving on to the description and analysis of the material, we consider that individual actors and structures are mutually constructed, and structures influence individual ecological action space (Skill, 2008). Structures contribute with ways to interpret what is possible and doable, like ideas about the responsibility for the environment as well as suggestions for what to do. This is what makes it possible to find patterns in the ways people reason about their responsibility.

Everyday life as process – contextualizing environmental practices

In this chapter we argue that individual environmental activities can not be separated from the ongoing process of living everyday life, and that this has to be taken into account when discussing ecological citizenship. This argument is put forth by illustrating how activities take place in structures and how structures guide what activities are performed by individual actors (Giddens, 1989).

Even if it is possible to argue that most human activities have environmental consequences of one sort or another, there are only some activities that are labelled 'environmental activities'. Several researchers have attempted to deal with the idea of 'sustainable lifestyles' and concluded that there are no evident ways to conceptualize what defines a sustainable lifestyle (Brand, 1997; Hallin, 1999; Spaargaren, 2003). We argue that the difficulty implied in attempting to define a complete 'lifestyle' is due to the continuous performance of activities, and also bifurcation. We use the word bifurcation to highlight that each decision or activity, when examined closely, tends to divide into further decisions like a big tree with many branches. It is only when focusing on a specific and narrowly defined activity that it is possible to measure if it is environmentally friendly or not and, as we will show later, it also depends on what it is compared to. After this introduction we will now move on to illustrate our arguments with examples from the interviews from the study.

In everyday life different goals and demands may imply that environmentally friendly activities that the householders know of and can talk about are put aside to reach other more immediate or what may seem as more important goals. This can be characterized as to muddle through everyday life, and to get different goals to come together. A typical illustration of this was Beatrice and Burt, a couple with three children, who discussed environmental policies in the following way. We consider that it illustrates how responsibility is constructed and distributed among actors:

> Beatrice: [The environmental policy] should make things easier for people. It shouldn't be a hassle. There is so much pressure on people these days. I feel the schools put a lot more responsibility on parents these days than they did when we were kids. And you are supposed to have a career and a beautiful, well-kept home. There is just so much. And then you are supposed to be environmentally aware too, so it really has to be easy. Recycling stations have to be nearby, and there shouldn't be such big price differences. Maybe more sustainable products could be subsidized. Making active choices shouldn't affect families so much. You shouldn't be in the position of not being able to afford to make the choice.

> Burt: Exactly, it all depends on time and money.

What they focus on is the state structure that they as individuals and householders act in. They also give attention to the relationship between unpaid household tasks like recycling waste, and economic aspects, which seem common in environmental studies. These individual environmentally friendly activities have to be understood in relation to everyday life as a complex whole.

In line with what especially feminist scholars, in particular, have emphasized, it is important to highlight the unpaid aspects of everyday activities and requirements to perform environmentally friendly activities. Someone has to perform the activities, and responsibilities are distributed among actors. As was discussed in the theoretical section above, studies have indicated how certain activities tend to be gendered, and how unpaid household duties are performed to a larger extent by women (MacGregor, 2006). In our study we found that while women tend to perform unpaid household activities indoor, like maintaining the home and keeping it clean, and be responsible for the grocery shopping and involved in environmental decisions, the men performed unpaid activities outdoor like maintaining the car, or taking recyclable goods to the recycling station, and were responsible for energy decisions and the maintenance of the house. We did thus not find that men or women perform more or less environmentally friendly activities, but that the responsibility for different environmental activities is gendered. However, both men and women stated that it requires time to keep up to date on different consequences, and to perform the environmental friendly activities.

COMPLEXITY

Ecological citizenship can be considered to be a holistic political condition that requires consistency in practices across different contexts (Barry, 2006). An example of this way of thinking is the demand to change whole lifestyles and adapt to be more environmentally friendly. But is it possible to change just some practices, or is it a question of 'all or nothing'? In this section we will discuss complexities like how to choose between different activities or to abstain; how to know which is a 'better' alternative, and in relation to what; and the difficulties involved in monitoring the environmental consequences of everyday activities.

Through the case study with the householders, complexity proved to be a central issue in several ways. Firstly, it is difficult to monitor the environmental consequences of individual activities due to complex consumption and production processes. Secondly, complexity plays a role as a challenge to decide what environmental activities that the householders decide to perform, and what rationale those decisions are based on.

Several of the householders mentioned that they could purchase organic products or environmentally labelled products. Women, in particular, said that they buy organic fruit and vegetables with the motivation that they believe it is healthier for their children. Lucy, a woman in her early 30s, was among the few who reasoned about the relationship between consuming environmentally labelled products and the quantities used:

> Lucy: You wonder anyway, when I use a lot of detergent, and it has an environmental label, is it still 'good' for the environment?

It is a minor example, which, however, emphasizes the discussion of what individual activities are compared to, and what queries are involved in taking environmental responsibility through everyday decisions.

Another equally important issue to examine in this chapter is the relationship between abstract and general descriptions and what we described as bifurcation above, such as 'doing laundry', and specific details, which is where many environmentally friendly suggestions fit, such as the type of washing machine, how much energy it requires, at what temperature the laundry is washed, what detergent and softener are used, how full the machine is, whether the wet laundry is dried by hanging it or putting it in a tumble dryer, whether the dryer is energy efficient, what energy source is used, and finally who does the activity. Such *specification* and *concretization* make everyday life very complex when it comes to investigating practices that support sustainable development, since almost every detail of an activity has an alternative. This plays a part in deciding what is a better alternative, something that is discussed in the following section.

How to know which is a 'better' alternative, and in relation to what?

There has been a debate going on within environmental studies in relation to green theories and the deliberative turn to asking for more public participation, and a central question that has been raised is 'what happens if democratic processes produce the "wrong" environmental outcomes?' (Dobson and Bell, 2006:14). However, the fear that people will take the 'wrong' decisions, implicitly assumes that there is a 'right' decision. What we want to argue here is that the idea of – at least just one – right decision is a chimera.

Just like Barry argues, the requirement to keep up to date can be considered a part-time job (Barry, 2006). But stating that it is a part-time job doesn't emphasize enough that no matter how much the householders search for an answer, there might not be just one single answer for how to behave environmentally friendly since different values and different rationalities can be involved. An individual activity can be measured in the long perspective, or the immediate perspective like saving the polar ice for future generations or getting the kids home from kindergarten, help combating structures that create poverty or having a snack to stave off the immediate hunger. Of course there are plenty examples of win–win activities, which in turn are dependent on how society is organized, and what enabling structures exist, which we mentioned above.

Recycling household waste was the most commonly mentioned environmental household activity in our study that the householders said that they performed. The fact that the householders pondered on its relevance was therefore not very surprising. The complexity involved in what might seem like a simple decision – to recycle or not recycle, however, reveals what we consider to be an example of complexity. The complexity concerned expressions like – is it better to use hot water, which requires energy, to clean the containers that are to be taken to the recycling station, what is lost when taking the recyclable containers to the recycling station by car, is it better to burn newspaper or cardboard in municipalities where it becomes district heating, and what is the relation between using new natural resources and the energy required for the recycling process? A common way to calculate whether recycling was efficient or not was illustrated by Regina:

> **Regina:** If you wash a can made of aluminium, and use hot running water, then you have spent the energy savings you would have acquired if you had walked with it to the station, apart from the fact that a can is made of raw material. Just a thing like that. You should not wash the cans too thoroughly, and with cold water. But who wants to keep containers at home that are not thoroughly cleaned?

This example relates to the difficulties in deciding whether it makes sense to recycle and how values collide when different issues are included in the calculation. Because different rationalities (e.g. economic, environmental, energy related and cleanliness) can be used, these conflicts can be difficult to solve. Furthermore, the concern with keeping the home nice and clean was mainly raised by the female participants in this study.

In several of the municipal policies that have been analysed in this study an environmentally friendly suggestion for individuals is to reduce trips by car. This was also expressed by the householders as an environmentally friendly activity that they knew of, and which they said that they possibly could do. However, it is obvious that the car was used to organize everyday life, and reducing trips by car seemed to be difficult. Using the car implied further considerations. This illustrates how an environmental ideal can be neglected when everyday life is lived.

> **Burt:** We were looking and now I have found one [recycling station] on the way to work, which I pass anyway. Because, if you have to make an extra trip with the car, you lose what you have gained. [laughs] And then it is not that environmentally friendly anymore. Then you might just as well throw it in the regular waste.

The householders often paid attention to the relationship between activities, and in this case Burt was estimating what was most efficient.

Another issue to discuss in relation to complexity concerned who to trust, and how to judge information that is used to make up one's opinion in order to take decisions for environmentally friendly activities.

> **Michael:** You don't really know that much … This is a problem – should one act in line with what one believes or what one knows? If you only act in line with what you know, then perhaps you shouldn't act at all. Then you can't do anything, because how much does one know?

This illustrates how complexity, questions of whom one can trust, and variability of information even can result in passivity. It is easy to make comparisons to the concept 'hypercomplexity' that Luhmann (1998) has suggested.

Since there are hardly ever any 'once and for all good' practices, it comes as no surprise that the householders have decided to perform (a few of) what they consider environmentally friendly activities, like recycling domestic waste. This is part of simplifications that we will talk about later in the chapter.

Another issue that deals with complexity is the difficulty involved in measuring the environmental consequences of activities. It is obvious that this has to do with those descriptions and visualizations of environmental consequences that the householders trust, even if this was not mentioned by the householders themselves. One specific expression of this was when Roger, a man in his early 50s, said that:

Roger: There is a large step between taking recyclable goods to the recycling station and to notice any improvements in the environment.

Our last point of discussion in relation to complexity therefore is concerned with the fact that it is hard to notice any immediate improvements in the environment. It is also difficult to measure the individual contribution, for example to the general air quality by bicycling to work instead of taking the car. In the following section we will discuss how the householders gave expression of what we call compensatory practices in their everyday life.

COMPENSATORY PRACTICES AND DOING WHAT IS REASONABLE

The demand for consistency will be discussed in this section by using illustrations of how the householders argued about what we have termed compensatory practices. These compensatory practices are in line with the householders not wanting to abstain from certain activities, at the same time as they want to contribute by doing something for the environment, and thereby show that they take responsibility.

As described above, all the householders in the case studies proved to be aware of what they called environmental friendly activities, and they could discuss the environmental consequences of various everyday practices. They also described how they perform some of these activities. These practices are motivated by guilty conscience, and the desire to be a good citizen, and are related to how they navigate among different activities when living everyday life. In short, it contextualizes the environmentally friendly activities in the wider everyday life.

An illustrative example of what we call a compensatory practice was to argue like Vanda, a 40-year-old woman, and mother of two, living in Växjö municipality:

Vanda: I feel a little like a villain sometimes because I drive so much, but we recycle as much as we can.

This way of reasoning about recycling, and the central position that recycling had in the study, can be considered as a way to excuse other less environmentally benevolent practices. It concerns what is reasonable to do, and what environmentally motivated activities are incorporated in the householders' everyday life. This illustration has to be understood in relation to the expressed limit to what the householders are willing to do among the environmentally friendly activities that they know of. While it is possible to argue that it is environmentally better to abstain from performing certain activities, like flying by airplane or consuming large amounts of meat, often the choice is made between two or more alternatives where one might have a lesser environmental impact, i.e. be less bad. The morally influenced idea of abstinence has a central position in many green theories, which consider 'desires' a prime reason for the ecological crisis (Naess, 1981). This has been expressed through the slogan 'small is beautiful' (Schumacher, 1974) which was possible to detect in the municipal policies for sustainable development that were examined in the current study. An example of this is the policy as expressed by Växjö municipality:

> Commit yourself to quality: do not choose poor quality goods that soon need to be disposed of or semi-manufactured articles. Commit yourself to quality of life: go to the movies and dine out instead of purchasing products. (Växjö, 2006)

To abstain from certain environmentally negative activities was discussed by the householders, often spontaneously, which indicates that the notion is part of a social norm that they related to. Often the householders expressed that they were not willing to sacrifice their 'quality of life' by abstaining from activities that they knew could have a bad environmental influence. Several of the householders stated that 'there is a limit to what I am willing to do'. This is where we find it interesting to contextualize their everyday in relation to their environmental consciousness and knowledge. Taking this as a point of departure our argument – along with several other environmental researchers – is that information and becoming aware is never enough for changing peoples practices, they need systems and enabling structures to act within, and some 'conflicts' simply seem difficult to deal with due to other values in life.

SIMPLIFICATIONS

The overall aim of this chapter is to discuss how the householders deal with their environmental responsibility or, expressed differently, how they understand and manage general expectations to be good (ecological) citizens. We argue that it is possible to detect similar norms in the ways that the householders reason, as in the discussions that are found among scholars. Using Giddens' terminology this can be considered as an example of the hermeneutic circle between social sciences and society (Giddens, 1989).

It would be practically impossible to reflect on the environmental consequences of all everyday activities. In the section about complexity above we discussed how the intricacies of everyday life can make it difficult to compare which activities are 'better'. In one way systems like environmental labels or recycling stations help to facilitate the decisions for what environmental activities to perform. They simplify complexity.

Ulla described how she gets anxious about the excessive number of issues that she needs to understand to reach the ideal of being environmentally friendly. Again it is fruitful to keep the notion of hypercomplexity in mind. Ulla and Ulrik discussed in the following way about the expectation to keep up to date:

Ulrik: That's the thing about 'development', it can be positive or negative, but now we have such a wide range of choices that it requires more time [to make up one's mind].

Ulla: I know what you mean. I long for the old grocery stores with a limited range of products that have just about what I need. I don't want to be confronted with shelves filled with different products. I feel like screaming at all the different brands of cornflakes. This one has a lot of sugar, that one has a little, and all the additives. And you try to find the place of origin of the cookies and can't find it.

The way that Ulla discusses the labels of contents and how she attempts to judge a product depending on what it contains can be related to the descriptions of how environmental labels on food are simplifications.

Another issue concerning complexity is that what at a first glance may seem like better alternatives, such as recycling or buying an eco-car, can turn out to be complex and difficult to decide on. This dilemma was illustrated when Anna said the following:

Anna: We could exchange our car for an ethanol car, but they too have problems.

Her argument points to the complexity implied in determining what the most environmentally friendly alternative is. Since it is almost impossible to evaluate all possible options, the householders referred to certain symbolical or typical activities that they know of.

Some social scientists who have focused on the environmental challenge have predicted that our current complex society will cause people to *doubt* and be concerned about environmental risks; the other side of the coin is that since we cannot comprehend everything, we need to *trust* other actors (Beck, 1995, 1996; Giddens, 1998). Trust is a way to deal with, or manage, instability and unpredictability. How Paul responded to a question about his energy system is informative on this point:

Paul: Well, with all the choices that exist nowadays, it is a bit too much. One can't spend time investigating everything.

Here he referred to his limited time, opportunities and interest to find and scrutinize different options when taking environmentally informed decisions in his everyday life. His way of dealing with complexity was to imitate his neighbours, by installing district heating, thereby handing over the judgment to others. In a way, the discussion about trust is similar to what we call simplification, since it deals with how people manage and relate to environmental complexities and choices.

A field that relates to trust as well as simplification is the way several women discussed organic labels on fruit and vegetables. An illustration of this common way of reasoning among the women was given by Ylva, when the interviewer asked a follow-up question in relation to her mentioning that she found organic products important:

Interviewer: What do you think is the motivation for buying KRAV or organic products?

Ylva: I imagine that they are healthier and better quality, though of course I haven't checked up on that. I mean, we don't read everything; it is more like one trusts that they are better. Especially for the kids – it feels a lot better to give them an organic-labelled banana.

Like Ylva, some other women claimed that they trusted the labels, though they had never checked them out. The labels were generally trusted even by the men, and the purchase of them was mentioned as an important way to act environmentally friendly.

Perhaps it is impossible to lead an ecologically sustainable everyday life; one can only lead a less environmentally negative everyday life. Thereby ecological sustainability can be seen as a *stage* or *process* that is in line with considering everyday life as ongoing. The householders have tended to focus on a specific set of activities or what is possible to describe as 'symbolic activities' as a practice to deal with complexity since it is impossible to comprehend everything. As Giddens has emphasized, anyone who attended to environmental risks all the time would most likely be considered to have a mental disorder (1996). Subduing risks and trusting others, such as experts, officials or a household partner, is thus a viable way in contemporary society.

ANALYSIS – IMPLICATIONS OF AN EVERYDAY LIFE APPROACH FOR CITIZENSHIP

Everyday life is made up of a multitude of activities and each and everyone can have more or less benevolent consequences for the environment when placed under the magnifying glass. By using the word bifurcation we have discussed how many choices about environmental consequences tend to lead to more choices. This is why we have argued that a person who constantly evaluated the environmental consequences of each individual activity would not have time for anything else. This is where routines and habits play a role, something which has only been discussed briefly, however.

Since this text is activity focused we have argued that politics and citizenship is practiced through everyday life where individual citizens may attempt to create new structures or recreate existing ones, concerning for example environmental responsibility or ideas about the right to a safe environment. We consider structures to be made up of discursive and material relations that are interconnected through feedback loops. To give an example, a person can act environmentally friendly without expressing motivations for the action or considering it as 'environmentally friendly'. Similarly a person can be motivated to perform a specific activity by it being 'environmentally friendly' even if they are necessarily motivated in this way by another person. This is what we call the relationship between 'said and done' and how people are motivated, interpret, reflect on or excuse their individual activities and responsibilities for the environment. An activity that is 'excused' is most probably based on something that is not socially acceptable, there is a social norm surrounding it. It is also fundamental in activity focused studies to recognize that people recreate structures through actions and discourses; a person can attempt to influence others by showing them, or attempt to be a role model. This is why it is important to highlight that existing systems like recycling stations or ecological labels on products communicate a message to people, and when people are using or ignoring them they are (re)created. We have argued for a political model that not only takes expressed intentions and motivations into account, but also recognizes unintended consequences and behaviour, and how politics is done and practiced, i.e. the collective outcome of individual efforts and actions.

In the chapter we have focused on expressions of environmental responsibilities. The attention given to responsibilities rather than rights is based on the fact that responsibilities are both central in ecological citizenship theories and the right to a safe environment was more or less absent in the interview material. The participants in this study have expressed that they do have a responsibility for the environment through their everyday activities like what they decide to purchase in the grocery store, how they decide to travel, and how they care for their household waste among other things. However, when we have analysed how the participants in this study discuss their responsibility and how they decide on how to act we have found three important aspects that in many ways concern complexity and the challenges that are posed in deciding what the most environmentally friendly practice is. This in turn is interpreted to be due to the fact that decisions for how to act can be based on different rationalities, and different values and goals.

- Complexity: there are several aspects of complexity. Activities can have several meanings and rationalities, which mean that one activity can be viewed from different perspectives. There is further complexity in the sense that it is difficult to monitor all environmental consequences, and decide how to measure one against the other, what we call point of comparison – it depends on whether an individual activity is judged against abstaining from performing it, consequences in the long or short term etc.
- Householders can apply 'compensatory practices' in their everyday life and exchange one environmental friendly activity with another in order to contribute with something. We argue that this is done in relation to the perceived idea that they need to show that they actually do take responsibility, and are 'conscious' and show that they know the environmental consequences of their everyday activities.
- 'Simplifications' – which is another way to deal with complexity, to muddle through the complexity of everyday life, i.e. it is not possible to be conscious or reflect about everything.

In line with our theoretical framework (Giddens, 1989) the focus has been on the everyday practices. We argue that it is not only important to give attention to pro-environmental attitudes, but also to how the householders describe their practices. The householders' everyday practices can create or recreate social structures, which in turn interact with material struc-tures and environmental conditions. This is a way to extend the feminist argument that the 'private is political' to environmental studies, since the individual activities have conse-quences for the collective environment.

The policy implications of our study indicates that since the participants in the study express moral responsibility for the environment and others, aiming at increasing people's feelings of responsibility (awareness or consciousness about environmental consequences of household activities) should not be the focus for environmental policies. We suggest that policies directed to house-holders should focus on comparisons between different activities in order to help out with the simplification of complex issues, which further acknowledges that there is not just one correct practice. As emphasized through the text, it is only when everyday life is fragmented into separate activities that it is possible to judge whether an activity is 'better or worse' in environmental terms. Since everyday life makes up a complex whole it is difficult to talk about 'sustainable lifestyles'. Our findings further indicate that individuals need supporting struc-tures, which they of course always can contribute to, or help to create, which is why we talk about householders as both users of, and (re)creators of, structures in order not to individualize the responsibility. This is in line with what many political theorists have recognized, namely that the ability to perform one's duty as a citizen often depends on a set of enabling conditions (Yuval-Davis, 1997; MacGregor, 2006). To meet the complexity we further support 'progres-sive' policies where householders who already perform certain activities are suggested to try out new environmentally friendly ones.

CONCLUDING REMARKS

The aim of this chapter has been to focus on the everyday practices of house-holds and how environmental activities are integrated in their everyday lives, and then analyse how these practices are connected to the rights and responsi-bilities of environmental citizenship. In the chapter we have also examined what a household is and how to think about the individualization of environmental responsibility in citizenship theory. By using the structuration theory we discussed the requirements for changing individual practices towards more sustainable development, and showed that individuals always act within struc-tures. These structures are both material and social and can influence the recreation of unsustainable practices, but by giving individuals agency, the possi-bility for change exist. What we have discussed at length is the complexity that is involved in the individualization of environmental responsibility, and how the householders manage this.

Three themes emerged through the examination of in-depth studies of daily life in Swedish households with a specific focus on environmentally friendly activities: complexity, compensatory practices and simplifications. We have argued that with a comprehensive understanding of the everyday context where different activities are performed by householders, it is possible to understand the obstacles and opportunities for implementing sustainable development and environmental responsibilities in the household sphere. The three themes concern how environmental responsibility is understood by the householders in an everyday context, and how they manage the complexity involved in taking environmentally informed decisions. These conclusions contributed to suggestions for policies to attempt to create comparisons between the environmental impact of different activities in order to help out with the simplification of complex issues. It is further relevant to acknowledge that there is usually not just one correct practice. In order not to individualize the environmental responsibility it seems important to create and maintain enabling systems.

NOTE

1   Dobson (2003) has argued for a distinction between environmental and ecological citizenship. He relates environmental citizenship to liberal and republican models of democracy/citizenship, while ecological citizenship is distinct from these two models. A common distinction between the ecological and environmental has been to view ecological movements as wanting to *reform* the modern industrial society, and environmental movements as wanting simply to *mitigate the negative impacts* of industrial society (Bennulf, 1994, p. 64).

REFERENCES

Aarhus Convention (1998) *Convention on Access to Information, Public Participation in Decision-making and Access to Justice in Environmental Matters*, Internet: www.unece.org/env/pp/, accessed August 18, 2008.

Åberg, H. (2004) *Boendeperspektiv på hushållsavfall och på system för insamling och behandling i Västra Hamnen, Malmö* [The Householders' Perspective on Waste and Systems for Collection and Treatment in Västra Hamnen, Malmö], Research Report No. 37, Department of Home Economics, Gothenburg University.

Ahrne, G. (1994) *Social Organizations: Interaction Inside, Outside and Between Organizations*, Sage Publications, London.

Ahrne, G., and C. Roman (1997) *Hemmet barnen och makten. Förhandlingar om arbete och pengar i familjen* [The Home, the Children and Power. Negotiation about Work and Money in the Family], Fritzes, Stockholm.

Barry, J. (2006) 'Resistance is Fertile: From Environmental to Sustainability Citizenship', in A. Dobson, and D. Bell (Eds.), *Environmental Citizenship*, MIT Press, Cambridge.

Beck, U. (1995) *Ecological Politics in an Age of Risk*, Polity Press, Cambridge.

Beck, U. (1996) *Att uppfinna det politiska: Bidrag till en teori om reflexiv modernisering* [Inventing the Political: Contributions to a Theory of Reflexive Modernization], Daidalos, Uddevalla.

Bennulf, M. (1994) *Miljöopinionen i Sverige* [Public Opinion about the Environment in Sweden], Dissertation, Dialogos, Lund.

Bladh, M. (2005) *Hushållens elförbrukning: utvecklingen totalt och i detalj 1980-2000* [The Use of Electricity in Households: The Development in Total and in Detail 1980–2000], Working Paper 291, Tema Technology and Social Change, Linköping University.

Brand, K.-W. (1997) 'Environmental Consciousness and Behaviour: The Greening of Lifestyles', In M. Redclift and G. Woodgate (Eds.), *The International Handbook of Environmental Sociology*, Edward Elgar, Cheltenham.

Cohen, J. (1999) 'The Artisan's Society of Santa Ana del Valle, Oaxaca, Mexico: Household Competition and Cooperative Management', In D. Small and N. Tannenbaum (Eds.), *At the Interface: The Household and Beyond*, University Press of America, New York.

Dobson, A. (2003) *Citizenship and the Environment*, Oxford University Press, Oxford.

Dobson, A., and D. Bell (Eds.) (2006) *Environmental Citizenship*, MIT Press, Cambridge.

Ellegård, K., and E. Wihlborg (2001) 'Metoder för att studera och analysera vardagen', [Methods to Study and Analyse Everyday Life], In K. Ellegård and E. Wihlborg (eds.), *Fånga vardagen ett tvärvetenskapligt perspektiv* [Catching Everyday Life from an Interdisciplinary Perspective], Studentlitteratur, Lund.

Fenstermaker Berk, S. (1985) *The Gender Factory: The Apportionment of Work in American Households*, Plenum, New York.

Forssell, J. (2002) *Hushållsproduktion och föräldraledighet: Att städa, tvätta och laga mat – med och utan barn* [Household Production and Parental Leave: To Clean, Cook and Wash With and Without Children], Dissertation, Linköping University.

Gardiner, M. (2000) *Critiques of Everyday Life*, Routledge, London.

Giddens, A. (1989) *The Constitution of Society: Outline of the Theory of Structuration*, Polity Press, Cornvall.

Giddens, A. (1991) *Modernity and Self-identity: Self and Society in the Late Modern Age*, Polity Press, Cornwall.

Giddens, A. (1996) *Modernitetens följder* [Consequences of Modernity], Studentlitteratur, Lund.

Giddens, A. (1998) *The Third Way: The Renewal of Social Democracy*, Polity Press, Cambridge.

Hallin, P. O. (1999) 'Miljöforskningen och det problematiska livsstilsbegreppet', [Environmental Research and the Problematic Concept of Lifestyle], In L. J. Lundgren (Ed.), *Livsstil och miljö: värderingar, val och vanor* [Lifestyle and Environment: Values, Choices and Habits], Swedish Environmental Protection Agency, Stockholm.

Highmore, B. (2002) *Everyday Life and Cultural Theory: An Introduction*, Routledge, London.

Hook, N., and B. Paolucci (1970) 'The Family as an Eco System', *Journal of Home Economics*, Vol. 62, pp315–318.

Linnér, B.-O. (1998) *The World Household: George Borgström and the Postwar Population-Resource Crisis*, Dissertation, Kanaltryckeriet, Motala.

Lister, R. (2003) *Citizenship: Feminist Perspectives*, Palgrave Macmillan, Basingstoke.

Luhmann, N. (1998) *Observations on Modernity*, Stanford University Press, Stanford.

MacGregor, S. (2006) 'No Sustainability without Justice: A Feminist Critique of Environmental Citizenship', In A. Dobson and D. Bell (Eds.), *Environmental Citizenship*, MIT Press, Cambridge.

Mies, M., and V. Shiva (1993) *Ecofeminism*, Zed Books, London.

Moore, H. (1994) *A Passion for Difference: Essays in Anthropology and Gender*, Polity Press, Cambridge.
Naess, A. (1981) *Ecology, Community and Lifestyle: Outline of an Ecosophy*, Cambridge University Press, Cambridge.
Noorman, K. J. and T. Schoot Uiterkamp (Eds.) (1998) *Green Households? Domestic Consumers, Environment and Sustainability*, Earthscan, London.
Oslo Declaration of Sustainable Consumption (2005) Internet: www.scorenetwork.org/files/-OsloDeclaration.pdf#search=%22oslo%20declaration %20sustainable%20consumption%22, accessed August 21, 2006.
Pennartz, P., and A. Niehof (1999) *The Domestic Domain: Chances, Choices and Strategies of Family Households*, Ashgate, Aldershot.
Schumacher, E. F. (1974) *Small is Beautiful: A Study of Economics as if People Matter*, Sphere, London.
Segerberg, A. (2005) *Thinking Doing: The Politicisation of Thoughtless Action*, Dissertation, Elanders Gotab, Stockholm.
Shanahan, H. (2003) 'Hushållet – navet i livssystemet' [The Household as the Hub of the Life System]. In K. Ellegård, and L. Sturesson (Eds.), *Konsumenterna och makten: att använda och bevara resurserna* [The Consumers and Power: To Use and Conserve Resources], Carlsson, Stockholm.
Shanahan, H., A. Carlsson-Kanyama, and M. Pipping Ekström (2002) "Exploring Opportunities for Eco-sound Food Habits. Households and Research in Partnership," *Kappa Omicron FORUM*, Vol. 14, No 1, pp1–15.
Shove, E. (2003) *Comfort, Cleanliness and Convenience: The Social Organization of Normality*, Berg, Oxford.
Skill, K. (2008) *(Re)Creating Ecological Action Space: Householders' Activities for Sustainable Development*, Dissertation No 449, Linköping University.
Smith, D. E. (1987) *The Everyday World as Problematic – A Feminist Sociology*, Northeastern University Press, Boston, MA.
Sontag, S., and M. Bubolz (1996) *Families on Small Farms*, Michigan State University, East Lansing, MI.
Spaargaren, G. (2003) 'Sustainable Consumption: A Theoretical and Environmental Policy Perspective', *Society and Natural Resources*, Vol. 16, pp687–701.
Szerszynski, B. (2006) 'Local Landscapes and Global Belongings: Toward a Situated Citizenship of the Environment', In A. Dobson and D. Bell (Eds.), *Environmental Citizenship*, MIT Press, Cambridge.
UNCED (1993) *Agenda 21 Förenta Nationernas konferens om miljö och utveckling* [The United Nation's Conference on Environment and Development], Vol. II, Nordstedts Tryckeri AB, Stockholm.
Växjö (2006) 'Du behövs för ett hållbart Växjö' [You are needed for a Sustainable Växjö], and 'Miljötips för vardagen' [Environmental Suggestions for Everyday Life], Internet: www.vaxjo.se/vaxjowww/utsidan/omraderubrik_under.asp? rubrik=2839&omrade=125&meny=1963, accessed August 3, 2006.
Wendt Höjer, M., and C. Åse (2001) *Politikens paradoxer: en introduktion till feministisk politisk teori* [Paradoxes of Politics: An Introduction to Feminist Political Theory], Academia Adacta, Lund.
Wihlborg, E., and K. Skill (2004) *Jämställd hållbar framtid: Idéer och vardag i samspel* [Gender Equal Sustainable Future: Ideas and Everyday Life in Interplay], Report 5422 Swedish Environmental Protection Agency, Stockholm.
Wilk, R. (Ed.) (1989) *The Household Economy: Reconsidering the Domestic Mode of Production*, Westview Press, Boulder, CO.

Yanagisako, S. J. (1979) 'Family and Household: The Analysis of Domestic Groups', *Annual Review of Anthropology*, Vol. 8, pp161-205.
Yuval-Davis, N. (1997) *Gender and Nation*, Sage Publications, London.

4

Sticks, carrots and legitimate policies – Effectiveness and acceptance in Swedish environmental public policy

Simon Matti

INTRODUCTION

As already has been noted in the introductory chapters, a basic premise for this book is that current environmental policy objectives are unique in that a significant responsibility for performing pro-environmental activities and attaining political goals is found at the household level, especially in the many choices and activities that shape daily life. There is broad political and scientific consensus that the causes of current environmental problems, and thus many of the solutions to them, are found not only in the general policy decisions made by politicians at various levels or by the business community, but also in myriad everyday deliberations of individuals. The household, and ultimately the individual members who make up the household, thus hold a key role also in the practical effort towards achieving ecologically sustainable development. This 'individualistic turn' of environmental politics, however, also implies new challenges for political government. Increasingly, it highlights the necessity for policy-makers on all levels of government to construct new public policies that effectively initiate and sustain collective pro-environmental action on the individual level, and in a long-term perspective.

This challenge certainly requires that technical policy aspects, such as the selection, design and functioning of policy tools, are considered in both the decision-making and implementtation stages. However, for political government to successfully combat environmental degradation, by integrating environmental considerations as a social-choice mechanism determining individuals' lifestyles and selection of daily activities, I here propose that public policies to this effect need also to enjoy a certain measure of *legitimacy*. It is imperative that the public, towards whom these political aspirations are directed, views policy goals, as well as the tools used to attain these goals, as morally acceptable in the sense that they build on or can be justified by reference to core values and beliefs established in society (see, for examples Lipset, 1981; North, 1990; Beetham, 1991; Maio and Olsen, 1995; Widegren, 1998). Thus, effectiveness and efficiency when implementing political programmes must, in the endeavour of mediating or overcoming the collective-action problem, be complemented by a fundamental legitimacy for the public policy itself. In other words, policy performance is not only a question of decision-makers and implementators doing things right, but concerns also the question of them doing the right thing in the first place.

In this chapter, I therefore approach Swedish household-oriented environmental public policy from a perspective of legitimacy. I set off by proposing how the concept of policy legitimacy should be thought of and empirically explored, including its significance for environmental policy performance. Thereafter, I turn to the case of Sweden, examining the current degree of legitimacy for household-oriented environmental policy as well as the prospects and prerequisites for designing more legitimate policies in the future.

THREE ASPECTS OF THE POLICY LEGITIMACY PROBLEM

Political government can ensure behavioural change through the use of several different policy tools. Vedung (1998), for instance, broadly categorizes these as the stick, the carrot and the sermon, respectively. And true enough, contemporary environmental politics abounds with judicial-regulative economic and informative policy tools in use to make societal actors behave according to political sustainability aspirations. However, regardless of whether behavioural change is perceived as requiring a coercive power regulating daily activities or some form of 'indirect steering' (cf. Lundqvist, 2001b), a further necessary component in the process of governing individual environmental responsibility-taking in a long-term perspective is the legitimacy of the public policy itself. Any attempt to ensure public compliance with a policy's requirements will become less successful as the degree of legitimacy for the policy decreases. Thus, designing legitimate policies presents a core challenge for policy-makers, in particular those dealing with environmental issues requiring a broad and continuous public participation, and focusing legitimacy in the policy-making process might be a key to solving or at least reducing other problems related to policy efficiency and outcome.

In its most basic connotation, legitimacy refers to the normative, moral grounds underpinning the rightfulness or justifiability of political power. For example, Lipset (1981, p. 64) defines it as 'the capacity of the [political] system to engender and maintain the belief that the existing political institutions are the most appropriate ones for the society'; Hanberger (2003, p. 268) refers to legitimacy broadly as 'citizens' support for a policy order and a regime'; and Coicaud (2002, p. 10) defines legitimacy as 'the recognition of the right to govern'. In studies of the legitimacy of regimes, an important relation between the concepts of political *legitimacy* and political *authority* has also been suggested, where the former underpins the latter and, thus, creates the right for, e.g. a state or a government to expect obedience from its citizens when exercising its power (Buchanan, 2002, 2003). Legitimacy here connects to the normative acceptability of collective decisions, and the understanding of them as morally binding even though they might conflict with immediate personal preferences or interests. This connotation turns slightly away from explicit questions on the mere existence or stability of a regime, and towards a focus on the functioning of political government. Defining legitimacy as a measure of acquiescence indicates the instrumental importance of a regime's legitimacy for its exercise of political power, where a government enjoying a high level of legit-imacy has considerably lower costs associated with monitoring and enforcing public compliance with its decisions. For instance, ' government that is regarded as legitimate should not have to use force over more than a very small minority of its citizens, just as army officers should not have to constantly put their men on disciplinary charges and police officers should not often have to use their batons' (Birch, 2001, p. 57; see also Stoker, 1998; Parkinson, 2003). A range of empirical studies has also pointed towards this connection between high levels of legitimacy and correspondingly higher levels of voluntary compliance (Tyler, 1990; Hønneland, 1999; Rova, 2004; Fell, 2006; Stern, 2008). Similarly, Beetham (1991, p. 29, emphasis added) acknowledges this line of reasoning by concluding that...

> *...legitimacy is significant not only for the maintenance of order, but also for the* degree *of cooperation and* quality *of performance that the powerful can secure from the subordinate; it is important not only for whether they remain 'in power', but for* what their power can be used to achieve.

When exchanging the prefix of legitimacy, from political (i.e. the legitimacy of regimes) to policy, a similar functional argument applies. The legitimacy of public policies, therefore, affects both whether a government achieves its polit-ical aspirations within a specific policy area, as well as its possibilities for achieving a high level of policy performance in future decisions. In the first place, the issue of *ex-post legitimacy* calls to attention the effect legitimacy has on the performance of already decided-on policy, in particular in those instances where the exercise of political power is in need of continuous public support or voluntary acceptance. Legitimacy affects the way in which policy goals and strategies are understood, received and responded to by the public, and is thereby expected to induce a moral foundation for compliance. To a certain extent, governments can introduce new legislation to ensure policy compliance, but the effectiveness and efficiency of legal rules, and thereby their ability to govern behaviour in a long-term perspective, nevertheless depends on the extent to which the underpinning policy enjoys legitimacy among the public. For example, following March and Olsen (1989, 2004), legislation expressed preferred norms of behaviour, and in this they also embody a specific set of values and beliefs. Legitimacy of the rule, where people share the values making up its underpinning principles reduces the cost for monitoring and enforcing compliance, as people will follow the rule as it is seen as 'natural, rightful, expected and legitimate' (March and Olsen, 2004, p. 3; see also Beetham, 1991). On the other hand, if people find the formal rules in use to be in some way or another inappropriate, unjust or disproportional, the cost for monitoring will rise rapidly, making it increasingly difficult for the state to maintain a cooperative situation (Widegren, 1998; Ostrom, 2005).

To consider also the legitimacy of new rules is therefore an imperative task when designing public policy, as it can be reasonably assumed that an implementation of new formal institutions does not automatically change either values or behaviour among the public. Nor do they have an immediate impact on existing societal structures. Rather, when formal rules are implemented, they unavoidably have to negotiate what is already in place. In their seminal work on public policy failure, *Implementation*, Pressman and Wildavsky (1973; see also Rose, 1990) point towards the fact that new policy unavoidably bumps into, and needs to deal with, the effects and consequences of previously implemented political programmes. However, this is far from the only obstacle new public policy is faced with, neither is it the most difficult to deal with. The process of policy implementation also meets (perhaps even clashes?) with informal rules already established among the members of society in the shape of routines, customs, traditions and conventions (North, 1990). In the ideal situation, informal institutions in use constitute the foundation for the development of formal rules, thereby granting them legitimacy. But, as previous research has shown, if inadequate consideration is taken to already established informal rules during the policy-making process, traditions, diverging values and ghost-like remnants of old public policies may also contradict or undermine formal rules, rendering them inefficient (Fell, 2008; see also Knight, 1992; Nee, 2001). In essence, if most people are unwilling to voluntary conform to the new rules based on their inherent legitimacy, resorting to a coercive situation where 'fear is larger than greed' (Rothstein, 2000, p. 481) is the only means by which cooperation can be successfully regulated, and this in turn presents yet another dimension of legitimacy problems. Thus, in democratic states, relying on formal legislation for resolving the dilemma of increased individual environmental responsibility also requires that the substantive elements of the public policy underpinning the rules correspond with the values established among the general public.

Policy legitimacy, however, is not only relevant for the immediate effective-ness and efficiency of political programmes and policy tools in use with the aspiration of remedying collective action problems. Legitimacy also has a signif-icant effect also on the foregoing decision-making process and, thus, on the ability of political government to reach political aspirations. The effect of *ex-ante legitimacy* constrains, or, for that matter, constitutes a driving force in the policy-making process (i.e. impacts policy before the decision is taken). In particular, what is considered legitimate sets the boundaries for actors partici-pating in the process of deciding on and designing public policy. For example, the limitations of the traditional command-and-control approach for governing individuals' contribution to ecological sustainability have sparked an increasing use of policy tools that do not impose direct regulation on individual activities, but rather has a more voluntary image about them. As social dilemmas are viewed as emanating from the conflict between individual and collective rationality, public choice theory suggests the application of market-based policy instruments in order to transform the context in which actors make their behav-ioural choices. Strictly following the logic of consequences rather than one of appropriateness (cf. March and Olsen, 1989), economic (dis)incentives are designed to address the individual's self-interest, and therefore not directly associated with the simultaneous need for a moral motivation bolstering action. Nevertheless, market-based policy tools also presuppose a certain measure of legitimacy, but at a higher level (Widegren, 1998, p. 77). First things first, the functions embedded in the notion of representative democracy means that democratically elected governments are unlikely to risk unpopularity by intro-ducing command-and-control policies that are believed to lack a fundamental support among the majority of the citizenry (Stimson et al, 1994; Jacobs et al, 1999; Lundqvist, 2004c). A public policy suggesting the introduction of market-based tools for realizing its goals must, consequently, be legitimate in itself. If not, public support for a redistribution of governmental resources in the form of subsidies, or for raised taxes and levies on certain activities, should not be expected. Neither should the introduction of such tools, at least not if we agree that politicians, although sometimes driven by a desire to implement contested policies in the service of a broader public interest, also are rational, vote-maximizing, re-election seekers. The same argument holds, of course, for other types of policy instruments. For legislation, or indeed for the public policy underpinning it, to be decided on, in the first place a certain measure of public support is required. Considering the scope for change that the notion of individ-ual environmental responsibility suggests (i.e. transformation of whole lifestyles and consciousnesses), this might, again, prove to be a significant challenge for effective environmental protection in the democratic state. Although rules and regulations can be seen as necessary for structuring cooperation among individ-uals, not all activities, in particular those within the private sphere of the household, might be open for strict regulation and extensive monitoring within the normative framework of the contemporary democratic state.

In this sense, public policy-making in general and household-related environmental policy-making in particular (see, for instance, the reasoning in

Chapter 2 above) are faced with a *legitimacy/effectiveness dilemma* strongly discouraging contemporary political government from effectively demanding or promoting comprehensive changes in individual lifestyles and social structures. In the environmental context, this dilemma argues, the state is simply caught between the dual imperatives of effectively protecting the environment on the one hand, and promoting other, perhaps more politically rewarding, societal goals (e.g. continuous economic growth or individual freedom and autonomy) on the other (cf. Frickel and Davidson, 2004). Thus, policy legitimacy is not only understood to be a significant factor for the effectiveness and efficiency of already implemented public policy and for policy tools in use. Legitimacy is significant for the selection of discourses, symbols and motivational appeals applied to describe both policy problems and overarching political aspirations, as well as for the design of political strategies for solving policy problems and the distribution of responsibilities they imply. Just as specific institutions created to deal with single aspects of the environmental situation become embedded in structures containing already established beliefs, traditions and practices, the introduction of new public policy brings questions on its legitimacy to the foreground and the policy-making process itself thereby becomes deeply intertwined with the values and attitudes already established among the public. It therefore seems reasonable to assume that legitimacy both constitutes the limits and provides the opportunities for the policy-making process itself. In practice, a perceived lack of public support for certain categories of political measures results in these being either avoided entirely or in attempts to rhetorically frame them in a manner that encourages broad support (Baumgartner and Jones, 1993; Rein and Schön, 1993; Gilbert et al, 1998). The main question for policy-makers, then, is where these *ex-post* limits of legitimacy are to be drawn – both in practice (e.g. for re-election) and in theory.

To these empirical attributes, legitimacy, *thirdly*, unavoidably brings with it theoretically founded questions relating to democracy and democratic government, as the very definition of these concepts implies at least some sort of correspondence between public values and public policy. The very basics of representative democratic rule are founded on the notion that policy-makers represent collective interests (e.g. Dahl, 1985). Public policy, therefore, expresses what governmental actors (wishes to) do as well as why and how they (wish to) do it as *representatives* of their citizens. From this perspective, a minimum requirement for the legitimacy of democratic political government is that also policy content itself, not only the institutional arrangements for deciding on it, to some extent align with the basic values established in society, at least when considering collective decisions on broad societal issues (Williams and Edy, 1999; Mehrtens, 2004; Wallner, 2008). Although dissonant policies do not necessarily present any core democratic problems, there are, so to speak, certain limits on what this dissonance should be allowed to concern. Conflicts regarding short-term objectives or personal habits are commonplace in the democratic political debate and may certainly affect the amount of initial support a policy receives. This, however, is not to say that all contested or unpopular policies should be dismissed as being undemocratic. In a representa-

Table 4.1 *Three aspects of the policy legitimacy problem*

Type of legitimacy	Consequences	Conditions for legitimacy
Legitimacy *ex-post* (policy outcomes)	The degree of policy legitimacy affects the performance, effectiveness, efficiency and long-term stability of political programmes and policy tools in use.	The selection of (and rhetorical communication surrounding) policy tools builds on values and beliefs shared by the public.
Legitimacy *ex-ante* (policy decisions)	The legitimacy/effectiveness dilemma in political practice. Legitimacy constitutes the limitations for (and exerts pressure on) the policy-making process. Certain decisions are perceived as a political impossibility, others a political necessity.	Political aspirations and goals, including value priorities, strategies and motivations for reaching them, align with publicly established values and beliefs.
The democratic legitimacy of public policy	The level of policy legitimacy affects the democratic standing (and future performance) of political government.	Collective decisions on broad social issues made by political representatives can be justified by reference to values and beliefs held by the citizens.

tive system, where decisions are made through majority rule, a complete agreement on all aspects of policy would be difficult, not to say impossible, to achieve and the democratic system therefore rather relies on acceptance despite disagreement (Dahl, 1985). This is where policy legitimacy becomes significant. In order for a policy to enjoy a fundamental acceptance by the public, thus being viewed as morally obligatory to obey even though it might conflict with immediate personal preferences, policies need to be legitimate in the sense that they keep within the framework of core values or beliefs established in society. The same requirement is valid from a perspective of democratic theory (e.g. Dahl, 1989; Held, 1996). In political practice, it is therefore imperative for policy-makers to work to ensure that the policies made indeed are publicly acceptable, judged by the normative foundations of their content, and in this also to acknowledge the significant differences between illegitimacy (based on non-corresponding values and beliefs) and other forms of dissonance (based on shallower factors). In political and policy research, the connections between public policy content and legitimacy should therefore not be understated. In Table 4.1 above, these three (i.e. ex-post; ex-ante; and democratic) aspects of the policy legitimacy-problem are summed up.

EXPLORING POLICY LEGITIMACY

Over these introductory sections, I have aimed at outlining in more detail the nature of the general problem addressed in this thesis, and thus my rationales for granting it attention: the consequences that legitimacy amounts to for the design, performance and long-term stability of contemporary environmental policy. Summing up the chapter's discussion so far on the relation between public policy and legitimacy, we can identify three distinct types of legitimacy issues or problems facing policy-makers in this respect. As illustrated by Table 4.1, policy legitimacy concerns, in a general sense, the moral justification of public policy and the provision of publicly acceptable reasons for compliance. Legitimacy is thereby a highly significant component affecting the outcomes of public policy in several ways. *First*, when implementing public policy or governmental programmes, legitimacy affects the effectiveness of policy tools and determines the amount of external factors needed to initiate and sustain patterns of collective action. As such, legitimacy influences performance both in the short and in the long term. Illegitimate policies, unable to install a feeling of moral obligation and desire for voluntary responsibility-taking among the public, can be expected to be strongly reliant on external incitement structures and therefore increasingly vulnerable to the long-term volatile workings of politics. *Second*, taking the shape of a legitimacy/effectiveness dilemma, legitimacy is also expected to have an impact on political decision-making itself, by setting the limitations for (and exerting pressure on) decision-makers. Although decisions on public policy predominately are seen as being shaped by the desires and preferences held by actors participating in the process, certain outputs are still perceived as a political impossibility (or a political necessity), due to the established belief systems in society. Thus, legitimacy not only amounts to an *ex-post* factor affecting policy success and failure, but can also assist in explaining why some political choices are made (or not) in the first place, thereby suggesting an *ex-ante* effect on policy performance. *Third*, apart from the risk of unsuccessful implementation of a single policy or programme due to its legitimacy deficit, policy-makers need also to consider the legitimacy of their decisions from a point of view of both democracy and, perhaps more politically rational, re-election. In a normative perspective, democratic theory tells us that elected representatives of the public, in keeping with the democratic framework that has brought them to power, should take care to make decisions that at least align with a number of socially established, basic values and beliefs. In the real world of democratic politics, introducing an illegitimate policy rarely leads to revolution, but it may well be expected to curb both the future performance of the particular government as well as its possibility for remaining in power after the next election.

How, then, should the degree of policy legitimacy be evaluated? Evident from the above outlined tripartite effects of legitimacy on public policy performance, the empirical study of policy legitimacy essentially amounts to a study of belief-system (incorporating both abstract and general values as well as empirically oriented beliefs about the world) correspondence. In other words, policy legitimacy amounts to the extent to which the normative foundations of political goals and strategies expressed through the content of public policy aligns with the dominant values, beliefs and attitudes in society (cf. Connolly, 1984; Beetham, 1991). It focuses the analysis on the extent to which public policy and public systems of belief aligns and how this correspondence in turn amounts to a possibility for moral justification of a decision. As such, however, policy legitimacy delineates a specific role for values and beliefs shared between policy and public. It is not equal to the expressed support of, or volatile opinions on a policy, which can be triggered by any number of factors. Legitimacy instead digs deeper and focuses the values and beliefs lying behind an expression of opinion, whether it be in the form of acceptance or discontent. As Beetham (1991, p. 100) puts it, studies on legitimacy involve 'reproducing the reasoning of people within [...] society, and reconstructing the logic of their own judgements'. Nor is legitimacy equal to a policy's rightfulness according to some external standard, as proposed by the concept of normative legitimacy, as this approach exclusively focuses on drawing up guidelines for when a policy or institution *should* be considered legitimate, not when it actually is so in the eyes of the public. Thus, when conducting an evaluation of policy legitimacy the relatively enduring belief systems, rather than opinions or theoretically derived constructions, should constitute the analytical focus.

It should also be noted that defining legitimacy as belief-system correspondence, and thus dependent on the extent to which public policy aligns with publicly established values and beliefs, also explicates that illegitimacy does not always result from policy-makers going too far in their decisions, for example by making too strong a policy infringing on a basic value such as freedom or autonomy (although this is a popular notion, we remember the discussions on both the legitimacy/effectiveness and the freedom/security dilemmas from above). Since the frames of legitimacy are determined by people's values and beliefs, whichever they may be, illegitimacy can also be the result of policy-makers not going far enough, or moving in a completely different direction. It can, for example, be the result of too weak a policy, not adequately addressing a mutually experienced problem or of a policy resting on a view of the world and of basic causal relationships completely different from those established among the public. These situations may, for example, arise if policy-makers misconceive the nature of the established belief systems (perhaps by taking expressions of negative opinion at face value as a sign of illegitimacy) and attempt to avoid introducing an illegitimate policy. Putting this problem in terms of a legitimacy/effectiveness dilemma, if effectiveness in fact is legitimate, choosing another way will be illegitimate. For policy-makers, the fact that illegitimacy can be the result also from situations like these further accentuates the necessity of considering the public/policy interplay in the process of designing policy.

As illustrated in Figure 4.1 below, exploring policy legitimacy requires a three-tiered study, where policy content, in terms of basic values and empirically oriented beliefs, are compared and contrasted with the corresponding belief system established among those subject to the policy. It thus requires analytical tools for exploring both fundamental values and policy-specific beliefs held by individuals, as well as underpinning policy decisions.

Correspondence among systems of belief, then, holds a key role in the exploration of policy legitimacy. But this also means that reliably exploring the degree of legitimacy requires, using the words of Sabatier and Jenkins-Smith (1999, p. 154), public policies to be mapped on the same canvas as an individual's system of belief. An analysis of correspondence needs, in order to be meaningful, the two main objects of study to hold some common characteris-

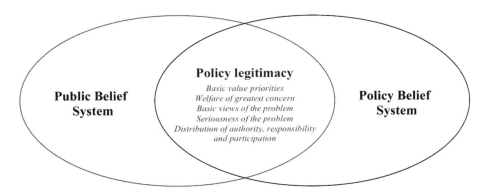

Figure 4.1 *A general framework for studying policy legitimacy*

tics that make them possible to compare in a reliable manner. Turning towards well-tested approaches to the empirical study of public belief systems, the hierarchical structure of values and beliefs suggested by the Value-Belief-Norm (VBN) theory (e.g. Stern et al, 1999; Stern, 2000) serves as an adequate tool for measuring both basic values and more empirically oriented beliefs among individuals. This in particular when concerned with the environmental policy domain as the VBN theory captures those values and cognitive elements that are deemed to be of significant importance for the formation of a range of attitudes, opinions and behaviours in the specifics of the environmental context. Thus, public systems of beliefs are elucidated through mass surveys including questions on basic value priorities (derived from the Schwartz [1992] value survey); general environmental beliefs (as outlined in the New Ecological Paradigm (NEP) scale [e.g. Dunlap et al, 2000]); as well as more specific beliefs on environmental consequences, distribution of authority and responsibility, and personal norms towards pro-environmental action taking.

Similar to these models' focus on both very basic value priorities and conceptions of reality related to the policy domain in question, a number of established approaches to the analysis of public policy focus the significance of belief systems as underpinning its formation and design. Policy decisions comprise both basic values (expressed as the selection of political aspirations and policy goals) as well as empirically oriented beliefs (manifested through the framing of the nature of the policy problem at hand and in the outline of preferred strategies for solving it). The highly influential and well-tested checklist of Sabatier's (e.g. 1988, 1998; Sabatier and Jenkins-Smith, 1993, 1999) Advocacy Coalition Framework (ACF), for example, clearly diverges from previously applied rational goal-selection models of elite and mass beliefs, where actors' positions regarding specific policy options are inferred directly from their very fundamental normative or ideological orientations valid across policy-domains (cf. Sabatier and Hunter, 1989). Instead, similar to the concept of personal values and beliefs in social psychology (cf. Rohan, 2000); and departing from previous research on public opinion and political behaviour (e.g.

Table 4.2 *An outline of topics for studying belief systems*

	Main topics	Defining questions
Fundamental normative principles	Basic value priorities	Which basic values are emphasized as important guiding principles, in individuals' lives and as determining policy goals?
		How do these values relate to each other, i.e. when making trade-offs which basic values are prioritized?
	Welfare of greatest concern	Which group's or entity's welfare is the most important?
Policy-domain specific beliefs	Basic views of the problem	Which are the basic causes of the problem?
		What types of solutions are necessary for moving development in the opposite direction?
	Seriousness of the problem	How serious is the policy problem?
		For whom does the identified problem present a threat?
	Distribution of authority, responsibility and participation	Who is responsible for amending the policy problem (e.g. citizens, municipal or state authorities)?
		How, and by whom, should decisions on the distribution of responsibility be taken?
		What is the individual's ability to make a personal impact in remedying the policy problem?

Converse, 1964; Putnam, 1976; Peffley and Hurwitz, 1985), beliefs in the ACF are nested in a three-tiered hierarchical structure, where beliefs in the policy core represent what actors aspire to translate into public policy and thus constitute the relevant focus for a study of policy content. By comprising both fundamental principles expressing the underpinning normative goals for the policy domain, as well as empirically oriented problem descriptions and suggestions for strategies, policy core beliefs also serve to bridge the divide between core values and issue-specific opinions in a way similar to the individual's belief system. Applying this checklist for studying policy belief systems is therefore believed to be an adequate point of departure also when the overarching aim is to explore policy legitimacy.

Table 4.2 summarizes the five main topics by which the exploration of belief systems in policy as well as among the public is constructed. Starting at the highest level of abstraction, the first topic outlined in the analytical framework concerns *basic value priorities*, as expressed both among the public and in policy. Most studies concerned with public belief systems take their point of departure in the analysis of very basic, cross-situational values, for example the relative importance assigned to freedom, to equality or to security. Following theory, the importance ascribed to basic values draws on their centrality for understanding a number of more situational-specific beliefs, attitudes, opinions and actions. How priorities among core values are made determine which issues are granted explicit concern, express the basic motivation to take action and underpin the construction of overarching (personal or political) goals. Value priorities have therefore been applied as a point of departure for predicting a range of political preferences and choices as well as more specific environmental attitudes and behaviour (e.g. Steg et al, 2005; Davidov et al, 2008). Also within frameworks for analysing policy, basic value priorities constitute the critical foundation of policy beliefs, expressing the basic policy goals and guiding more empirically oriented understandings and preferences related to their achievement (e.g. Sabatier and Jenkins-Smith, 1999, p. 132). As values are conceived as generally applicable across policy domains, and not specifically related to environmental issues, the exploration of value priorities is believed to capture basic political–ideological preferences (or broad ideological attitudes, cf. Free and Cantril, 1968; Coughlin, 1980). In particular, and following the horizontal value dimension outlined by Schwartz, the basic values explored within this topic relate to different conceptions of the proper state/individual relationship by focusing the balance between individual rights and responsibilities; between individualism and collectivism as guiding social principles; and between liberalism and conservatism as the basic ideological guide. As such, and in line with the hierarchical structure of belief systems, they are also believed to constitute the foundation for more empirically oriented beliefs regarding the distribution of decision-making authority and public participation in the specific environmental context explored in this thesis.

The list of fundamental normative principles also includes basic values pertaining to *welfare of greatest concern*. In other words, which groups or entities that are singled out for their welfare being of significant priority, basically ranging between a self- and an other-regarding orientation. To its essence, values addressing welfare priorities have a strong political–ideological bearing as they underpin understandings of economic egalitarianism, and guide the individual to different political preferences on this issue (cf. Barnea and Schwartz, 1998; Caprara et al, 2006). Within the environmental policy domain, how the importance between personal and social context outcomes is rated is of course of significant relevance. One reason is that the attainment of positive environmental outcomes might entail both economic and social costs for the individual (hence the framing of them as collective-action dilemmas), another that environmental problems may be conceptualized as threats to a number of different groups (self, in-group, out-group) the significance of which is determined by these values. The egoism/altruism demarcation that this value dimension elucidates has therefore been widely applied to characterize both the sources of the environmental problem as well as the necessary change of individuals' consciousness in the process of amending it (cf. Dobson, 2003). In this endeavour, Sagoff (1988, p. 8; see also Berglund and Matti, 2006), for example, highlights the egoism/altruism divide by distinguishing between the motivational differences behind the two roles of citizen and consumer: 'As a *citizen*, I am concerned with the public interest, rather than my own interest; with the good of the community, rather than simply the well-being of my own family. [...] In my role as a *consumer*, [...] I concern myself with personal or self-regarding wants and interests; I pursue the goals I have as an individual.' Values expressing welfare priorities thus lie at the core of how the relationships both between human beings and nature (e.g. a moral sphere expanded also to other species or entities), and between state and individual (e.g. non-territorial or global duties for the citizen) are understood.

Following on from the analysis of fundamental normative principles, the exploration of policy-domain specific beliefs initially addresses how the (environmental) policy problem is understood and expressed. This approach draws inspiration from the constructivist notion of problem representation as the key for public policy formulation. It has causal effects for subsequent political strategies, and, following the understanding that an event or process is only understood as a problem if it challenges the dominating discourse, serves to highlight basic value priorities. The focus for the first topic addressing policy-domain specific beliefs is placed on the *basic views of the problem,* i.e. how the basic causes as well as necessary solutions to the problem are expressed. Focusing on how the causes to the problem are presented is an approach granted significant attention within different policy analytical approaches as understandings of causation lie at the core of a range of further beliefs. The framing of a particular situation, or the way in which a policy problem is perceived and constructed, is central to the subsequent process of selecting strategies and assigning responsibilities (e.g. Majone, 1989; Baumgartner and Jones, 1993; Kingdon, 1995; Bacchi, 1999; Fischer, 2003). Problem understanding thereby has significant bearings on resulting policy outputs as a policy alternative will only be advocated in those cases when it is seen as causally linked to the problem that is to be solved (Sabatier and Hunter, 1989, p. 232).

This is particularly salient in analyses of environmental policy discourses, where problem causes affect perceptions of alternative solutions (balancing technological optimism and pessimism, or the roles of government and market); the proper distribution of costs and benefits for amending the problem (e.g. zero-sum competition or mutual accommodation of environment and growth); as well as the responsibility for different actors to participate in solving the problem (Sabatier, 1988; Dryzek, 2005). As demonstrated by, among others, Hobson (2003) and Macnaghten and Urry (1998) also how people in general understand the basics of an environmental problem strongly affect their further views on necessary solutions as well as responsibilities for implementing these. In its essence, therefore, exploring basic views of the problem relates to how the relationship between human beings and nature are understood; if the environmental problem is perceived either as internal or as external to the basic social structure, and therefore requiring either fundamental social restructuring or increased technological inventiveness.

Strongly related both to the above-discussed perceptions of causes to the problem as well as to values capturing basic welfare priorities are beliefs on the *seriousness of the problem* and, not least, its direction. How the magnitude of the problem is perceived certainly affects the necessity to properly amend it and to utilize societal (or personal) resources for this endeavour. It seems reasonable to assume that a problem believed to be highly serious also will be seen as requiring radical and immediate solutions, whereas minor amendments might suffice for a problem considered less severe. Furthermore, beliefs about the direction of the problem, that is the identification of those groups or entities primarily affected by it, certainly have an affect of how basic values on welfare priorities are transformed into empirically oriented beliefs on the necessity for problem solving. In policy analysis, for instance, exploring the distribution of costs and benefits resulting from a particular policy is an essential component as this provides an initial indication on how different interests might react to it (Wilson, 1995; Sabatier and Jenkins-Smith, 1999; Birkland, 2005). It is therefore necessary to elucidate not only how the basic problem is described, but also the policy's rhetorical construction of those interests benefiting from the policy (or those explicitly threatened by the problem addressed).

As a final topic, beliefs related to the *distribution of authority, responsibility and participation* are explored. Regardless of whether the object of study concerns a single specific case of policy development or the politics of sustainability in a broad perspective, questions on the extent and reach of political authority's decision-making power and the individual's responsibilities have been deemed critical to be included in any comprehensive analysis of environmental policy beliefs. Even in cases when the existence of a basic public consensus on, and legitimacy for, the representative democratic system and the legislative function of parliament can be assumed, the question of what political authority should be allowed to decide upon is still very much an open question. From a general political–theoretical perspective, views on the proper societal distribution of participation, responsibility and authority constitute basic factors when discriminating between different interpretations of the state/individual relationship. We recall that these issues are, for instance, fundamentals in traditional theories of citizenship, ranging between the classic liberal notion of a passively rights-claiming, autonomous individual enabled by a fundamentally neutral state, and the duty-bound, socially conditioned civic-republican citizen (e.g. Held, 1996). As such, beliefs on the role of the individual vis-à-vis the state have a considerable relevance also for the specifics of environmental politics. As mentioned on several occasions above, diverging trade-offs made between the values of (state mandated) pro-environmental obligations and individual autonomy constitutes one primary source of potential legitimacy deficits within environmental public policy. Put most simply, governments prescribing reformed institutions and an increased civic day-to-day responsibility for the environment must consider the possibility that 'not all people wishes to become involved in such political action' (Rydin, 1999, p. 477). However, for an evaluation of legitimacy it is not sufficient to merely consider how public opinion responds to the question *if* individual participation should be mandated to or not. In line with the critique directed towards the concept of social legitimacy, dichotomous pro and con statements are certainly valuable for elucidating the direction of public opinion, but they provide little guidance to the complex, sometimes highly context dependent, processes underpinning a person's expressed preferences and thus only convey a limited image of publicly established values and beliefs (e.g. Beetham, 1991; Glynn et al, 1999). It therefore seems reasonable to take an analysis of legitimacy further, by considering also beliefs pertaining to *why* public participation (if at all) is necessary, *what* form it should take, and *how* this participation should be decided on.

THE LEGITIMACY OF SWEDISH
HOUSEHOLD-RELATED ENVIRONMENTAL POLICY

Advancing towards a more comprehensive understanding of household-related environmental policy legitimacy in Sweden, the empirical analysis elucidates, compares and contrasts the normative foundations (i.e. the moral justification) of Swedish environmental public policy with those values and beliefs held by Swedish citizens, thus significantly affecting how policy requirements are received and reacted to. As a first instance, a qualitative, belief system oriented analysis of official policy documents from the period 1994 to 2006 was conducted with the purpose of mapping the normative content of Swedish policy. Secondly, a dominant public belief system was distilled from a quantitative analysis of two mass surveys, conducted in the years 2004 and 2006, respectively, tapping values and beliefs established among the Swedish public (cf. Matti, 2009).

In the following correspondence analysis, the five analytical topics outlined in the framework above are divided into two categories highlighting both their level of abstraction, their generality, as well as how salient they are believed to be for making decisions in specific policy domains. Fundamental normative principles, comprising both basic value priorities and conceptions of groups whose welfare is of greatest concern, are located at the highest level of abstraction. These represent the basic guiding principles in an individual's life as well as the key goals towards which a policy aspires.

Comparing the results from our empirical studies, we note that the two belief systems build on a relatively similar set of core values. We remember that Swedish environmental policy, in describing the overarching goals for the political sustainability aspirations, draws strongly on the values of security, stability and tradition. The main policy problem outlined is finding ways to bring the Swedish welfare state into the new century, thus ensuring that the traditional values of the Swedish model are kept intact now as well as in the future. This value-base aligns rather well with conservation being the dominant value orientation in the public belief system, expressing a preference for stability, conformity and collectiveness rather than individualism and change. Furthermore, security is, among our respondents, the single value item enjoying the strongest support as a guiding principle in life, and framing the policy

Table 4.3 *Comparing basic value priorities*

Basic value priorities	
Policy belief system	*Public belief- system*
Welfare, security, stability and tradition	Security and freedom most important guiding principles. Conservation slightly more dominant value orientation: a preference for stability, conformity and collectiveness over individualism and change.

Table 4.4 *Comparing conceptions of distributive justice*

Welfare of greatest concern *Policy belief system*	*Public belief system*
An anthropocentric ethic, incorporating some streaks of green. Nature subordinate to human needs. Ability of human ingenuity to expand or negotiate natural limits. Narrow-scope altruism, extending welfare first to the present generation (growth and economy) and second to future generations (a long-term stable welfare and prosperity – the generation goal) of Swedes.	Self-transcendence significantly more important than self-enhancement. Universal altruism signalling welfare beyond the own in-group, to a global (and even environmental) perspective.

problem as an issue of security, threatening both to values and entities of greatest concern, ensuring its further legitimacy among the public. Perhaps, one can argue, is this correspondence in very basic, core values more or less unsurprising? These types of fundamental cognitive frames are very stable, develop early in a person's life and are therefore, at least to some extent, bound by cultural socialization processes. As such, it seems reasonable to expect that a broad social agreement on basic values, particularly when taken at face value, would be more readily found than a similar agreement on more empirically oriented beliefs.

Considering the second topic within our fundamental normative principles (Table 4.4), however, this correspondence between policy and public is not as evident. Admittedly, both belief systems agree that the sphere of interest for the highly valued issues of welfare and security is wider than the own person. Altruism, that is the care for others, is the guiding principle both when settling on policy goals as well as when forming reactions and responses to social objects. Nevertheless, despite this basic alignment, we should note here some significant differences between the two systems of belief. Whereas policy, in a majority of statements addressing the issue of welfare priorities either directly or indirectly, clearly expresses a perspective of territorially bound, narrow-scope altruism, established values among the public instead convey a strong universalistic stance, extending the welfare priorities further than the own in-group (or, in this case, nation state). Although those subject to the policy, and those who subsequently are expected to change their day-to-day behaviour as a result of it, state that they are predominately motivated in their actions by a care for others in a global perspective, policy, following the ideal type of a discourse of ecological modernization, primarily draws on the value of a common national good for instituting collective action. Put in other words, it is a policy building on a traditional, territorial conception of citizenship, but directed towards post-cosmopolitan (even ecological) citizens.

Certainly, we could argue these statements not to be mutually exclusive (Sweden is of course a part of the global community) and therefore not an issue. But they are not the same. When contemplating the issue of distributive justice, a more fundamental difference is also noted in how the benefits from the suggested environmental policy are presented. The issue of reciprocity holds a central place for motivating action in the policy documents, and although this reciprocity is interpreted as denoting a common (even intergenerational, extended to future generations of Swedes), rather than personal, good, it clearly diverts from the value of social justice and global concern expressed by the respondents. This in particular, seen as the opposing value orientation express-ing the individual's role as a rational, self-interested and motivated by personal benefits, i.e. self-enhancement, receives an overwhelmingly low support among the respondents. Thus, our two systems of belief clearly diverge in this aspect. It reveals either that policy-makers and the public basically hold different views as to whose welfare is most threatened by the problem addressed in policy, and who consequently benefits from the strategies outlined, or that policy-makers (mistakenly) believe that the public in general are motivated by interests closer to their own person. In any case, this divergence in conceptions of distributive justice is problematic as it conveys that policy does not apply those motivations towards which a majority of the public will respond positively, as it frames the policy problem as an opportunity for reciprocity rather than as a problem of global social justice.

When moving beyond the relationship between individuals and instead approaching those values concerning welfare distribution that more specifically addresses our policy domain, we also find that the public and the policy belief system display slightly diverging understanding on the human beings/nature relationship. A broader moral sphere, extended also to the non-human world, is clearly evident among the respondents. This is suggested by their strong prefer-ence for the universal value orientation (incorporating, we remember, also a care for nature) and even more pronounced when considering their answers on the environmental values and beliefs in the NEP scale. In my surveys, as well as in several previously conducted studies, the extension of rights to the non-human world proves to be an established understanding among the Swedish public. This is further explicated both in the respondents' general pro-environ-mental orientation as well as in their outright rejection of human exemptionalism. The policy rhetoric, on the other hand, accentuates both nature's subordination to human needs and wants as well as its primary value as a provider of human goods. As evident from our conclusions on the expectance of reciprocity permeating the policy discourse, motivational statements focus primarily on the necessity for action in order to ensure present and future human prosperity, not upholding or protecting the rights of nature.

In sum, it is possible to conclude that although the divergences concerning fundamental normative principles are not of an all-encompassing kind, our two belief systems still display some differences, primarily pertaining to concep-tions of welfare priorities. These, in turn, I believe are quite significant also for questions of legitimacy and policy performance. *First*, welfare priorities, in this case the difference between a broad, non-territorial altruism (even incorporat-ing non-human entities) and a territorially bound care for the own in-group or community, as well as between global justice and expectance of reciprocity, constitute starkly different motivational concerns. Thus, we cannot expect people falling into the former category to be as motivated to voluntary responsibility taken by arguments drawing on the latter. *Second*, these values are of significance as they set the frames for how beliefs relating more specifically to the policy area, or policy problem, in question are both formed and interpreted. A strong concern for global justice and environmental protection, which is clearly displayed in the public belief system, thus highlights the significance of also amending more abstract or distant problems of environment and development, in addition to those problems threatening the (predominately economic) welfare of the own in-group. The second set of topics in our analytical framework leaves the generally held values for a focus on beliefs related specifically to the nature of the policy problem: how its causes are understood; how serious it is perceived to be; as well as how the responsibility for amending (and for deciding on this amendment) is distributed in society. When contemplating similarities and differences related to the overall image of the policy problem, we should remember that Swedish environmental policy is not a policy exclusively addressing environmental protection (see Table 4.5). Rather, it is primarily devoted to building the ecologically sustainable society, thus incorporating a range of societal concerns and perspectives. Now, although the public belief system rests on core values well in line with the aspiration to update the Swedish welfare state for the 21st century (e.g. collectiveness, security, stability and tradition), a closer comparison of beliefs regarding the problem reveals a number of potentially difficult divergences.

First, although the environment certainly holds a place in policy's broad definition of the general problem addressed, the environmental dimension of sustainability in this is clearly subordinate to both the economic and the social development dimension, as the overall goals towards which the Swedish

Table 4.5 *Comparing basic views of the problem*

| Basic views of the problem | |
Policy belief system	Public belief system
Building the ecologically sustainable society. The economic dimension of sustainability dominates. Main problems address the furthering of welfare and Swedish economy. Environment-as-growth, where environmental adaptation is the tool for furthering a broad range of societal goals. Unsustainable patterns of consumption (and thereby production) presented as a main cause of the problem at the individual level – the individual has the ability to impact positive development through active responsibility, primarily on the market. Strategies: sector integration (an all-inclusive responsibility); top-down administration; public investments; partnerships; and market-based policy tools. Social restructuring as modernization rather than as radical change.	Strong pro-environmental orientation. General awareness of environmental problems. Human activities as significant contributors to environmental degradation. Weak trust in human ingenuity and technological development as solutions to problem. An acknowledgement of natural limits and need for social change – lifestyles and development.

environmental policy predominately aspires are expressed in terms of welfare, prosperity and growth. Protecting the environment, and taking steps towards a transition to a more ecologically rational development, is instead framed as a strategy, or a tool, for reaching these goals (e.g. new export and employment opportunities; development of new technology; an increase in government investments). The environmental protective parts of the policy are thereby to be negotiated so as not to curb development in other areas and, we can at least hypothesize, given the evident environment-as-a-tool-for-growth perspective, are up for replacement when their role in driving socio-economic development has passed. With this in mind, we should consider that the overall pro-environmentalism and the awareness of environmental problems (as well as the universal value orientation containing both the goal of protected environment and of social justice) among the respondents is strongly pronounced. This, in turn, suggests a motivation for environmental protection as a value of its own, rather than as a means to a different end. Furthermore, the respondents clearly acknowledge the structural base of environmental problems, agreeing that addressing current human practices in a broad perspective (e.g. lifestyles and development) and the effects of further industrialization are at the core of solving the problem. This, again, seems counter to the belief in top-down administrated modernization and further investments in industrial development expressed in policy.

Second, as policy primarily revolves around furthering goals other than environmental protection, its views on what is required in terms of strategies for change also follow this path. The analysis of policy belief systems concluded that Swedish environmental policy draws strongly on a strategy for societal modernization, where all actors are required to take part in the transitory work but where the efforts needed primarily are framed as a natural next step, as following an already chosen track, and thus as developments where no agonizing trade-offs between ends are required. This discourse of reassurance is

Table 4.6 *Comparing views of problem seriousness*

Seriousness of the problem	
Policy belief system	*Public belief system*
Environmental degradation not the main focus for policy. The environmental situation needs amendment, also on the individual level, but not in terms of an imminent crisis requiring radical and immediate measures. Rather a natural, gradual reformation of current structures. Policy primarily depicts possibilities (for further development) rather than (environmental) problems. A highly optimistic view of the future where a modernized society leads to future prosperity, and natural limits to growth can be overcome through government-led initiatives and human ingenuity.	High sense of risk-awareness. The environmental problem as highly serious – eco-crisis or catastrophe approaching – need for immediate measures. The environmental situation as a global problem (less local or personal) for both human beings and other living entities. Connection between private activities and global problems. Household-related activities a serious environmental threat.

further emphasized when considering the views of problem seriousness (Table 4.6) expressed in the policy documents.

Here we noted the environmental-threat rhetoric, following the discursive transition from environmental protection to sustainability, being strongly downplayed in preference to an optimistic framing of how the current challenges can be turned into positive opportunities for future growth. As opposed to this, however, established among the public is not only an acknowledgement of the very existence of an environmental problem, but a strong belief in it as a serious threat or even an imminent crisis (descriptions never found in the policy documents) in need of both immediate and large-scale measures for its amendment. As opposed to the modernized environment-growth rhetoric found in policies, one of the main features of the public environmental beliefs is the notion that humanity, through its current practices, both are severely abusing an environment too fragile to cope with the pressure from further industrialization and growth, as well as approaching natural limits. A belief that, in prolongation, also stands in stark contrast to the ecologically modernized policy strategies of top-down administered investments in technological development as a way of counteracting limits and remedying the negative effects of the environment on prospects for further growth. In fact, the respondents place little or no faith in the prospects for human ingenuity to be able to control natural developments and instead express a belief that these types of endeavours commonly result in more or less disastrous consequences.

Third and last, we also conclude that divergences among the belief systems are found when comparing beliefs related to the responsibilities for implementing change, and the roles for different actors in this endeavour (Table 4.7).

In both policy and among the public is the need for a common responsibility for all actors in society clearly displayed, and subsequently also the necessity to involve individuals in the transition, amending lifestyles and counteracting the broader effects of their private activities. However, we also see that the image of the individual provided in policy does not align with the one derived from our mass surveys. In policy, the role of the individual is primarily framed as one of changing behaviour in the market in response to external (fiscal) incitements and top-down instructions from the government. The individual, although being willing to conform, requires that the state both informs them of the direction of change necessary as well as provides, or at least clearly displays, the benefits arising from these changes. Addressing the consumer role is thus understood as being highly relevant for the promotion of individual level responsibility-taking in Sweden, and for reaching political sustainability aspirations. The reasons for this dominant consumer focus in policy are multifaceted. It is certainly related to the overall framing of the problem, where the prospects for Swedish economic development are a main target. This certainly requires a strong private consumption, but also that patterns are changed to drive industrial renewal and making Sweden a leading nation in exporting green goods, knowledge and technology. It is also an effect of the ambition to successfully demonstrate the viability of protecting the environment while simultaneously

Table 4.7 *Comparing views of authority, responsibility and participation*

Distribution of authority, responsibility and participation	
Policy belief system	*Public belief system*
Partnerships: an all-inclusive participation in all sectors of society required for achieving the ecologically sustainable society. The individual has a responsibility, even duty, to further the common good by amending unsustainable lifestyles and take an active part in the work. Citizens are environmentally aware, but lack knowledge and ability. The citizen as a consumer: motivated by economic rationality and reciprocity, as well as passively reacting to governmental instructions. The state governs changes (societal as well as individual) through top-down administration and dissemination of information/education.	Shared responsibility between all major societal actors. Single individuals hold a large responsibility for causing and amending the environmental situation. Civic environmental responsibility as a moral duty. Responsibility for all to change lifestyles and actively support protection of the environment. Environmental protection trumps freedom: environmental responsibility not open for self-determination or majority will. Strong sense of personal responsibility and ability to make a difference. Strong feeling of personal norm to take action.

ensuring continuous economic growth and a preservation of traditional practices (i.e. a gradual reformation and modernization through amendments of policy rather than radical changes). This requires that environmentally protective measures are devised so as not to curb growth or infringe on individual freedom and autonomy. Lastly, it is an effect of the belief that individual's primary motivation for action lies in a commitment to benefits for the own person, either directly or by the way of a common Swedish good.

However, when scrutinizing the results of our surveys we observe that the policy envisioned needs to deal with individuals as rational consumers, promoting individual environmental action through the use of fiscal (dis)incentives and the promise of reciprocity, should not be taken for granted. The public, we instead found, holds a strong sense of social and environmental justice, and are strongly concerned with the spread of negative effects from their personal, household-related activities in a global perspective. As a response, guided by their basic value orientations, they also express a strong feeling of moral obligation to actively counteract these negative effects. This obligation is of such magnitude that environmental protection, according to the respondents, trumps the value of personal autonomy and the state legitimately can mandate an all-inclusive responsibility-taking. Lastly, as we previously noted, the values most clearly associated with the role of a rational consumer, i.e. those collected under the label self-enhancement, only receive marginal support among the respondents. This, again, is in stark contrast to the policy-beliefs that instead targets consumer role and presenting assurances for reciprocity in order to accomplish broad participation at the individual level.

CONCLUSIONS: THE LEGITIMACY PROBLEM IN SWEDISH ENVIRONMENTAL PUBLIC POLICY

The objective for the above exploration of belief system correspondence in Swedish environmental public policy has been to draw together the results of my two empirical studies, thereby advancing towards an answer to the question of whether the studied policy suffers from a legitimacy problem. Furthermore, in the case of an affirmative answer, my ambition has been to outline which aspects, pertaining to which values or beliefs, policy and public systems of belief diverge. This is in order to enable also a presentation of suggestions for how to amend the problem and how to avoid or at least reduce legitimacy problems in the future.

The short answer to this overarching research question is that a legitimacy problem is present in Swedish environmental policy, affecting its performance and, thus, ultimately, hampering its possibilities for success. However, studying policy legitimacy, we noted above, is more a question of determining the degrees of legitimacy than of making dichotomous either/or statements, and it should indeed be noted that shared values and beliefs are found within all our analytical topics. My assertion that a legitimacy problem nevertheless permeates environmental policy in the Swedish case builds on the indisputable fact that policy and public still diverge on several aspects. In particular, policy and public draw on fundamentally different beliefs when outlining the nature, seriousness, and direction of the problem. In this chapter, I argued that a significant part of the policy-making process amounts to a struggle between different overall problem frames, held by different actors and interests. Applying this notion agrees that policy problems indeed are socially constructed and thus can vary between groups of actors, dependent both on their more fundamental beliefs about causal relationships in the world and on the basic values they wish to promote. What is more, problem framing amounts to a critical aspect of any policy as it governs decisions and activities downstream, for example the selection of policy strategies for addressing the problem, the preference policy tools, and the motivations applied to promote (collective) action. Therefore, although a failure to align with public beliefs on the nature and seriousness of the problem may seem as a minor problem compared to, for example, a fundamental difference in basic value priorities, this nevertheless amounts to a significant issue in terms of legitimacy.

Just as a common view of the problem is anticipated to be an important factor in bringing and holding policy coalitions together, problem framing in our case serves to set policy and public apart. What, then, are the policy implications arising from this divergence in problem framing? As I see it, it presents, first, a problem of governmental *credibility*. A basic point of departure for this study of policy legitimacy has been that public policy is, or at least should be, the method for forwarding collectively held values and solving collective problems. Now, since the established public belief system holds that the environmental situation amounts to a highly serious problem, in need of immediate measures to avoid an imminent crisis, it seems reasonable to conclude that the practice of directing environmental public policy towards solving other types of societal problems will be understood as unsatisfactory in the eyes of the public. On the one hand, it can be viewed as the government ignoring, or failing to notice, a pressing issue. On the other, it could also be viewed as a more fundamental conflict of values, regardless of the fact that the overall goals for policy, as we have noted they do, align with other basic values held by the public as guiding principles in life. From Chapter 3, we remember that the rationale for settling on belief systems, that both conceptions of the desirable and of reality, as the unit of analysis is that abstract and general values need a connection to empirically oriented beliefs in order to be interpreted, bestowed meaning and, finally, activated. This dual connection between core values and beliefs is highly relevant also for our present analysis of legitimacy. Consider, as an example, that the value item security is an important guiding principle in the public belief system. Although policy can be said to address issues of security (framed in terms of sustained future welfare, growth and employment), it does not address environmental security, which, seen in the context of public beliefs on the current environmental situation and the necessity to take immediate action in response to it, can be reasonably assumed a similarly significant issue. Thus, although the prima facie discrepancy concerns problem-related beliefs, this also amounts to a divergence of very basic policy goals.

Diverging beliefs concerning the nature of the environmental problem also amounts to a *motivational* problem, where diverging views on the world make it increasingly difficult to present acceptable, or at least efficient, arguments for individual environmental responsibility-taking. For one, framing the policy problem in terms of the economy and opportunities for prosperity is expected to have less an effect on behavioural predispositions. This is particularly the case as the established beliefs among the public tell us that the major motivations for action draw on a sense of global justice and moral responsibility, rather than reciprocity. From previous research, we also remember that the application of external (in particular market-based) motivations can even have a reverse effect on the intended activities. In particular when considering the structure of the established public belief system, we should note that research in the field of economic psychology point towards the danger of turning behavioural patterns into commodities as this might 'crowd out' a pre-existing sense of moral obligation (e.g. Berglund and Matti, 2006). Furthermore, framing the policy problem in positive terms as an opportunity for the common Swedish good, and not as an imminent global catastrophe, can reasonably be expected to be less convincing as an argument for voluntary lifestyle changes. This is both for those without pronounced pro-environmental beliefs (if it is not a serious problem, it is not important!) and for those who view the environmental situation as a pressing global problem (why make an effort if policy does not properly address the environmental situation, but rather is a tool for ensuring further growth).

Lastly, the divergence in problem framing also represents a problem for *policy decisions*, and in prolongation of the outcomes of the decided policy (e.g.

an *ex-ante* legitimacy problem). Considering the way in which the belief systems diverge, we can conclude that the pre-existing legitimacy problem is not due to policy-makers proposing too strict a policy, or too extensive measures. Rather the opposite. The problem we encountered can be described as a reversed legitimacy/effectiveness dilemma, where established public beliefs actually align with taking stronger measures for the sake of environmental protection. Nevertheless, across the entire period studied here, policy continuously de-emphasizes the seriousness of the environmental problem and focuses instead on the modernized strategy of value accommodation, thus avoiding trade-offs between environmental protection and radical changes in contemporary ways of life. At this stage, we can only hypothesize about the reasons for these divergences. They might be an expression of a fundamental difference in world views between policy-makers and public, but they might also be the effect of policy-makers attempting to steer clear of an *ex-post* legitimacy problem by aligning policy to an ideal type of the economically rational citizen-consumer. Given that policy-makers also are a part of the broader public, and therefore should be expected to share significant parts of society's dominant belief-system, it perhaps seems more reasonable to expect the divergences to be connected to the rationality of the decision-making process (and of the role as a decision-maker), rather than to the beliefs of the people being part of them. In either case, however, I conclude that policy-makers, given the values and beliefs of those subordinate to policy, certainly have the opportunity for going further in terms of environmental protection than what presently is the case.

Prospects and prerequisites for future environmental policy legitimacy

One of the ambitions of this thesis has been to encourage policy-makers and public policy scholars alike to consider also the legitimacy of a policy when evaluating and explaining its performance, as well as to grant legitimacy a central role in the processes of public policy design. In this endeavour, I initially presented the theoretically founded rationales for applying legitimacy as a unit of analysis, and subsequently attempted to apply these lessons for exploring the legitimacy situation of contemporary Swedish environmental policy. The result of my empirical analysis was presented in the section above. I concluded that Swedish environmental policy indeed is characterized by a legitimacy problem, affecting performance in a number of different ways: pertaining to credibility for political government, to the prospect for motivating collective action, as well as to initially settling on policy decisions that have good prospects for addressing the environmental problems. We can thereby conclude that I, at this stage, have both created a problem and defined its nature. But, as Wildavsky tells us, public policy analysis is essentially about problem solving; providing solutions to the identified problem presents an equally (or even more) important task for any study. In this section, I will therefore attempt to provide some suggestions as to how the legitimacy problem of Swedish environmental public policy might be amended; how policy-makers in the future can avoid the pitfalls of designing and deciding on policies characterized by a legitimacy problem; as well as, consequently, how the performance of environmental policy in Sweden can be enhanced. This task is captured by the second half of the thesis' aim, to *analyse the prospects and prerequisites for designing future environmental policies that hold a high(er) degree of legitimacy.*

Conceiving legitimacy as belief-system correspondence, the prospects and prerequisites for a high degree of policy legitimacy can be seen as ultimately residing both with policy-makers and with the public. On the one hand, policy legitimacy is determined by the extent to which policy aligns with public values and beliefs, and its legitimacy therefore becomes a question of policy-makers considering established systems of belief when designing policy. On the other hand, legitimacy is conferred to policy by the public, based on shared values and beliefs. Seen in this way, policy legitimacy is, in each specific case, determined by the nature of the publicly established belief system and the opportunities and constraints this places on political decisions. In my view, then, whereas policy-makers need to take certain steps to ensure that the basic requirements, the prerequisites, for policy legitimacy are fulfilled (that is, by ensuring that policies are in fact addressing the right thing), the public ultimately determines the prospects for each policy's legitimacy by setting the frames within which legitimate policy decisions must keep. In other words, the public, through their values and beliefs, determine what this 'right thing' amounts to. Consequently, just because one holds the political *power* to make decisions within the existing legal framework, this does not mean that all possible outputs from the decision-making processes automatically will hold a high degree of legitimacy. And just because a political decision is legitimate in one context, this does not mean that it will be so in another. I acknowledge that this lack of absolutes certainly means some policies, addressing certain issues, will never have the prospect of reaching a high degree of legitimacy in a particular context, as they will be at odds with established public belief systems. If this is positive or negative is a highly subjective question, the answer to which is, again, dependent on each person's basic values and beliefs. Some policies, we may find, are best avoided as they are counter to our own conceptions of the desirable. But legitimacy, seen in this way, may also hinder the decision on, or performance of, policies to which we personally attribute high importance.

In my present case of environmental public policy in Sweden, we remember that the comparison of policy and public belief systems concludes that the present legitimacy problem best can be characterized as a reversed legitimacy/effectiveness dilemma. Overall, the dominant public belief system displays a range of key features that we normally associate with a strong and long-term stable policy for environmental protection: altruism; the primacy of global social justice; a pronounced pro-environmental stance; as well as an awareness of the problem and its consequences. These results indicate that the prospects for making future *environmentally protective* policies with a high degree of legitimacy are good, even if these policies include an increased responsibility-taking (even comprehensive changes in lifestyle) on the part of the individual. Considering the question of prospects for legitimacy, it is certainly of further interest to note that Sweden, despite what above has been concluded on the overall goals, direction and, ultimately, legitimacy of its environmental policy, is still seen as an international forerunner in the environmental domain. In part, this might be an effect of the high level of basic environmental awareness among its citizens. Nevertheless, we cannot evade the hypothetical question of what the status of the Swedish environmental work would be had the prospects for increasing the degree of environmental policy legitimacy been fully utilized.

However, increasing the degree of policy legitimacy indeed requires efforts also on the part of the policy-makers. We know that the basic prerequisite for policy legitimacy is the alignment of belief systems. The task for policy-makers is, consequently, to make sure that decisions are made based on, or at least framed in a way that corresponds to, publicly established values and beliefs. As we have seen above, this concerns both the basic goals towards which policy ultimately aspires, as well as how the nature of a specific policy problem addressed is presented. Realizing a high level of policy legitimacy therefore requires, *first*, that policy-makers are familiar with the prospects for legitimacy in each particular policy context, and, *second*, that they allow this knowledge to be guiding in the process of deciding on policy and framing its message. Although these prerequisites might be interpreted as pointing towards a strengthening and formalizing of the relationship between the powerful and the subordinate, and thus promoting an increased public participation in decision-making processes, I will leave the suggestions for institutional restructuring as a response to legitimacy problems for others to make. Suffice to say that, in those cases where this is a practical possibility, increasing the participatory elements can certainly be one tool for reaching policy decisions that enjoy higher degrees of legitimacy.

Turning towards the case of Swedish environmental policy legitimacy, we noted that the legitimacy problem primarily emanates from Swedish policy not adequately aligning with established beliefs pertaining to the nature, seriousness and direction of the environmental problem. Being more specific, policy neither matches the public's strong pro-environmental beliefs and high sense of risk awareness, nor their sense of moral motivation building on a non-territorial and non-reciprocal sense of social justice. The challenge for policy-makers is therefore to, paraphrasing a well-known expression, speak truth to the public. Rather than framing the environmental problem as an opportunity for increased growth and welfare in Sweden, calling for top-down administration; technological innovation; and transformed market behaviours in expectance of reciprocity, environmental policy legitimacy in Sweden requires, based on what we have learned from the two surveys of public values and beliefs, quite the opposite. Given the strong environmental awareness among the respondents, the dominating broad-scope altruism and the concern for the impact private, household-related activities have on global problems, there are no reasons for policy-makers to hide these facts in political discourse. If the public willingly state that there are more important values that those drawing on self-enhancement, more pressing needs than those of their own in-group, and more in the relationship with nature than merely resource extraction, these beliefs should also be presented to the public as motivations in policy. Therefore, I conclude, not until the environmental situation is framed as a serious (security) problem placed in a global context, as a situation that we therefore by necessity must, and indeed also hold a *moral* obligation to, properly amend, will the degree of legitimacy for Swedish environmental public policy increase.

REFERENCES

Bacchi, C. (1999) *Women, Policy and Politics. The Construction of Policy Problems*, Sage, London

Barnea, M. F. and S. C. Schwartz (1998) 'Values and Voting', *Political Psychology*, 19(1): pp17–39

Baumgartner, F. and B. Jones (1993) *Agendas and Instability in American Politics*, University of Chicago Press, Chicago, IL

Beetham, D. (1991) *The Legitimation of Power*, Macmillan Press, London

Berglund, C. and S. Matti (2006) 'Citizen and Consumer: The Dual Roles of Individuals in Environmental Policy', *Environmental Politics*, 15(4): pp550–571

Birch, A. H. (2001) *Concepts and Theories of Modern Democracy*, Routledge, London

Birkland, T. A. (2005) *An Introduction to the Policy Process: Theories, Concepts, and Models of Public Policy-making*, M.E. Sharpe, Armonk, NY

Buchanan, A. (2002) Political Legitimacy and Democracy. *Ethics*, 112(4): 689–719

Buchanan, A. (2003) *Justice, Legitimacy and Self-Determination: Moral Foundations for International Law*, Oxford University Press, Oxford

Caprara, G. V., S. Schwartz, C. Capanna, M. Veccione and C. Barbanelli (2006) 'Personality and Politics: Values, Traits, and Personal Choice', *Political Psychology*, 27(1): pp1–28.

Coicaud, J.-M. (2002) *Legitimacy and Politics – A Contribution to the Study of Political Right and Political Responsibility*, Cambridge University Press, Cambridge

Connolly, W. E. (1984) Introduction: Legitimacy and Modernity, in W. E. Connolly (ed) *Legitimacy and the State*, pp1–19, Basil Blackwell Ltd, Oxford

Converse, P. (1964) The Nature of Belief Systems in Mass Publics. In D. Apter (ed.) *Ideology and Discontent*, pp206–261, Free Press, New York, NY

Coughlin, R. (1980) *Ideology. Puhlic Opinion and Welfare Policy*, University of California Press, Berkeley, CA

Dahl, R. A. (1985) *A Preface to Economic Democracy*, Yale University Press, New Haven, CT

Dahl, R. A. (1989) *Democracy and its Critics*, Yale University Press, New Haven, CT

Davidov, E., P. Schmidt and S. H. Schwartz (2008) 'Bringing Values Back In. The Adequacy of the European Social Survey to Measure Values in 20 Countries', *Public Opinion Quarterly*, 72(3): pp420–445

Dobson, A. (2003) *Citizenship and the Environment*, Oxford University Press, Oxford

Dryzek, J. S. (2005) *The Politics of the Earth* (2nd edition), Oxford University Press, Oxford

Dunlap, R. E., K. D. Van Liere, A. G. Mertig and R. E. Jones (2000) 'Measuring Endorsement of the New Ecological Paradigm: A Revised NEP Scale', *Journal of Social Issues*, 56(3): pp425–442

Fell, P. T. (2006) *Legitimacy and Conflict – Explaining Tension in Local Swedish Hunting Policy*, Doctoral Thesis, Luleå University of Technology

Fell, P. T. (2008) 'Conflict and Legitimacy: Explaining Tension in Swedish Hunting Policy at the Local Level', *Environmental Politics*, 17(1): pp105–114

Fischer, F. (2003) *Reframing Public Policy: Discursive Politics and Deliberative Practices*, Oxford University Press, Oxford

Free, L. A. and H. Cantril (1968) *The Political Beliefs of Americans*, Simon & Schuster, New York

Frickel, S. and D. J. Davidson (2004) 'Building Environmental States: Legitimacy and Rationalization in Sustainability Governance', *International Sociology*, 19(1): pp89–110

Gilbert, D. T., S. T. Fiske and G. Lindzey (1998) *The Handbook of Social Psychology*, Oxford University Press, Oxford

Glynn, C. J., S. Herbst, G. J. O'Keefe and R. Y. Shapiro (1999) *Public Opinion*, Westview Press, Boulder, CO

Hanberger, A. (2003) 'Public Policy and Legitimacy: A Historical Policy Analysis of the Interplay of Public Policy and Legitimacy', *Policy Sciences*, 36: pp257–278

Held, D. (1996) *Models of Democracy*, Polity Press, Cambridge

Hobson, K. (2003) 'Thinking Habits into Action: The Role of Knowledge and Process in Questioning Household Consumption Practices', *Local Environment*, 8(1): pp95–112

Hønneland, G. (1999) 'The Stories Fishermen Tell: Themes from the Barents Sea Fisheries', *Human Ecology*, 27(4): pp621–626

Jacobs, L.-R., C. J. Glynn, S. Herbst, G. O'Keefe and R. Y. Shapiro (1999) 'Public Opinion and Policymaking', in C. J. Glynn, S. Herbst, G. O'Keefe and R. Y. Shapiro (eds), *Public Opinion*, pp299–340, Westview Press, Boulder, CO

Kingdon, J. W. (1995) *Agendas, Alternatives and Public Policies* (2nd edition), HarperCollins, New York

Knight, J. (1992) *Institutions and Social Conflict*, Cambridge University Press, Cambridge

Lipset, S. M. (1981) *Political Man: The Social Bases of Politics*, Johns Hopkins University Press, Baltimore, MD

Lundqvist, L. J. (2001) 'A Green Fist in a Velvet Glove: The Ecological State and Sustainable Development', *Environmental Values*, 10: pp455–472

Lundqvist, L. J. (2004) *Sweden and Ecological Governance: Straddling the Fence*, Manchester University Press, Manchester

Macnaghten, P. and J. Urry (1998) *Contested Natures*, Sage, London

Maio, G. R. and J. M. Olsen (1995) 'Relations between Values, Attitudes, and Behavioural Intentions: The Moderating Role of Attitude Function', *Journal of Experimental Social Psychology*, 31: pp266–285

Majone, G. (1989) *Evidence, Argument and Persuasion in the Policy Process*, Yale University Press, New Haven, CT

March, J. G. and J. P. Olsen (1989) *Rediscovering Institutions*, Free Press, New York

March, J. G. and J. P. Olsen (2004) The logic of appropriateness, *ARENA Working Papers: WP 04/09*. ARENA (Centre for European Studies), University of Oslo

Matti, S (2009) *Exploring Public Policy Legitimacy: A Study of Belief-System Correspondence in Swedish Environmental Policy*, Doctoral Thesis, Luleå University of Technology

Mehrtens III, F. J. (2004) 'Three Worlds of Public Opinion? Values, Variation, and the Effect on Social Policy', *International Journal of Public Opinion Research*, 16(2): pp115–143

Nee, V. (2001) 'Sources of New Institutionalism', in V. Nee and M. C. Brinton (eds) *The New Institutionalism in Sociology*, pp1–17, Stanford University Press, Stanford, CA

North, D. C. (1990) *Institutions, Institutional Change and Economic Performance*, Cambridge University Press, Cambridge

Ostrom, E. (2005) *Understanding Institutional Diversity*, Princeton University Press, Princeton, NJ

Parkinson, J. (2003) 'Legitimacy Problems in Deliberative Democracy', *Political Studies*, 51: pp180–196

Peffley, M. and J. Hurwitz (1985) 'A Hierarchical Model of Attitude Constraint'. *American Journal of Political Science*, 29: 871–890

Pressman, J. L. and A. Wildavsky (1973) *Implementation: How Great Expectations in Washington Are Dashed in Oakland*, University of California Press, Los Angeles

Putnam, R. (1976) *The Comparative Study of Political Elites*, Prentice-Hall, Englewood Cliffs, NJ

Rein, M. and D. Schön (1993) 'Reframing Policy Discourse', in F. Fischer and J. Forester (eds) *The Argumentative Turn in Policy Analysis and Planning*, pp145–166, Duke University Press, Durham, NC

Rohan, M. J. (2000) 'A Rose by Any Name? The Values Construct', *Personality and Social Psychology Review*, 4(3): 255–277

Rose, R. (1990) 'Inheritance Before Choice in Public Policy', *Journal of Theoretical Politics*, 2: pp263–291

Rothstein, B. (2000) 'Trust, Social Dilemmas and Collective Memories', *Journal of Theoretical Politics*, 12(4): pp477–501

Rova, C. (2004) *Flipping the Pyramid. Lessons from Converting Top-down Management of Bleak-roe Fishing*, Doctoral Thesis, Luleå University of Technology

Rydin, Y. (1999) 'Can We Talk Ourselves Into Sustainability? The Role of Discourse in the Environmental Policy Process', *Environmental Values*, 8: pp467–484

Sabatier, P. A. (1988) 'An Advocacy Coalition Framework of Policy Change and the Role of Policy-oriented Learning Therein', *Policy Sciences*, 21: pp129–168

Sabatier, P. A. (1998) 'The Advocacy Coalition Framework: Revisions and Relevance for Europe', *Journal of European Public Policy*, 5(1): pp98–130

Sabatier, P. A. and H. C. Jenkins-Smith (eds) (1993) *Policy Change and Learning. An Advocacy Coalition Approach*, Westview Press, Boulder, CO

Sabatier, P. A. and H. C. Jenkins-Smith (1999) 'The Advocacy Coalition Framework: An Assessment', in P. A. Sabatier (ed) *Theories of the Policy Process*, pp117–166, Westview Press, Boulder, CO

Sabatier, P. A. and S. Hunter (1989) 'The Incorporation of Causal Perceptions into Models of Elite Belief Systems', *The Western Political Quarterly*, 42(3): pp229–261

Sagoff, M. (1988) *The Economy of the Earth*, Cambridge University Press, Cambridge

Schwartz, S. H. (1992) 'Universals in the Content and Structure of Values: Theoretical Advances and Empirical Tests in 20 countries', *Advances in Experimental Social Psychology*, 25: pp1–65

Steg, L., L. Dreijerink and W. Abrahamse (2005) 'Factors Influencing the Acceptability of Energy Policies: A Test of VBN theory', *Journal of Environmental Psychology*, 25: pp415–425

Stern, M. J. (2008) 'Coercion, Voluntary Compliance, and Protest: The Role of Trust and Legitimacy in Combating Local Opposition to Protected Areas', *Environmental Conservation*, 35(3): pp200–210

Stern, P.C. (2000) 'Toward a Coherent Theory of Environmentally Significant Behaviour', *Journal of Social Issues*, 56: pp407–424

Stern, P. C., T. Dietz, T. Abel, G. A. Guagnano and L. Kalof (1999) 'A Value-belief-norm Theory of Support for Social Movements: The Case of Environmental Concern', *Human Ecology Review*, 6: pp81–97

Stimson, J. A., M. B. MacKuen and R. S. Erikson (1994) 'Opinion and Policy: A Global View', *PS: Political Science and Politics*, 27(1): pp29–35

Stoker, G. (1998) 'Governance as Theory: Five Propositions', *International Social Science Journal*, 50(155): pp17–28

Tyler, T. (1990) *Why People Obey the Law: Procedural Justice, Legitimacy and Compliance*, Princeton University Press, Princeton, NJ

Vedung, E. (1998) 'Policy Instruments: Typologies and Theories', in M-L. Bemelmans-Videc, R. C. Rist and E. Vedung (eds) *Carrots, Sticks and Sermons: Policy Instruments and their Evaluation*, pp21–58 Transaction Publishers, New Brunswick, NJ

Wallner, J. (2008) 'Legitimacy and Public Policy: Seeing Beyond Effectiveness, Efficiency, and Performance', *The Policy Studies Journal*, 36(3): pp421–443

Widegren, Ö. (1998) 'The New Environmental Paradigm and Personal Norms', *Environment and Behaviour*, 30(1): pp75–100

Williams, B. and J. A. Edy (1999) 'Basic Beliefs, Democratic Theory and Public Opinion', in C. J. Glynn, S. Herbst, G. J. O'Keefe and R. Y. Shapiro (eds) *Public Opinion*, pp212–248, Westview Press, Boulder, CO

Wilson, J. Q. (1995) *Political Organizations*, Princeton University Press, Princeton, NJ

5

Barriers and facilitators for pro-environmental behaviour

Annika Nordlund, Louise Eriksson and Jörgen Garvill

INTRODUCTION

To what extent we as individuals and members of a household live a sustainable life depends on the choices we make in our everyday life. This means that the products we consume, the way we travel, the kind of appliances we use in our household, and the way we handle our household waste are all examples of behavioural choices with serious implications for the environment. In Chapter 2, the important relationship between the individual and the state was discussed. This relationship is important since much of the everyday pro-environmental behaviours households are expected to execute are policy directed. If the households perceive that they are left without support, that is, left to fend for themselves when it comes to the dos and don'ts within the realm of environmental behavioural choices, this might affect the degree of willingness for change. In order to achieve a change in a sustainable direction there is therefore a need to understand the diversity of factors important for the daily behaviours of citizens. For example, why do some people buy only organic foods and others don't and what are the reasons for choosing to go by bicycle instead of taking the car? The complexity of everyday life in households has been discussed in depth in Chapter 3. Knowledge of different important factors for daily behaviour is important for the understanding of under what conditions different pro-environmental behaviours are carried out or not by individuals in households. In addition this accentuates the importance of knowledge about barriers and facilitators for policy-makers having to deal with issues of effectiveness and legitimacy, in the design of, for the public, acceptable pro-environmental policies.

The human–environment relationship is a complex one, in which behaviour is both a function of the person and their environment. In addition, pro-environmental behaviour is based on self-interest as well as a concern for other people (Bamberg and Möser, 2007). In order to clarify the multifaceted nature of pro-environmental behaviours, there is a need to include a variety of different factors important for these behaviours, in a structured fashion. The present chapter draws on Stern's (2000) review of four types of causal variables influencing environmentally significant behaviour. The first type is termed *contextual factors* and includes variables such as the physical, economic and social context in which the individual acts. *Personal capabilities* including the knowledge, time and money available to the individual, are the second type of factors acknowledged by Stern. The third category is labelled *attitudinal factors* including the values, beliefs, attitudes and norms the individual holds. Finally, the fourth type is *habits or routines*. The importance of these four types of factors varies between different environmentally significant behaviours. In addition, there are several examples of how factors interact in determining behaviour (see e.g. Guagnano et al, 1995). Overall, these four types of factors constitute a general framework for understanding environmentally significant behaviour. In order to clarify how these factors influence behaviour there is moreover a need to highlight different theoretical approaches used within this field of research, for example the relationship between attitudes and behaviours. In the present chapter, the four types of factors are reviewed and theoretical perspectives explaining the processes by which these factors influence behaviour are described. Empirical evidence will mainly be taken from three domains of everyday behaviour, that is, consumption, waste management and transportation. Finally, the way in which these factors may function as facilitators or barriers for environmentally sustainable behaviour is discussed.

CONTEXTUAL FACTORS

The context in which the individual performs environmentally significant behaviours specifies the extent to which it is feasible to carry out different behaviours. Hence, the context may be more or less facilitating or hindering for various pro-environmental behaviours. According to Stern (2000), contextual factors are, for example, the physical environment, social and societal norms, regulations and monetary incentives and costs, and the broader social, economic and political context. Stern and others (e.g. Clitheroe et al, 1998) label contextual factors as external factors. In addition, how individuals perceive the context may also provide information on how contextual factors influence behaviours (see Stokols, 1987).

Within psychology, two approaches, the instrumentalist and the spiritualist perspectives, highlight the importance of considering contextual factors when examining behaviour (Stokols, 1990). According to an instrumentalist view the context is mainly perceived to be a means for achieving certain goals (e.g. influence the behaviour of individuals). In contrast, the spiritual perspective views the context as an end in itself and highlights both its effect on behaviour and inherent psychological and socio-cultural meanings. Both the instrumentalist and the spiritual perspectives are valuable for an understanding of contextual factors important for pro-environmental behaviour. For example, in an instrumental sense, contextual factors may be changed by means of different policy measures (e.g. reducing the price on public transport) in order to achieve a more pro-environmental behaviour. This perspective is often highlighted in policy discussions. However, for a deeper understanding of motives and barriers for pro-environmental behaviours, there is also a need to understand the psychological and socio-cultural meanings of the context (e.g. the cultural value associated with fast and flexible mobility). According to Stokols (1987), an essential aspect of examining contextual factors is to identify the effective context, that is, the most important contextual factors for a specific behaviour (see also Clitheroe et al, 1998). Even though it would be impossible to identify all potentially relevant factors there is a need to single out the most important factors and their relative importance. In this section, a few examples of contextual factors important for different pro-environmental behaviours within the areas of consumption, waste management and transportation will be reviewed.

For different consumption behaviours, the shops providing the products are the context in which more or less pro-environmental consumer choices are made. One pro-environmental consumer decision concerns whether or not to purchase organic food. Studies have shown that several situational factors, such as the price, availability, marketing strategies and quality of the products are important contextual factors (see e.g. Padel and Foster, 2005; Hughner et al, 2007). For example, Magnusson et al (2001) found that compared to conventional food, organic products were perceived to be more expensive, and in a study by Padel and Foster (2005) high prices were identified as an important barrier for not buying organic food. Moreover, lack of availability has been mentioned as a barrier for buying organic products (Zanoli and Naspetti, 2002), although to what extent it is easy or difficult to find different products may vary. For example, Magnusson et al (2001) demonstrated that while organic milk was perceived to be relatively easy to find organic meat and bread were more difficult.

Households' waste management is carried out inside the home (washing and sorting the waste fractions) as well as leaving the waste to property-close bins or public bins and/or shops. Contextual factors of importance for recycling behaviour are, for example, physical proximity to recycling facilities and storage facilities in the home (see e.g. Ludwig et al, 1998; Do Valle et al, 2004). Ludwig et al (1998) showed that proximity to recycling bins for aluminum cans was important. When the recycling bins were placed in classrooms, where the majority of beverages were consumed, the percentage of cans recycled increased as compared with when the bins where placed in a central location. In addition, the social context (e.g. others' recycling behaviours and others' expectations) has been found to influence recycling (Vining and Ebreo, 1992). In intervention studies, where curbside recycling may be perceived as facilitating recycling through a more favourable physical and social context, recycling behaviour has increased (see e.g. Guagnano et al, 1995).

Travel behaviour often starts at home but is carried out in the external rural or urban setting on public roads or paths using own or public transportation modes. Studies of travel behaviour have demonstrated the importance of both spatial aspects of the travel context, for example, density (Giuliano and Dargay, 2006; Dargay and Hanly, 2007) and social aspects of the travel context, for example, others' travel behaviour (Heath and Gifford, 2002). In many Western countries, these factors facilitate a continued car use. Furthermore, the car has a generally positive symbolic value in our culture (Gatersleben, 2007), even if there are indications that car commuters find their journey more stressful than other mode users, mainly due to delays and other road users (Gatersleben and Uzzell, 2007). Although travel behaviour may be modified by changing the cost for travelling (Goodwin et al, 2004; Paulley et al, 2006; Dargay, 2007) or the service frequency of the public transportation (see Evans, 2004) the behavioural changes are generally modest. Since our perception of the context may influence our travel behaviour, studies have also examined subjective evaluations of the context. McCormack et al (2008) showed that people in general over- or underestimated distances to different locations, that is, overestimated the distance to close destinations and underestimated the distance to destinations farther from the home. This overestimation will for instance influence the willingness to walk or bicycle for shorter trips close to home.

The context is often highlighted when they act as a barrier for pro-environmental behaviours. In order to understand the role of contextual factors in relation to pro-environmental behaviours both an instrumentalist and a spiritualist perspective is useful (cf. Stokols, 1990). The review of studies shows that both physical and socio-cultural factors are important for different pro-environmental behaviours. Among the physical factors, availability (e.g. to find eco-labelled products in the shop, to have room to store recycling materials in the home, or to have access to alternative travel modes), spatial issues (e.g. distance to recycling facilities and distance to important destinations), quality (e.g. quality of eco-labelled products, of recycling stations and of public transportation), and the economic cost of acting (e.g. the cost of purchasing eco-labelled products) are important to consider. Fewer studies have examined socio-cultural factors, even though studies in different behavioural domains have showed that, for example, social norms play an important role when it comes to pro-environmental behaviours. These factors may be considered an initial attempt to summarize the effective context of pro-environmental behaviours (cf. Stokols, 1987). More structured analyses are, however, needed in order to compare the importance of different factors in relation to different behaviours. Moreover, there is a lack of theoretical models clarifying the process by which different contextual factors influence behaviour, for example, the relationship between the objective context and subjective evaluations of the context.

PERSONAL CAPABILITIES

Several resources and abilities are needed in order to perform different pro-environmental behaviours. Personal capabilities including the individual's knowledge, available time and money, social status and power constitute the second type of variables essential for an understanding of pro-environmental behaviours. According to Stern (2000), different socio-demographic variables, for example, age, educational attainment and income may be used as indicators of personal capabilities. Numerous studies have shown that there exists a relationship between personal capabilities, assessed by socio-demographics, and environmental concern and behaviour (e.g. Zelezny et al, 2000; Kemmelmeier et al, 2002; Rimal et al, 2005; Giuliano and Dargay, 2006; Gelissen, 2007; Karpiak and Baril, 2008); however, there are studies in which background demographic factors, including income, education, gender and age, had little effect on self-reported pro-environmental behaviours (Widegren, 1998). Hence, the results of socio-demographics-based investigations are still far from conclusive (Straughan and Roberts, 1999).

In general, studies have shown that people with higher education and income are more likely to have more pro-environmental attitudes (Shen and Saijo, 2008) and to engage in pro-environmental behaviours (Diamantopoulos et al, 2003). Income is said to be positively related to environmental sensitivity, since a higher income level makes it possible for the individual to bear increases in costs that could be associated with some types of pro-environmental behaviours (Zimmer et al, 1994; Kemmelmeier et al, 2002). In contrast, a higher income may also be associated with acting less pro-environmentally. For example, studies have shown that a higher income is associated with driving the car to a larger extent (Giuliano and Dargay, 2006; Dargay and Hanly, 2007). A personal capability closely related to education is knowledge. A heightened level of knowledge would arguably lead to stronger, or more positive, beliefs about a specific behaviour and it has been shown that the knowledge of causes of climate change is greater than that of the climate state and of future consequences of climate change (Sundblad et al, 2009). Moreau et al (2001), also point to knowledge as a central factor influencing new product adoption. More knowledgeable consumers may evaluate attributes differently, ask effective questions and identify for themselves relevant information to a greater extent than less knowledgeable consumers (e.g. Wood and Lynch, 2002). Moreover, age differences in pro-environmental behaviour has been studied (e.g. Van Liere and Dunlap, 1981; Dietz et al, 1998) showing that younger individuals tend to display stronger pro-environmental attitudes. An explanation for this is that those who have grown up when environmental concerns have become or been salient would be more sensitive to environmental issues. Gender is another demographic variable examined in relation to pro-environmental concern and behaviour (e.g. Stern et al, 1993; Dietz et al, 1998; Zelezny et al, 2000; Eisler et al, 2003; Grønhoj and Ölander, 2007). Research has shown that women are more likely than men to hold pro-environmental attitudes and to some degree also report more pro-environmental behaviour. A theoretical justification for this can be traced to Eagly (1987), stating that women are more prone to carefully consider the impact of their actions on others; this then is a result of social development and sex role differences.

Since different socio-demographic factors tend to be important for consumer behaviour in general, it is highly relevant to examine the effects of these factors for pro-environmental consumer behaviour. For example, early adopters of new innovations and products, in general, have higher income and education, and are thereby said to have a financial strength and a more open mindset and ability to learn in general. This is especially true for a high involvement product category such as consumer durables (Gatignon and Robertson, 1985; Martinez et al, 1998; Rogers, 2003). In addition, it has been shown that early adopters are younger and thereby less conservative (Labay and Kinnear, 1981; Wang et al, 2008). Both women and those of younger age have also been found to be more prone towards pro-environmental consumption in general (Dietz et al, 1998). With regard to organic food, women have been found to express more favourable attitudes (Ureña et al, 2008) and both women and the younger population have been found to buy organic food more regularly (Rimal et al, 2005; Onyango et al, 2007). Ureña et al (2008), however, showed that men were more willing to pay a higher price for organic food than women were. Moreover, while income was not important for buying organic food in some studies (see Onyango et al, 2007) other studies have identified an income effect indicating that a higher income is associated with buying organic food to a larger extent (Rimal et al, 2005).

Results from studies of personal capabilities in relation to recycling are not altogether conclusive. A number of studies have shown that income was important for recycling, that is, the higher the income the higher level of recycling (Schultz et al, 1995; Berger, 1997; Scott, 1999; Kurz et al, 2007), even if others have pointed to the reverse (Do Valle et al, 2004; Saphores et al, 2006). Studies on whether gender, age and education are important for recycling behaviour also show mixed results, some pointing to these factors as important while others point to their lack of importance (Schultz et al, 1995; Berger, 1997; Scott, 1999; Do Valle et al, 2004; Saphores et al, 2006). On the other hand there are results showing that recycling is considered too time-consuming and therefore avoided (Vining and Ebreo, 1990; McCarty and Shrum, 1994; Werner and Makela, 1998; Ebreo et al, 1999). One type of recycling is composting household waste, and Edgerton et al (2009) showed that there are several different determinants for this behaviour, two being the degree of knowledge about home composting and the household structure in terms of the family life cycle. Taylor and Todd (1997) studied waste management and found that attitude was positively influenced by societal relative advantage and negatively influenced by personal relative advantage and complexity.

With regard to travel behaviour, the importance of different socio-demographic factors has been examined extensively. In general, gender, age, income and car access have been found to influence travel behaviour (e.g. Giuliano and Dargay, 2006). Women travel shorter distances and use the car less compared to men, express more criticism of auto-mobility, are more positive towards proposals that reduce or eliminate the environmental impact of car use, and express more willingness to reduce their use of the car than men (Polk, 2003). The higher level of subway use among women may be explained by women's stronger ecological norm and weaker car use habit (see also below, Matthies et al, 2002). Furthermore, older people tend to travel shorter distances and use their car less compared to younger people (Steg et al, 2001; Giuliano and Dargay, 2006). Several studies have also demonstrated that individuals with a higher income travel more and use the car more compared to individuals with a lower income, and access to a car is related to travelling longer distances (e.g. Giuliano and Dargay, 2006; Dargay and Hanly, 2007). We know that available time is a personal capability factor that may influence behaviour, but commuting time is to some extent estimated. Fujii et al (2001) showed that drivers who commuted by automobile overestimated commuting time by public transport. If the person, however, gains direct experience with commuting with public transportation, this may result in more accurate estimates of route distances (Thorndyke and Hayes-Roth, 1982; Fujii et al, 2001), which could have an effect on the travel mode choice.

Overall, there is a tendency for women, young people, people with more knowledge and people with a higher educational level to express stronger pro-environmental attitudes and display more frequent pro-environmental behaviours. However, the results are mixed. For example, while there is a tendency for women to display more pro-environmental consumer behaviour and more pro-environmental travel behaviour, the importance of gender for recycling is uncertain. Moreover, a higher income may lead to a more pro-environmental behaviour in one behavioural domain (for example buying organic products to a larger extent) while in a different domain the effect may be reversed (for example a higher level of car use).

In addition, several studies have found that these factors have limited explanatory power (Diamantopoulos et al, 2003; Dietz et al, 1998). However, socio-demographic variables are of importance for certain behaviours and can be, and often are, used as control variables. In future studies, it is important to examine personal capabilities more directly, not only through socio-demographic factors, for example, time and money available for different types of pro-environmental behaviour and the status associated with for example bicycling or buying organic foods.

ATTITUDINAL FACTORS

According to Stern (2000), attitudinal factors include environmental and non-environmental attitudes, personal norms, beliefs and values. Several social psychological models include these factors in order to explain environmentally significant behaviour. One theory often used to explain relationships between attitudinal factors and pro-environmental behaviour is the theory of planned behaviour (TPB) (Ajzen, 1988; 1991). The TPB stipulates that attitudes towards the behaviour (i.e. whether the behaviour is evaluated positively or negatively), subjective norm (i.e. the perception of whether important people think the individual should or should not perform the behaviour), and perceived behavioural control (PBC) (i.e. the perception of control over the behaviour) influence the intention to perform a behaviour. In turn, the PBC and intention jointly predict behaviour. Moreover, beliefs about the consequences of the behaviour (i.e. behavioural beliefs) influence attitude, beliefs about the normative expectations of others (i.e. normative beliefs) influence subjective norm and beliefs about factors facilitating or inhibiting the behaviour (i.e. control beliefs) influence PBC. According to this theory, factors, such as personality, more general attitudes (e.g. awareness of environmental problems), education, gender, knowledge and the context are believed to have only indirect influences on behaviour and mainly influence the individual's beliefs, for example, in relation to general ecological behaviour (i.e. different types of pro-environmental behaviours, such as recycling and limiting car use), Kaiser and Gutscher (2003) found that attitude towards ecological behaviour, subjective norm and perceived behavioural control were all significant predictors of intention to perform ecological behaviour. In turn, intention (although not PBC) significantly predicted ecological behaviour.

In a different theory, the decision to act pro-environmentally is perceived to be a result of a norm activation process. An extensive meta-analysis by Bamberg and Möser (2007) demonstrate that the activation of a moral norm is based on interplay between cognitive, emotional and social factors. The mainstream of the research in this tradition is based on the theory of normative influences on altruistic behaviour proposed by Schwartz (1977) and specifically related to environmental issues, the value-belief-norm (VBN) theory of environmentalism (Stern et al, 1999). The VBN theory stipulates a hierarchy of values, environmental beliefs and personal norm to explain pro-environmental behaviour. Altruistic and biospheric values emphasizing others above one's own interests, a general awareness of the environmental problems measured by the New Ecological Paradigm (NEP) scale (see Dunlap et al, 2000), an awareness of the adverse consequences of human behaviour on the environment, and an ascription to oneself of a responsibility to act, activate a personal norm to save the environment. In turn, the activated personal norm influences pro-environmental behaviour. According to the theory, perceiving environmental problems as more or less severe or threatening depend on the value structure. Values were argued to function as the frame from within which available information about the state of the environment is interpreted, or as amplifiers of such information (Stern and Dietz, 1994; Stern et al, 1995). The amplifying function of values depends on whether the values are individually or collectively oriented. The activated personal norm is therefore a mediator between problem awareness and behaviour (Schwartz, 1977). Karpiak and Baril (2008) showed that moral reasoning correlated positively with belief in the intrinsic importance of nature (ecocentrism), however unrelated to belief that nature is important because it is central to human well-being (anthropocentrism), and negatively associated with environmental apathy. Environmental concern, such as ecocentrism or NEP does correspond with environmentally friendly behaviour, and is predicted by such moral reasoning. Hence, a personal norm to act may be activated among individuals with more collective values who are aware of the need to save the environment and perceive a personal responsibility to take action.

Kaiser et al (2005) found, when comparing the explanatory power of the TPB (Ajzen, 1991) and the VBN theory (Stern, et al, 1999) that both theories accounted for a large degree of variance in conservation behaviours. However, the researchers stated that the TPB has stronger predictive power and better depicted the determinants of conservation behaviour. Within the TPB framework, moral norms are not accounted for and Kaiser and Scheuthle (2003) showed that moral norms are not needed in the TPB in order to improve the already great explanatory power. Hübner and Kaiser (2006), however, demonstrated that moral considerations have a stronger effect on the behavioural intention when a conflict between the attitude and the subjective norm exists, pointing to the important moderating role of a moral norm in the TPB framework. Hence, examining factors stipulated both in the TPB and the VBN theory provide valuable insights to understand attitudinal factors important for pro-environmental behaviour in different behavioural domains.

Much research on pro-environmental consumption has been conducted and factors such as value orientation, environmental beliefs, attitudes and norms have been shown to influence the willingness to consume in a pro-environmental manner and the willingness to pay higher prices for environmentally friendly foods (Homer and Kahle, 1988; Widegren, 1998; Thøgersen and Ölander, 2002; Hughner et al, 2007; Tsakiridou et al, 2008). For example, collective values, such as self-transcendent values and environmental values have been shown to influence the willingness to consume in an environmentally responsible manner (Grunert and Juhl, 1995; Roberts and Bacon, 1997). Birgelen et al (2009) demonstrate that eco-friendly purchase of beverages is related to the environmental awareness of consumers and their eco-friendly attitudes. Consumers are willing to trade off almost all product attributes in favour of the specific attribute: environmentally friendly packaging of beverages. There is further research showing that there are emotional consumption experiences related to environmental products expressed as feelings of well-being from acting in an altruistic way (i.e. not counteracting your personal norms) and that the identification of ethical issues in consumption affects both attitudes and consumption choices (Hartmann, 2008; Michaelidou and Hassan, 2008). In line with the VBN theory, Widegren (1998) demonstrated that the personal norm was far more strongly correlated to the willingness to pay more for environmentally friendly foods, than was the NEP scale. Moreover, Thøgersen and Ölander (2006) found that in addition to the perceiving of organic products as less expensive, consumers with stronger personal norms to buy organic food products were more likely to change their purchase patterns in favour of organic products.

The extensive research on recycling clearly shows that factors such as value orientation, environmental beliefs and norms do influence recycling behaviour (Hopper and McCarl-Nielsen, 1991; Vining and Ebreo, 1992; McCarty and

Shrum, 1994; Thompson and Barton, 1994; McKenzie-Mohr et al, 1995; Thøgersen, 1996; Bratt, 1999). In a study by Taylor and Todd (1997), an integrated model of waste management was found to explain a large share of the variance in behaviour. The model combined different environmental beliefs and factors stipulated by the TPB, showing that the attitude concept was the key determinant of the behavioural intention. Studies have also demonstrated the possibility to increase the level of recycling with interventions aiming to produce attitude and behaviour change (Burn and Oskamp, 1986; Wang and Katzev, 1990). Koestner et al (2001) showed that if the individual is recycling foremost as a result of a personal norm, meaning that the person recycles to avoid feelings of guilt, this person is more prone to listen to counter-attitudinal information, especially coming from an attractive source (Koestner et al, 2001). Attitudes have in addition been shown to be the most important determinants of whether a household chooses to compost household waste, which means it is important to have a favourable attitude towards what home composting involves if composting behaviour is to be carried out (Edgerton et al, 2009).

In relation to travel behaviour, both the VBN theory and the TPB have been found to be useful theoretical approaches. For example, studies have verified a relationship between a personal norm on one hand and car use (Bamberg and Schmidt, 2003), willingness to reduce car use (Matthies et al, 2002; Nordlund and Garvill, 2003) and the use of transport modes other than the car (Harland et al, 1999; Hunecke et al, 2001; Matthies et al, 2002; Matthies et al, 2006; Bamberg et al, 2007; Beale and Bonsall, 2007) on the other hand. In addition, the TPB constructs, and more specifically intention, have been found to be related to car use (Bamberg and Schmidt, 2003), restricting car use (Kaiser and Gutscher, 2003), changing travel mode (Bamberg, 2006; Bamberg et al, 2007), and the use of transport modes other than the car (Bamberg and Schmidt, 2001; Heath and Gifford, 2002). It has been shown that collective values, such as values transcending the self, influences willingness to reduce car use positively (Garvill, 1999). People with a cooperative value orientation have in addition been found to prefer public transportation to car use (van Vugt et al, 1995). Wall et al (2007) compared Schwartz's (1977) norm-activation theory (NAT) and Ajzen's TPB in relation to the intention to reduce car use for commuting. The results showed that the NAT explained more variance than the TPB when tested independently, while a model combining the NAT and TPB explained a larger share of the variance. In the combined model, the personal norm from the NAT and the perceived behavioural control from the TPB influenced the intention to reduce car use.

Overall, the review shows that attitudinal factors in relation to different pro-environmental behaviours have been examined extensively. In general, studies demonstrate that different attitudinal factors, such as values, environmental beliefs, personal and subjective norms, attitudes and perceived behavioural control are important direct or indirect predictors of pro-environmental intentions and behaviours. Hence, the individuals' beliefs about environmental issues and beliefs about the specific behaviour are crucial for an understanding of pro-environmental behaviours. A general conservation stance can be seen to exist, in that environmental values that people hold foster feelings of behavioural choices in many settings. When people start to act in an environmentally friendly way in one area this behaviour is to some degree also related to other types of environmentally behaviour (Thogersen and Ölander, 2006).

HABIT OR ROUTINE

Even though contextual factors, personal capabilities and attitudinal factors are important for environmentally significant behaviour, Stern (2000) highlights the need to consider a fourth factor, that is, habit or routine. Since much environmentally significant behaviour is performed repeatedly in a relatively stable context they tend to evolve into behavioural habits, that is, past behaviour guides future responses (Aarts et al, 1998; Ouellette and Wood, 1998). According to Verplanken and Aarts (1999), habits are characterized by automaticity (e.g. efficiency and lack of awareness), functionality and situational constancy. Hence, habits develop if a certain behaviour has rewarding consequences and is repeated in a stable context. For example, if the car is used to go to work for a long period of time and it is experienced as an effective transportation mode, it is likely that the individual uses the car automatically and no longer considers other travel options. Habit has been defined as an automatic link between a goal (i.e. an intention to act) and a certain behaviour (Verplanken and Aarts, 1999; Aarts and Dijksterhuis, 2000a, 2000b) or a behavioural script stored in memory (Gärling et al, 2001; Fujii and Gärling, 2003).

The traditional perspective on consumer choice is that these choices are based on conscious information processing. However, others propose that many consumer choices are made unconsciously and are strongly affected by cues in the environment (Dijksterhuis et al, 2005; Ji and Wood, 2007). When getting people to start buying organic foods consumers' old consumer habits must be broken and the new experience must be sufficiently rewarding to establish a new organic purchasing routine (Thøgersen and Ölander, 2006), otherwise there is a risk that habitual consumer behaviours will continue even if alternative intentions are present (Ji and Wood, 2007). Since our consumption behaviour is prone to develop into habits, studies have been conducted with the aim of suppressing the distracting influence of past food purchase habits (Dahlstrand and Biel, 1997; Thøgersen and Ölander, 2006). In response to interventions, such as monetary incentives and stimulation to plan for a new behaviour, an experimental group was significantly more likely to enact the goal intention to test organically produced food, compared to the control group (Bamberg, 2002). Hence, interrupting the habitual behaviour resulted in a greater probability of actually performing the new behaviour. Moreover, Dahlstrand and Biel (1997) highlight a series of processes important for establishing a pro-environmental habit in the realm of consumption. First, there is a need to activate environmental values in order to interrupt old habits, subsequently attend to the present behaviour and consider alternatives, to plan for a new behaviour as well as testing and evaluating the new behaviour.

Only a few studies have examined the role of habit within the realm of recycling behaviour, for example regarding past recycling behaviour but also the lack of habit as a reason for failing to recycle (Knussen et al, 2004; Knussen and Yule, 2008). However, the importance of habit has been a much more prominent issue when it comes to transportation behaviour. In line with the proposition that habit strength should influence the elaborateness of choice processes, studies have shown that those who had a strong habit towards choosing a particular travel mode did acquire less information and were less elaborative in their choice strategies (Aarts et al, 1997; Verplanken et al, 1997). When travel behaviour is habitual, the activation of a travel goal automatically activates a travel mode in memory, and this habitual response is difficult to suppress under conditions of cognitive load (Aarts and Dijksterhuis, 2000a). Since habitual behaviour is characterized by a lack of awareness, studies of the effects of increased awareness on travel mode choice is of interest. In a field experiment it was shown that in an experimental group, in which a more deliberate choice of travel mode was induced, a temporally extended decrease in car use was observed (Garvill et al, 2003).

Even though behaviours in the domains of consumption, recycling and transportation have been considered a result of deliberate decisions for a long time, recent research indicates a need to highlight the habitual quality of these everyday behaviours. For example, the way in which habits should be interrupted in order for a new behaviour to be enacted has been demonstrated. While contextual factors, personal resources and attitudinal factors have been found to be significant direct predictors of pro-environmental behaviours, the relationship between habit and behaviour is more complicated. Even though certain studies have found that habit is a significant direct predictor of behaviour (see e.g. Bamberg and Schmidt, 2003), several researchers describe habit as a moderator of the attitude–behaviour relationship (see Triandis, 1980). Hence, habit and attitudinal factors interact in order to determine behaviour. The interaction between different causal factors will be dealt with in the coming section.

INTERACTIONS BETWEEN CAUSAL FACTORS

The four factors proposed by Stern (2000) are certainly related in various ways. For example, personal capabilities as well as the context in which the individual act are important for the formation of attitudes and norms. Furthermore, these different types of factors may not only influence behaviour separately, they may also interact in determining behaviour. In this section, the interactions between contextual factors, personal capabilities, attitudinal factors and habits will be highlighted.

The ways in which attitudinal factors and contextual factors interact have been examined to some extent and different accounts of this relation have been proposed. According to the Attitude, Behaviour and Context/external conditions (ABC) theory proposed by Guagnano et al (1995), the relationship between attitude and behaviour is strong only when the contextual factors are neutral. In strongly inhibiting and in strongly facilitating conditions the relationship between attitude and behaviour is weaker (i.e. an inverted U-shaped function). For example, when it is very easy to act pro-environmentally there is no need for favourable attitudes and when it is very difficult to act pro-environmentally even very favourable attitudes cannot influence behaviour because of the contextual constraints. Hence, attitudinal factors influence behaviour only when the context neither facilitates nor inhibits the behaviour. In a different attempt to describe under what conditions attitudinal factors influence behaviours, Diekmann and Preisendörfer (2003) proposed the low-cost high-cost hypothesis. According to them, the relationship between attitudinal factors and behaviour is stronger when the context is facilitating and weaker when the context is inhibiting (i.e. a linear relationship). Hence, only when it is very easy to perform the behaviour will the individuals' attitudes influence behaviour. In general, both the ABC theory and the low-cost high-cost hypothesis stipulate a boundary condition for the relationship between attitudes and behaviour so that attitudes are only related to behaviour in certain conditions.

When one defines what habits are and how they develop, the interaction between habits and the context is always present, since habits develop in stable contexts. Habit has been found to interact with intention when the context is stable but intentions guide behaviour when habits are weak or the context unstable (Danner et al, 2008). Interactions between different attitudinal factors and habit in predicting pro-environmental behaviour have been examined in several studies. The main argument is that when a behavioural habit is strong the influence of various attitudinal factors, such as, intentions (Triandis, 1980; Verplanken et al, 1998; Staats et al, 2004), attitudes (Verplanken et al, 1994) and norms (Klöcker et al, 2003; Klöckner and Matthies, 2004) on environmentally significant behaviours are weaker. Hence, attitudinal factors mainly influence behaviour when the behaviour is not habitual, while habit is the most important predictor when a strong habit has developed. Consequently, in the same way as the context, habits have a boundary effect on the attitude–behaviour relationships.

Consumption

Also in our everyday consumption our choices are prone to be affected by different causal factors. Dahlstrand and Biel (1997) showed that habits affect consumer choices. Results from their study demonstrated that environmental values and a sense of responsibility for the environment was more influential in an early phase rather than in a later phase of changing established habits regarding pro-environmental purchases. In later phases specific beliefs about the product were more influential. Hence, different beliefs were found to be important at different stages in the process towards establishing a new habit.

Recycling

In studies of recycling and composting kitchen waste, interactions between attitudinal and contextual factors have been examined. In these studies, a facilitating condition was to have curb side pickup of recycling goods, while an inhibiting condition was when recycling goods had to be taken to a public container. In line with the low-cost high-cost hypothesis (Diekmann and Preisendörfer, 2003), attitudinal factors, such as environmental concern, were found to be correlated with recycling in facilitating situations and not in inhibiting situations (Derksen and Gartrell, 1993; Diekmann and Preisendörfer, 2003). After an intervention involving storage equipment for compostable kitchen waste as well as biweekly pickups Ölander and Thøgersen (2005) found that attitude became a more important predictor of recycling compared to before. Hence, in line with the low-cost high-cost hypothesis, attitudinal variables were mainly important for recycling in a facilitating context. However, an empirical test of the ABC theory in relation to recycling found that awareness of responsibility (i.e. an attitudinal variable) was correlated with behaviour in inhibiting situations but not in facilitating situations (Guagnano et al, 1995). The results indicate that the context interacts with attitudinal variables in determining behaviour, although the exact nature of this relationship is uncertain. Moreover, one could see in a study by Katzev et al (1993) that the self-reported recycling level in multi-family residences where a recycling system had been installed was positively associated with income, education and cleanliness of the recycling system. Thus, what can be called 'user friendliness' of the recycling system and its spatial location accounted for a large degree of the variance in recycling behaviour.

Knussen et al (2004) showed when studying recycling intentions that the TPB components (not subjective norm however), past recycling behaviour and recycling habits had independent effects on recycling intentions. Moreover, the results suggested that the relationship between perceived behavioural control and recycling intention was weaker when facilities were perceived to be lacking, indicating the important role of the contextual factor.

Transportation

With regard to travel mode choice, studies have used different ways to operationalize facilitating and inhibiting situations when examining the importance of contextual variables. For example, a free ticket on public transport and a short distance to a destination have been used as indicators of contexts facilitating a more pro-environmental travel mode choice. In these studies, however, no support was found for the moderating effects of context. While Hunecke et al (2001), found that personal norm and travel mode choice was correlated both in a low-cost situation (with a free ticket to use public transport) and in a high-cost situation (without a free ticket), Diekmann and Preisendörfer (2003) found that environmental concern was not a significant predictor of shopping without a car in neither a low-cost group (i.e. individuals with less than one kilometre to the shop) nor in a high-cost group. In a few studies, the perception of how facilitating or inhibiting the context is perceived to be (e.g. the perceived behavioural control) was used as an indicator of contextual factors. For example Wall et al (2005) found that the correlation between a measure including awareness of responsibility combined with personal norm and car use was lower, but significant, when perceived behavioural control was low compared to when the perceived behavioural control was high. Hence, no strong support for the moderating role of context was found in that study. In a slightly different approach, Corraliza and Berenguer (2000) found that in situations where there is a conflict between personal variables and the situation, for example a weak personal norm in a situation where control over the behaviour is high or a strong personal norm in a situation where the possibility to perform the behaviour is low, less variance in restricting vehicle use is explained by attitudinal factors compared to when there is no conflict. It has been shown that there exists a positive relationship between income and car use (e.g. Giuliano and Dargay, 2006; Dargay and Hanly, 2007). There is, however, an adaptation taking place when car-use costs increase; a trade-off between minimizing travel costs and travel time was then observed in car users (Horeni et al, 2007).

Some research has been done on how attitudinal factors and habits interact within the field of travel mode choice. For example, Matthies et al (2006) showed that moral motivation is a relevant predictor for travel mode choices after an intervention (gift of a free ticket on public transportation), in a group of habitual car users. Moreover, the effects of attitude and habit on choice of travel mode have been studied in a number of experiments (Verplanken et al, 1994; Verplanken et al, 1997; Gärling et al, 2001). For example, Gärling et al (2001) found that when people have a positive attitude towards driving, this leads to a more frequent choice of driving and over time makes the choice script-based, that is, habitual. Results from these studies confirmed that when no car habit exists, information about contextual factors, such as the weather, distance, time, cargo and available alternatives and their consequences, for the trip is given more attention.

Bamberg et al (2003) showed that the choice of travel mode largely was a reasoned decision and that this decision can be affected by interventions aimed at changing attitudes, subjective norms and perceptions of behavioural control. In addition they showed that past travel choice contributes to the prediction of later behaviour only if circumstances remain relatively stable. Breaking habitual travel mode choice is thus related to contextual change (Bamberg, 2006). Moreover, Davidov (2007) showed that when the context changes, as a residential relocation, effect of habits on behaviour no longer exists and the use of public transportation increased. A finding further supported by Verplanken et al (2008) who found that individuals who had recently moved to a new home and were environmentally concerned used the car less frequently for commuting to work, compared to those who were environmentally concerned but had not recently moved. When a change in travel mode choice has been established, for example an increased use of public transportation due to a temporary freeway closure, this change may develop into a script-based travel mode choice enduring a longer period after the closure (Fujii and Gärling, 2003).

DISCUSSION

The review shows the complexity of human–environment relationships, in which behaviour is both a function of the person and their environment and based on self-interest as well as a concern for other people (Bamberg and Möser, 2007). Hence, a multitude of factors are important for these behaviours. In the present chapter research has been reviewed from the standpoint of Stern's (2000) four types of causal variables influencing environmentally significant behaviour. *Contextual factors* include variables such as the physical, economic and social context in which the individual act. *Personal capabilities* include the knowledge, time and money available to the individual. *Attitudinal factors* including the values, beliefs, attitudes and norms the individual holds and finally, *habits or routines*.

These causal factors may be viewed from different perspectives, that of factors as external versus internal to the individual, and the factors existing on different levels in society, close to the individual or more distant. In Figure 5.1, these different factors are ordered, seen from an individual perspective, from factors external from the individual to gradually more internal individual factors. The contextual factors constitute the external frame in which all environmentally significant behaviour takes place, while personal capabilities consist of both internal and external abilities and resources, and the two remaining factors, attitudinal factors and habits, are internal factors. The focal point within this line of research is the individual – an individual with a certain set of values, beliefs and norms. As shown in the large bulk of research these attitudinal factors can influence the willingness to act pro-environmentally with regards to recycling, consumption and transportation behaviours, in a directly positive as well as in a negative way. In addition, it has been shown that the individual may have developed habits or routines in his or her everyday life, which may counteract any influence of attitudinal factors. Our personal capabilities have been shown to both have an influence on the willingness to act in a pro-environmental manner, but also on our attitudes. Likewise the contexts we function within pose an influence on behaviour, on our attitudes and habits, and also on our personal capabilities. Figure 5.1, implies that the context is the frame from which we are able to act, meaning that in situations with a strong contextual support for pro-environmental behaviour there is less need for more personal factors to influence behaviour (Stern, 2005). However, in a very restricted context these personal factors do become important and salient as causal factors.

When trying to understand how we can eliminate barriers and instead facilitate pro-environmental behaviours, with different strategies or policies, Stern's (2000) four categories of causal factors is a viable point of departure. Even though pro-environmental behaviours are very different, much green behaviour entails some kind of sacrifice from the individual, that is, there are a number of costs attached to the green behaviour. The costs are often strongly dependent on time and context (for instance, in relation to recycling). People may for example feel green behaviour is expensive, inconvenient or an annoyance and those costs may act as a significant barrier to green behaviour in households. Since much everyday behaviour is regularly repeated in similar situations, habits are formed to make daily life easier. The behaviour then becomes automatic and the individual does not think deeply about his behaviour. Habitual sustainable actions thus make green behaviour easier for the individual. However, habitual non-sustainable actions constrain change because behaviour is then controlled by habit rather than inner motivation to act green. This thus shows that even if the individual is motivated to act green by reason of a personal norm, the perceived costs or strong habits of non-sustainable action may prevent the behaviour from actually being performed. Much behaviour is strongly determined by the context within which they are present, such as location of home and of workplaces, the availability of public transportation, and the availability of recycling facilities. Also our personal capabilities play a role, in that the knowledge, time and money available to the individual do influence our decisions at given times, such as when we are at the verge of buying a new car, or new kitchen appliances, or when we are relocating. In addition, we know that inducing personal and social norms in relation to different environmentally significant behaviours is one way to encourage behavioural change within the everyday context of households. We know that people are influenced by norms on one hand, but we also know that people do not necessarily act in accordance with their held norms, due to the fact that they often act out of habit, without reflection. Behavioural change is thus achieved to a larger extent by changing the context of behaviour, rather than by trying to change the behaviour directly. This is, however, not easily done since the context is often more or less set, such as the transportation infrastructure in most towns, regions and nations. Despite this, there is a need to find innovative ways of changing the context of behaviour in order to achieve a change towards the more pro-environmental.

Viewing the model of the causal factors in Figure 5.1, adapted from Stern (2000), together with the knowledge from previous research on the influence of these factors on intentions and behaviours, there are different policy implications to consider. One such consideration is that when policies are developed and implemented we need to know towards which causal factors they are aimed. A policy might be aimed at changing people's behaviour through their attitudes directly, without consideration of any contextual or personal capability barriers, by, for example, information campaigns evoking positive attitudes towards travelling by public transportation or recycling paper, plastics and metals. The aim of a policy can, on the other hand, take on a more overall perspective on behavioural change by considering people's attitudes and personal capabilities within their contextual boundary, by directed information to a town's inhabitants or city district. A policy may also be directed directly at the behaviour at hand, such as introducing a road toll to decrease carbon dioxide emissions in a city. Such a policy when implemented may change people's

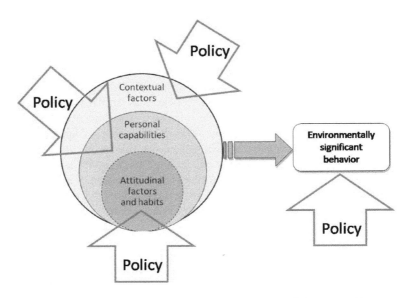

Figure 5.1 *Policy implications on the four causal factors influencing environmentally significant behaviour (adapted from Stern, 2000)*

attitudes towards using the car or public transportation, but this is not necessarily the aim of the policy. As Stern suggests, behavioural change is the result of a number of different causal factors (Stern, 2000), thus leading to the conclusion that we have to work with policies that tap on these different factors. In essence then, it is of importance to know at what level in the causal chain the policy is to be aimed, or towards which behaviours it is aimed, in order to fully understand the seen or unseen behavioural changes.

What characterizes most demands for personal environmental responsibility is that they require personal sacrifices of some kind in the form of money, time or perhaps less convenience. They benefit the common good in the form of a better environment, but the direct benefit to the individual is often minor. The facts then, that behaviour and its causal factors are complex in nature lend support to using multiple policies, or policy packages. Such policy packages should range over more than one causal factor and present the household with solutions presenting a facilitating perspective on the related costs of giving something of value up in their everyday life. We can by using multiple policies seize the opportunity given by the influence of the individual's own sense of a personal obligation to act pro-environmentally (personal norm) as we also contribute with necessary facilitators of the given behaviour.

CONCLUSIONS

The first important conclusion one can draw is that individuals' pro-environmental behaviours in the private sphere are important targets for behavioural change, since they have a large impact on the environment at an aggregated level. Problem awareness, a positive perception of one's own personal capacity to affect environmental outcomes, social influence and reasonable sacrifices are factors that – in combinations – induce people to take active individual responsibility for the environment and undertake any related activities. These results apply equally well to recycling, purchasing eco-labelled products and choosing modes of transport. The strength of these factors largely explains the wide variation in individual action across these three areas. It is, however, very important to realize that behaviours are more or less constrained by the context, and behavioural change may require a contextual change foremost. When this is not possible, powerful approaches can be developed that entail multiple influences on behaviour, presenting a 'carrot and stick' perspective on behavioural change in the environmental sphere. In the following chapter the causal factors reviewed and discussed in this chapter, that of context, personal capabilities, attitudinal factors and habits, will be analysed and discussed in the empirical setting of pro-environmental behaviours such as recycling, eco-consumption and sustainable travel behaviour in Swedish households, foremost in the present, but also from a historical perspective.

REFERENCES

Aarts, H. and Dijksterhuis, A. (2000a) 'The automatic activation of goal-directed behaviour: The case of travel habit', *Journal of Environmental Psychology*, vol 20, pp75–82

Aarts, H. and Dijksterhuis, A. (2000b) 'Habits as knowledge structures: Automaticity in goal-directed behavior', *Journal of Personality and Social Psychology*, vol 78, pp53–63

Aarts, H., Verplanken, B. and van Knippenberg, A. (1997) 'Habit and information use in travel mode choices', *Acta Psychologica*, vol 96, pp1–14

Aarts, H., Verplanken, B. and van Knippenberg, A. (1998) 'Predicting behavior from actions in the past: Repeated decision making or a matter of habit?', *Journal of Applied Social Psychology*, vol 28, pp1355–1374

Ajzen, I. (1988) *Attitudes, personality, and behaviour*, Dorsey Press, Chicago, IL

Ajzen, I. (1991) 'The theory of planned behavior', *Organizational Behavior and Human Decision Processes*, vol 50, pp179–211

Bamberg, S. (2002) 'Implementation intention versus monetary incentive comparing the effects of interventions to promote the purchase of organically produced food', *Journal of Economic Psychology*, vol 23, pp573–587

Bamberg, S. (2006) 'Is a residential relocation a good opportunity to change people's travel behavior?: Results from a theory-driven intervention study', *Environment and Behavior*, vol 38, pp820–840

Bamberg, S. and Möser, G. (2007) 'Twenty years after Hines, Hungerford, and Tomera: A new meta-analysis of psycho-social determinants of pro-environmental behavior', *Journal of Environmental Psychology*, vol 27, pp14–25

Bamberg, S. and Schmidt, P. (2001) 'Theory-driven subgroup-specific evaluation of an intervention to reduce private car use', *Journal of Applied Social Psychology*, vol 31, pp1300–1329

Bamberg, S. and Schmidt, P. (2003) 'Incentives, morality, or habit? Predicting students' car use for university routes with the models of Ajzen, Schwartz, and Triandis', *Environment and Behavior*, vol 35, pp264–285

Bamberg, S., Ajzen, I. and Schmidt, P. (2003) 'Choice of travel mode in the theory of planned behavior: The roles of past behavior, habit, and reasoned action', *Basic and Applied Social Psychology*, vol 25, pp175–187

Bamberg, S., Hunecke, M. and Blöbaum, A. (2007) 'Social context, personal norms and the use of public transportation: Two field studies', *Journal of Environmental Psychology*, vol 27, pp190–203

Beale, J. R. and Bonsall, P. W. (2007) 'Marketing in the bus industry: A psychological interpretation of some attitudinal and behavioural outcomes', *Transportation Research Part F: Traffic Psychology and Behaviour*, vol 10, pp271–287

Berger, I. E., (1997) 'The demographics of recycling and the structure of environmental behaviour', *Environment and Behavior*, vol 29, pp515–531

Birgelen, M., von., Semeijn, J. and Keicher, M. (2009) 'Packaging and proenvironmental consumption behavior', *Environment and Behavior*, vol 41, pp125–146

Bratt, C. (1999) 'The impact of norms and assumed consequences on recycling behavior', *Environment and Behavior*, vol 31, pp630–656

Burn, S. M. and Oskamp, S. (1986) 'Increasing community recycling with persuasive communication and public commitment', *Journal of Applied Social Psychology*, vol 16, pp29–41

Clitheroe, H. C., Stokols, D. and Zmuidzane, M. (1998) 'Conceptualizing the context of environment and behavior', *Journal of Environmental Psychology*, vol 18, pp103–112

Corraliza, J. A. and Berenguer, J. (2000) 'Environmental values, beliefs, and actions. A situational approach', *Environment and Behavior*, vol 32, pp832–848

Dahlstrand, U. and Biel, A. (1997) 'Pro-environmental habits: Propensity levels in behavioral change', *Journal of Applied Social Psychology*, vol 27, pp588–601

Danner,U. N., Aarts, H. and de Vries, N. K. (2008) 'Habit vs. intention in the prediction of future behaviour: The role of frequency, context stability and mental accessibility of past behaviour', *British Journal of Social Psychology*, vol 47, pp245–265

Dargay, J. (2007) 'The effect of prices and income on car travel in the UK', *Transportation Research Part A, Policy and Practice*, vol 41, pp949–960

Dargay, J. and Hanly, M. (2007) 'Volatility of car ownership, commuting mode and time in the UK', *Transportation Research Part A*, vol 41, pp934–948

Davidov, E. (2007) 'Explaining habits in a new context: The case of travel-mode choice', *Rationality and Society*, vol 19, pp315–334

Derksen, L. and Gartrell, J. (1993) 'The social context of recycling', *American Sociological Review*, vol 58, pp434–442

Diamantopoulos, A., Schlegelmilch, B. B., Sinkovics, R. R. and Bohlen, G. M. (2003) 'Can socio-demographics still play a role in profiling green consumers? A review of the evidence and an empirical investigation', *Journal of Business Research*, vol 56, pp465–480

Diekmann, A. and Preisendörfer, P. (2003) 'Green and greenback: The behavioral effects of environmental attitudes in low-cost and high-cost situations', *Rationality and Society*, vol 15, pp441–472

Dietz, T., Stern, P. C. and Guagnano, G. A. (1998) 'Social structural and social psychological bases of environmental concern', *Environment and Behavior*, vol 30, pp450–471

Dijksterhuis, A., Smith, P. K., van Baaren, R. B. and Wigboldus, D. H. J. (2005) 'The unconscious consumer: Effects of environment on consumer behavior', *Journal of Consumer Psychology*, vol 15, pp193–202

Do Valle, P. O., Reis, E., Menezes, J., and Rebelo, E. (2004), 'Behavioral determinants of household recycling participation – The Portuguese case', *Environment and Behavior*, vol 36, pp505–540

Dunlap, R. E., Van Liere, K. D., Mertig, A. G. and Jones, R. E. (2000) 'Measuring endorsement of the New Ecological Paradigm: A revised NEP scale', *Journal of Social Issues*, vol 56, pp425–442

Eagly, A. H. (1987) *Sex differences in social behavior: A social-role interpretation*, Lawrence Erlbaum Associates, Hillsdale, NJ

Ebreo, A., Hershey, J. and Vining, J. (1999) 'Reducing solid waste. Linking recycling to environmentally responsible consumerism', *Environment and Behavior*, vol 31, pp107–135

Edgerton, E., McKechnie, J. and Dunleavy, K. (2009) 'Behavioral determinants of household participation in a home composting scheme', *Environment and Behavior*, vol 41, pp151–169

Eisler, A. D., Eisler, H. and Yoshida, M. (2003) 'Perception of human ecology: Cross-cultural and gender comparisons', *Journal of Environmental Psychology*, vol 23, pp89–101

Evans, J. E. (2004) 'Traveler response to transportation system changes. Chap. 9: Transit scheduling and frequency', *TCRP Report* 95. Transportation Research Board

Fujii, S. and Gärling, T. (2003) 'Development of script-based travel mode choice after forced change', *Transportation Research Part F*, vol 6, pp117–124

Fujii, S., Gärling, T. and Kitamura, R. (2001) 'Changes in drivers' perceptions and use of public transport during a freeway closure: Effects of temporary structural change on cooperation in a real-life social dilemma', *Environment and Behavior*, vol 33, pp796–808

Gärling, T., Fujii, S. and Boe, O. (2001) 'Empirical tests of a model of determinants of script-based driving choice', *Transportation Research Part F*, vol 4, pp89–102

Garvill, J. (1999) 'Choice of transportation mode: Factors influencing drivers' willingness to reduce personal car use and support car regulations', in M. Foddy, M. Smithson, S. Schneider, and M. Hogg (eds) *Resolving social dilemmas. Dynamic, structural, and intergroup aspects*, Psychology Press, Philadelphia, PA

Garvill, J., Marell, A. and Nordlund, A. (2003) 'Effects of increased awareness on choice of travel mode', *Transportation*, vol 30, pp36–79

Gatersleben, B. (2007) 'Affective and symbolic aspects of car use', in T. Gärling and L. Steg (eds) *Threats from car traffic to the quality of urban life: Problems, causes, and solutions*, Elsevier, Amsterdam

Gatersleben, B. and Uzzell, D. (2007) 'Affective appraisals of the daily commute: Comparing perceptions of drivers, cyclists, walkers, and users of public transport', *Environment and Behavior*, vol 39, pp416–431

Gatignon, H. and Robertson, T. S. (1985) 'A propositional inventory for new diffusion research', *Journal of Consumer Research*, vol 11, pp849–867

Gelissen, J. (2007) 'Explaining popular support for environmental protection: A multi-level analysis of 50 nations', *Environment and Behavior*, vol 39, pp392–415

Giuliano, G. and Dargay, J. (2006) 'Car ownership, travel and land use: A comparison of the US and Great Britain', *Transportation Research Part A*, vol 40, pp106–124

Goodwin, P., Dargay, J. and Hanly, M. (2004) 'Elasticities of road traffic and fuel consumption with respect to price and income: A review', *Transport Reviews*, vol 24, pp275–292

Grønhoj, A. and Ölander, F. (2007) 'A gender perspective on environmentally related family consumption', *Journal of Consumer Behavior*, vol 6, pp218–235

Grunert, S. C. and Juhl, H. J. (1995) 'Values, environmental attitudes, and buying of organic foods', *Journal of Economic Psychology*, vol 16, pp39–62

Guagnano, G. A., Stern, P. C. and Dietz, T. (1995) 'Influences on attitude-behavior relationships. A natural experiment with curbside recycling', *Environment and Behavior*, vol 27, pp699–718

Harland, P., Staats, H. and Wilke, H. A. M. (1999) 'Explaining proenvironmental intention and behavior by personal norms and the theory of planned behavior', *Journal of Applied Social Psychology*, vol 29, pp2505–2528

Hartmann, P. (2008) 'Virtual nature experiences as emotional benefits in green product consumption. The moderating role of environmental attitudes', *Environment and Behavior*, vol 40, pp818–842

Heath, Y. and Gifford, R. (2002) 'Extending the theory of planned behavior: Predicting the use of public transportation', *Journal of Applied Social Psychology*, vol 32, pp2154–2189

Homer, P. M. and Kahle, L. R. (1988), 'A structural equation test of the value-attitude-behavior hierarchy', *Journal of Personality and Social Psychology*, vol 54, pp638–646

Hopper, J. R. and McCarl-Nielsen, J. (1991) 'Recycling as altruistic behavior. Normative and behavioural strategies to expand participation in a community recycling program', *Environment and Behavior*, vol 23, pp195–220

Horeni, O., Gärling, T., Loukopoulos, P. and Fujii, S. (2007) 'An experimental simulation of adaptations to increased car-use costs', *Transportation Research Part F: Traffic Psychology and Behaviour*, vol 10, pp300–320

Hübner, G. and Kaiser, F. G. (2006) 'The moderating role of the attitude-subjective norms conflict on the link between moral norms and intention', *European Psychologist*, vol 11, pp99–109

Hughner, R. S., McDonagh, P., Prothero, A., Shultz, C. J. and Stanton, J. (2007) 'Who are organic food consumers? A compilation and review of why people purchase organic food', *Journal of Consumer Behavior*, vol 6, pp94–110

Hunecke, M., Blöbaum, A., Matthies, E. and Höger, R. (2001) 'Responsibility and environment. Ecological norm orientation and external factors in the domain of travel mode choice behavior', *Environment and Behavior*, vol 33, pp830–852

Ji, M. F. and Wood, W. (2007) 'Purchase and consumption habits: Not necessarily what you intend', *Journal of Consumer Psychology*, vol 17, pp261–276

Kaiser, F. and Gutscher, H. (2003) 'The proposition of a general version of the theory of planned behavior: Predicting ecological behavior', *Journal of Applied Social Psychology*, vol 33, pp586–603

Kaiser, F. G. and Scheuthle, H. (2003) 'Two challenges to a moral extension of the theory of planned behavior: moral norms and just world beliefs in conservationism', *Personality and Individual Differences*, vol 35, pp1033–1048

Kaiser, F. G., Hübner, G. and Bogner, F. X. (2005) 'Contrasting the theory of planned behavior with the value-belief-norm model in explaining conservation behavior',

Journal of Applied Social Psychology, vol 25, pp2150–2170

Karpiak, C. P. and Baril, G. L. (2008) 'Moral reasoning and concern for the environment', *Journal of Environmental Psychology*, vol 28, pp203–208

Katzev, R., Blake, G. and Messer, B. (1993), 'Determinants of participation in multi-family recycling programs', *Journal of Applied Social Psychology*, vol 23, pp374–385

Kemmelmeier, M., Król, G. and Kim, Y. H. (2002) 'Values, economics, and pro-environmental attitudes in 22 societies', *Cross-Cultural Research*, vol 36, pp256–285

Klöckner, C. A. and Matthies, E. (2004) 'How habits interfere with norm-directed behaviour: A normative decision-making model for travel mode choice', *Journal of Environmental Psychology*, vol 24, pp319–327

Klöckner, C. A., Matthies, E. and Hunecke, M. (2003) 'Problems of operationalizing habits and integrating habits in normative decision-making models', *Journal of Applied Social Psychology*, vol 33, pp396–417

Knussen, C. and Yule, F (2008), '"I'm not in the habit of recycling" – The role of habitual behavior in the disposal of household waste', *Environment and Behavior*, vol 40, pp683–702

Knussen, C., Yule, F., MacKenzie, J. and Wells, M. (2004) 'An analysis of intentions to recycle household waste: The roles of past behaviour, perceived habit, and perceived lack of facilities', *Journal of Environmental Psychology*, vol 24, pp237–246

Koestner, R., Houlfort, N., Paquet, S. and Knight, C. (2001) 'On the risks of recycling because of guilt: An examination of the consequences of introjection', *Journal of Applied Social Psychology*, vol 31, pp2545–2460

Kurz, T., Linden, M. and Sheehy, N., (2007) 'Attitudinal and community influences on participation in new curbside recycling initiatives in Northern Ireland', *Environment and Behavior*, vol 39, pp367–391

Labay, D. G. and Kinnear, T. C. (1981) 'Exploring the consumer decision process in the adoption of solar energy systems', *Journal of Consumer Research*, vol 8, pp271–278

Ludwig, T. D., Gray, T. W. and Rowell, A. (1998) 'Increased recycling in academic buildings: A systematic replication', *Journal of Applied Behavioral Analysis*, vol 31, pp683–686

Magnusson, M. K., Arvola, A., Koivisto Hursti, U.-K., Åberg, L. and Sjödén, P.-O. (2001) 'Attitudes towards organic foods among Swedish consumers', *British Food Journal*, vol 103, pp209–226

Martinez, E., Polo, Y. and Carlos, F. (1998) 'The acceptance and diffusion of new consumer durables: Differences between first and last adopters', *Journal of Consumer Marketing*, vol 15, pp323–342

Matthies, E., Kuhn, S. and Klöckner, C. A. (2002) 'Travel mode choice of women: The result of limitation, ecological norm, or weak habit?', *Environment and Behavior*, vol 34, pp163–177

Matthies, E., Klöckner, C. A. and Preiner, C. L. (2006) 'Applying a modified moral decision making model to change habitual car use: How can commitment be effective?', *Applied Psychology: An International review*, vol 55, pp91–106

McCarty, J. A. and Shrum, L. J. (1994), 'The recycling of solid wastes: Personal values, value orientations, and attitudes about recycling as antecedents of recycling behavior', *Journal of Business Research*, vol 30, pp53–62

McCormack, G.R., Cerin, E., Leslie, E., Du Toit, L. and Owen, N. (2008) 'Obejctive versus perceived walking distance to destinations: Correspondence and predictive validity', *Environment and Behavior*, vol 40, pp401–425

McKenzie-Mohr, D., Nemiroff, L. S., Beers, L. and Desmarais, S. (1995) 'Determinants of responsible environmental behavior', *Journal of Social Issues*, vol 51, pp139–156

Michaelidou, N. and Hassan, L. M. (2008) 'The role of health consciousness, food safety concern and ethical identity on attitudes and intentions towards organic food', *International Journal of Consumer Studies*, vol 32, pp163–170

Moreau, C. P., Lehmann, D. R. and Markman A. B. (2001) 'Entrenched knowledge structures and consumer response to new products', *Journal of Marketing Research*, vol 38, pp14–29

Nordlund, A. M. and Garvill, J. (2003) 'Effects of values, problem awareness, and personal norm on willingness to reduce personal car use', *Journal of Environmental Psychology*, vol 23, pp339–347

Ölander, F. and Thøgersen, J. (2005) *The A-B-C of recycling*. Paper presented at the European Association for Consumer Research Conference, Gothenburg

Onyango, B. M., Hallman, W. K. and Bellows, A. C. (2007) 'Purchasing organic food in US food systems. A study of attitudes and practice', *British Food Journal*, vol 109, pp399–411

Ouellette, J. A. and Wood, W. (1998) 'Habit and intention in everyday life: The multiple processes by which past behavior predicts future behavior', *Psychological Bulletin*, vol 124, pp54–74

Padel, S. and Foster, C. (2005) 'Exploring the gap between attitudes and behaviour. Understanding why consumers buy or do not buy organic food', *British Food Journal*, vol 107, pp606–625

Paulley, N., Balcombe, R., Mackett, R., Titheridge, H., Preston, J., Wardman, M., Shires, J. and White, P. (2006) 'The demand for public transport: The effects of fares, quality of service, income and car ownership', *Transport Policy*, vol 13, pp295–306

Polk, M. (2003) 'Are women potentially more accommodating than men to a sustainable transportation system in Sweden?', *Transportation Research Part D. Transportation and environment*, vol 8, pp75–95

Rimal, A. P., Moon, W. and Balasubramanian, S. (2005) 'Agro-biotechnology and organic food purchase in the United Kingdom', *British Food Journal*, vol 107, pp84–97

Roberts, J. A. and Bacon, D. R. (1997) 'Exploring the subtle relationships between environmental concern and ecologically conscious consumer behavior', *Journal of Business Research*, vol 40, pp79–89

Rogers, E. M. (2003) *Diffusion of innovations*, (5 ed) Free Press, New York

Saphores, J. D. M., Nixon, H., Ogunseitan, O. A., and Shapiro, A. A. (2006), 'Household willingness to recycle electronic waste – An application to California', *Environment and Behavior*, vol 38, pp183–208

Schultz, P. W., Oskamp, S. and Mainieri, T. (1995) 'Who recycles and when? A review of personal and situational factors', *Journal of Environmental Psychology*, vol 15, pp105–121

Schwartz, S. H. (1977) 'Normative influences on altruism', *Advances in Experimental Social Psychology*, vol 10, pp221–279

Scott, D., (1999) 'Equal opportunity, unequal results – Determinants of household recycling intensity', *Environment and Behavior*, vol 34, pp267–290

Shen, J. and Saijo, T. (2008). 'Reexamining the relationship between socio-demographic characteristics and individual environmental concern: Evidence from Shanghai data', *Journal of Environmental Psychology*, vol 28, pp42–50

Staats, H., Harland, P. and Wilke, H. A. M. (2004) 'Effecting durable change. A team approach to improve environmental behavior in the household', *Environment and Behavior*, vol 36, pp341–367

Steg, L., Geurs, K. and Ras, M. (2001) 'The effects of motivational factors on car use: A multidisciplinary modelling approach', *Transportation Research Part A*, vol 35, pp789–806

Stern, P. C. (2000) 'Toward a coherent theory of environmentally significant behavior', *Journal of Social Issues*, vol 56, pp407–424

Stern, P. C. (2005) 'Understanding individuals' environmentally significant behavior', *Environmental Law Reporter: News and Analysis*, vol 35, pp10785–10790

Stern, P. C. and Dietz, T. (1994) 'The value basis of environmental concern', *Journal of Social Issues*, vol 50, pp65–84

Stern, P. C., Dietz, T. and Kalof, L. (1993) 'Values orientation, gender and environmental concern', *Environment and Behavior*, vol 25, pp322–348

Stern, P. C., Dietz, T., Kalof, L. and Guagnano, G. A. (1995) 'Values, beliefs, and pro-environmental action: Attitude formation toward emergent attitude objects', *Journal of Applied Social Psychology*, vol 25, pp1611–1636

Stern, P. C., Dietz, T., Abel, T., Guagnano, G. A. and Kalof, L. (1999) 'A value-belief-norm theory of support for social movements: The case of environmentalism', *Human Ecology Review*, vol 6, pp81–97

Stokols, D. (1987) 'Conceptual strategies of environmental psychology', in D. Stokols and I. Altman (eds), *Handbook of environmental psychology*, Wiley, NY

Stokols, D. (1990) 'Instrumental and spiritual views of people-environment relations', *American Psychologist*, vol 45, pp641–646

Straughan, R. D. and Roberts, J. A. (1999) 'Environmental segmentation alternatives: A look at green consumer behavior in the new millennium', *Journal of Consumer Marketing*, vol 16, pp558–575

Sundblad, E.-L., Biel, A. and Gärling, T. (2009) 'Knowledge and confidence in knowledge about climate change among experts, journalists, politicians, and laypersons', *Environment and Behavior*, vol 41, pp281–302

Taylor, S. and Todd, P. (1997) 'Understanding the determinants of consumer composting behaviour', *Journal of Applied Social Psychology*, vol 27, pp602–628

Thøgersen, J. (1996) 'Recycling and morality. A critical review of the literature', *Environment and Behavior*, vol 28, pp536–558

Thøgersen, J. and Ölander, F. (2002) 'Human values and the emergence of a sustainable consumption pattern: A panel study', *Journal of Economic Psychology*, vol 23, pp605–530

Thøgersen, J. and Ölander, F. (2006) 'The dynamic interaction of personal norms and environment-friendly buying behavior: A panel study', *Journal of Applied Social Psychology*, vol 36, pp1758–1780

Thompson, S. C. and Barton, M. A. (1994) 'Ecocentric and anthropocentric attitudes toward the environment', *Journal of Environmental Psychology*, vol 14, pp149–157

Thorndyke, P. W. and Hayes-Roth, B. (1982) 'Differences in spatial knowledge acquired from maps and navigation', *Cognitive Psychology*, vol 14, pp560–589

Triandis, H. C. (1980) 'Values, attitudes, and interpersonal behavior', in H. E. Howe Jr. and M. M. Page (eds) *Nebraska symposium on motivation* (vol 27), University of Nebraska Press, Lincoln, NE

Tsakiridou, E., Boutsouki, C., Zotos, Y. and Mattas, K. (2008) 'Attitudes and behaviour towards organic products: an exploratory study', *International Journal of Retail and Distribution Management*, vol 36, pp158–175

Ureña, F., Bernabéu, R. and Olmeda, M. (2008) 'Women, men and organic food: Differences in their attitudes and willingness to pay. A Spanish study', *International Journal of Consumer Studies*, vol 32, pp18–26

Van Liere, K. and Dunlap, R. (1981) 'The social bases of environmental concern: A review of hypotheses, explanations, and empirical evidence', *Public Opinion Quarterly*, vol 44, pp181–197

van Vugt, M., Meertens, R. M. and Van Lange, P. A. M. (1995) 'Car versus public transportation? The role of social value orientations in a real-life social dilemma', *Journal of Applied Social Psychology*, vol 25, pp258–278

Verplanken, B. and Aarts, H. (1999) 'Habit, attitude, and planned behaviour: Is habit an empty construct or an interesting case of goal-directed automaticity?', in W. Stroebe and M. Hewstone (eds) *European review of social psychology* (vol 10), Wiley, Chichester, England

Verplanken, B., Aarts, H. and Van Knippenberg, A. (1997) 'Habit, information acquisition, and the process of making travel mode choices', *European Journal of Social Psychology*, vol 27, pp539–560

Verplanken, B., Aarts, H., van Knippenberg, A. and Moonen, A. (1998) 'Habit versus planned behaviour: A field experiment', *British Journal of Social Psychology*, vol 37, pp111–128

Verplanken, B., Aarts, H., van Knippenberg, A. and van Knippenberg, C. (1994) 'Attitude versus general habit: Antecedents of travel mode choice', *Journal of Applied Social Psychology*, vol 24, pp285–300

Verplanken, B., Walker, I., Davis, A. and Jurasek, M. (2008) 'Context change and travel mode choice: Combining the habit discontinuity and self-activation hypotheses', *Journal of Environmental Psychology*, vol 28, pp121–127

Vining, J. and Ebreo, A (1990) 'What makes a recycler? A comparison of recyclers and nonrecyclers', *Environment and Behavior*, vol 22, pp55–73

Vining, J. and Ebreo, A. (1992) 'Predicting recycling behavior from global and specific environmental attitudes and changes in recycling opportunities', *Journal of Applied Social Psychology*, vol 22, pp1580–1607

Wall, R., Devine-Wright, P. and Mill, G. A. (2005) *'Psychological predictors in context: An empirical study of interactions between determinants of car use intentions'*, 18th Conference of the IAPES, Vienna, Austria, Designing Social Innovation: Planning, Building, Evaluation, pp117–126

Wall, R., Devine-Wright, P. and Mill, G. A. (2007) 'Comparing and combining theories to explain pro-environmental intentions: The case of commuting-mode choice', *Environment and Behavior*, vol 39, pp731–753

Wang, G. P., Dou, W. Y. and Zhou, N. (2008) 'Consumption attitudes and adoption of new consumer products: A contingency approach', *European Journal of Marketing*, vol 42, pp238–254

Wang, T. H. and Katzev, R. D. (1990) 'Group commitment and resource conservation: Two field experiments on promoting recycling', *Journal of Applied Social Psychology*, vol 20, pp265–275

Werner, C. M. and Makela, E. (1998) 'Motivations and behaviors that supports recycling', *Journal of Environmental Psychology*, vol 18, pp373–386

Widegren, Ö. (1998) 'The new environmental paradigm and personal norms', *Environment and Behavior*, vol 30, pp75–100

Wood, S. L. and Lynch, J. G. (2002) 'Prior knowledge and complacency in new product learning', *Journal of Consumer Research*, vol 29, pp416–426

Zanoli, R. and Naspetti, S. (2002) 'Consumer motivations in the purchase of organic food', *British Food Journal*, vol 104, pp643–653

Zelezny, L. C., Chua, P.-P. and Aldrich, C. (2000) 'Elaborating on gender differences in environmentalism', *Journal of Social Issues*, vol 56, pp443–457

Zimmer, M. R., Stafford, T. F. and Stafford, M. R. (1994) 'Green issues – Dimensions of environmental concern', *Journal of Business Research*, vol 30, pp63–74

Part II

Empirical Analyses of the Swedish Case

6

Walk the talk for sustainable everyday life: Experiences from eco-village living in Sweden

Hilde Ibsen

INTRODUCTION

Individual responsibility for the environment was set in the Swedish political agenda in 1986. When summing up the political environmental talk in Parliament, Minister of Environment Ingvar Carlsson claimed that the government had done a lot, but still environmental problems occurred all the time, and in many situations the government was a step behind. It was like curing 'gastric ulcer with plaster' (Prot. 1985/86:72, p. 34. Notes from the debate in the Swedish Parliament, February 6, 1986, Stockholm). As a general trend, policy-making was characterized by the state taking responsibility for environmental effects by the use of instruments like law-making, planning, regulations, taxes, etc. According to Ulrich Beck, environmental policy developed according to 'the empty slogan of an "ecological restructuring of industrial society"' (Beck, 1997, p. 7).

Carlsson on the other hand claimed that citizens, as consumers, were parts of the environmental problem. All citizens influenced the environment through everyday routines and activities. It was time, he said, not only to ask what society did, but also to ask about the role of personal responsibility. Citizens, as consumers, had to take personal responsibility and change their lifestyles. This was more urgent than ever, since environmental problems had got proportions one could not even dream about in the 1970s, and they had become more and more global in character. What could the individual do? Carlsson suggested that citizens should travel more on public transport, use cars with exhaust emission control, reduce the use of energy, increase recycling of waste and choose environmentally friendly batteries in order to minimize emissions of mercury to nature (Lundgren, 1992 p. 20).

The interrelationship between citizens' lifestyles and the environment, as expressed by Carlsson, was further developed in the official report on 'A better environment' in 1987 (SOU, 1987:32; Lundgren, 1992 p. 28). The report stated that in the future it was important for citizens to influence environmental issues and thus also political decision-making. One means to achieve this was to increase citizens' environmental awareness. 'When the environmental awareness is deeply anchored with the majority of citizens, then they can in their roles as consumers, professionals and members of associations, contribute to improve the environment by taking environmental concern in practical action' (SOU, 1987:32, p.148). This meant that it was crucial to highlight interaction between governmental policies and individual behaviour in everyday life.

Today researchers and policy-makers to a large extent agree that individual citizens within the household are responsible for both the causes and solutions to environmental problems. And researchers also stress that in order to understand individual behaviour in a given time and context we also need to understand the political contexts. The opportunities for behaving environmentally friendly are structured by the government, but in a relationship with individuals (Giddens, 1984, 1991).

In this chapter our focus is on the interaction between government environmental policy and individual attitudes and behaviour over a long time period. The historical approach is chosen in order to explore continuity and change as regards possibilities and obstacles for environmentally friendly action in everyday life. This approach is also useful when studying how decisions made in the past have long-term impacts on values and behaviour, limiting or postponing alternatives. Our point of departure is the political–ideological environmental debates in the 1970s when alternative movements grew up, arguing that development rooted in continued economic growth was unsustainable. The alternative movement in Sweden took a bottom-to-top approach for change, which involved both individual citizens, or grass root people, scientists and politicians. Together they set out to walk the talk for environmentally friendly everyday life, which resulted in the first eco-village in Sweden. In order to capture the individual experiences and also the transfer of attitudes and behaviour, interviews were done with the adult householders in five households and with one child from each household. Our purpose was to get detailed knowledge about everyday life activities. We chose five different households. Three of them represented families who were part of the formative group and among this category one was single when she moved to Tuggelite. Two householders moved to a flat that became available soon after the area was finished, and one householder was a single parent when she moved to the area in 1992. Two of the children were still living in the household, while the others had finished grammar school and moved. The parents themselves asked their children, and chose the one who was willing to participate.

The aim of this chapter is threefold. First, we seek to explore the history and development of the eco-village. Eco-villages have been an innovative form of settlement since the 1960s and the first one in Sweden was set up in 1984, in the municipality of Karlstad. The eco-village represents a micro society or structure with specific ecological preconditions the individuals interact with. The chapter is an illustrative case for how voluntary environmental action made by ordinary citizens was possible and discusses why a group of people chose alternative living. How can we explain the decision to set up an eco-village? The second aim is to study changes in everyday practices. Neither the eco-village nor the households living in it are static and environmental action might or might not adjust to changes in environmental awareness and practices in society at large. Have there been any substantial changes in householders' attitudes and behaviour since 1984? The third aim is to gain knowledge about transfer of attitudes and behaviour. How was it to grow up in an eco-village, and to what extent has this way of living influenced the children's environmental actions?

ALTERNATIVE LIVING

In order to understand the motives and ideological basis for choosing eco-village living, we need to go back to Sweden in the 1970s. The 1970s was a decade of mixed development trends. On the one hand the welfare state had matured, giving people a high material living standard in the Western world. The institutional and political model of development was rooted in economic growth and more material consumption in order to keep up with or create even more affluence. Mainstream development ideas were based on conventional wisdom: 'more and more of the same' (Bäckstrand and Ingelstam, 1975, p.1). The environmental policy was dominated by a top-to-bottom approach to the effects of environmental problems. It departed from environmental degradation as a by-product of production patterns (Eckerberg, 2000; Lundgren, 2005). On the other hand, the 1970s was a decade when alternative voices assumed that present development or lifestyles could not continue along the same lines. There was a trend in society of talking about people-driven processes, collective solutions and the causes behind environmental problems. Also, the political Sweden took part in the lifestyle debates. The role of citizens' responsibility was highlighted when the former Prime Minister Olof Palme stated that 'in reality it is the citizens themselves who can and must decide the future development of society' (SOU, 1972:19; Andersson, 2002, p. 7). The Social Democrats took the lead in discussing alternative futures and development paths by setting up the Swedish Secretariat for Future Studies. The Secretariat published studies critical of the emerging consumer society, which caused debate for some years (Bäckstrand and Ingelstam, 1975), but faded away when political and popular discussions about nuclear power became the hot issue in the late 1970s.

However, in line with alternative development ideas, a concrete initiative for change came up in 1974 by the Centre for Cross-disciplinary Research at the University of Gothenburg. The researchers claimed, with particular reference to the use of energy, that the government's housing policy in Sweden was unsustainable. 'The standards in Sweden for energy- and resource use today are non-sustainable from both a historical and a global point of view' (Olsson and Tengström, 1976, p. 6). In the large blocks of flats citizens felt alienated in their social life and ended up with consumption of non-necessities as a kind of consolation. Probably material consumption would decrease if citizens could satisfy their social needs instead. The time had come for alternative living along the vision of 'small is beautiful' in combination with new advanced technical methods that kept down the use of energy without compromising comfort.

The proposed alternative village challenged both Swedish housing policy and the existing political ideas about welfare. In the Swedish Peoples' Home, the Social Democrat Party made housing one of their core issues soon after the Second World War. Housing was partly linked to the political goal of full employment since construction of dwellings would give people work, and partly linked to the ambition of reducing housing famine. According to the Social Democrat's After War Programme, which formed housing policy until the 1970s, the goal was to build residences with one room available per person within the household. Part of the programme was 'the million programme' aiming at the construction of one million flats between 1964 and 1974. The programme was criticized for being resource intensive, sterile and gave the citizens no influence over their own living.

On paper the village was constructed for 800 people. It would function with low use of energy and low use of human resources. Included in human resources were both health and environment. The researchers suggested the use of direct sun radiation, warm pump and wind energy as supplements for energy supply (Olsson and Tengström, 1976, p. 7). Also, the citizens within the village would have responsibility for common organization of arrangements like hobby rooms, washroom with washing equipment, stalls, etc. The ambition was to construct common facilities with as much resource reduction as possible. In the model village, households were supposed to share, for instance, electrical equipment, tools, and also shop together and thus reduce transportation. There would also be less use of resources if households could reduce packaging and intermediate products and instead make food, based on raw materials, together. Last but not least there would also be social gains. The size of households had reduced with the trend towards one person households or one parent households. These changes had social consequences due to isolation and loneliness. When living in a collective setting, the social networks would be stronger than in ordinary residential areas and the children would grow up in safe surroundings having a group of adults among them.

The Gothenburg group wanted to test their theories and models in real life and in the autumn of 1974 they approached the municipality of Karlstad, in order to discuss how to plan for a model village. It was important for the research group to anchor the planning in municipal reality and within a municipality acknowledging the potential for construction of the village. Cross-disciplinary working groups with experts from natural science, architecture, sociology, economy and history were involved in the planning, and they all worked according to human ecological perspectives, which in Sweden has been a topic in universities since 1974. Also, students and other researchers from the Centre for Cross-disciplinary Research in Gothenburg participated with smaller studies of alternative resource use, both related to the construction of houses and to the running of them (Olsson and Tengström, 1976, p. 10.) After some years of planning the project was put on ice. Some key actors withdrew (Norbeck, 2009).

To live one's vision

Visions from the larger Välsviken project did not die, and there is an ideological continuity from this project to the first eco-village in Sweden, Tuggelite. Some members of the Välsviken group in Karlstad did not give up the idea of constructing a housing area based on ecological principles and social community. In 1981 they constituted an interest group with ten member households. Among them were three families that had been members of the Välsviken group, and most of the others who participated in the new group had some relation to them and to each other. Why did they continue? Housing policy in Sweden was influenced by a top-to-bottom structure based on strong bureaucratic planning ideology, and obviously there were many constraints for individual actors to succeed. But still they hang on to their vision.

According to Berglund and Matti (2006) citizens often express both internal and external motives for many environmental activities. This is also the case with the group of people who chose to set up Tuggelite. There was a mix of driving forces that can be singled out when looking at motives characteristic of the group per se and also among the individual householders. First, the group initiative departed from an active ideological choice combined with a strong wish to design a residential area on their own conditions. They had learnt from Välsviken and wanted to have control of all steps and decisions. Second, the environmental awareness within the group was strong. Most of the people had in common, activism in the anti-nuclear movement. In the aftermath of the Swedish referendum about nuclear power it was crucial to experiment with alternative energy sources, and the core question within the group was how to use alternative energy in everyday life. 'Energy supply is crucial as regards our own lifestyle and our relation to the environment. We seek low-energy consumption.'[1] But the project was also an alternative to 'the tear- and throw society' and the group wanted to economize with natural resources as well as human resources.[2] Third, there was a highly relevant competence within the group, which made it possible to drive a bottom-to-top process. Most of the actors had university and college educations, which provided the group with the necessary technical knowledge. Fourth, the social structure of the group was not irrelevant. Several members had experience of collective living and they shared the ideological basis. A statement from residents in Tuggelite has often been that the project was characterized by high energy. But what do the individual householders stress as their internal motivation? How much do the households differ? Interviews were carried out with three households that were part of the Tuggelite group from the start, one household moved to the area in 1985 and one moved there in 1991.

In three households they expressed that the key motive for taking the decision to live in an eco-village was the environment. When one couple met they discussed moving to the countryside and living according to ecological principles. But when the Tuggelite project became concrete they found this a better alternative, since they were expecting their first child. They were both members of environmental organizations in the 1970s and met each other through an association for organic vegetables that existed in Karlstad in the 1980s. Another couple moved to Karlstad from Gothenburg in 1980 and settled close to friends who also came to live in Tuggelite. The male householder talked about living his visions and his main focus was, and is, energy and energy saving. He still regards energy to be the core environmental issue in modern society. He also explained that he had always lived with a focus on nature and claimed that this was a heritage from his parents. The female householder stressed that environmental concern about lifestyles had always been part of her and was probably because she grew up in the countryside. Both of them were members of environmental organizations and also in the anti-nuclear movement. By joining the Tuggelite project, both household members wanted to 'walk the talk' – and not only talk about the environment. They wanted something concrete. In the third household there was particular interest in ecology and particularly the idea of building houses that use passive solar energy. When joining the project the household member was single and she also saw eco-village living as a way of living in a 'sense of coherence' and pointed at the interrelation between the ecological and social aspects of the project. Like several of her neighbours she was then a member of the anti-nuclear campaign and other environmental organizations. She was also committed to outdoor life without regarding herself to be in any way extreme.

The two families who were not part of the formative group stressed that their motivation first of all was the social aspect of the project and they already had experience of collective living. One family had befriended other families that were part of it. When asked in the late phase of the construction of Tuggelite to participate they first said no. They found the project expensive and did not want to take out a loan. They had had their first child and were also offered a municipal apartment in another part of Karlstad. However, when their friends had moved in and as they gradually spent more time with friends living in Tuggelite, they changed their mind and rented a flat that became available. But they sympathized much with the ecological and resource friendly model. To move to an area with a focus on the possibility of environmentally friendly everyday life was a deliberate choice, but it was a coincidence that they ended up in Tuggelite. The last family, which was a single mother with one son, had been thinking of more ecological alternatives together with her former husband.

Some time after he died she moved to Karlstad with her son and she already knew people living in Tuggelite. She got the opportunity to rent a room in one of the houses, but the same week she planned to move in, one family had decided to sell their flat and asked her if she wanted to buy it. Her main reason for choosing Tuggelite was the collective model, but she was also concerned about the environment. Earlier she had struggled with explaining why she sorted her waste, but in Tuggelite this was an everyday practice. It was a deliberate choice of lifestyle to take this decision, and it was important that the area was close to the forest.

According to ecological modernization theory, however, individual decisions are not enough in order to establish ecological activities (Spaargaren and Vliet, 2000). The individual interacts with surroundings and there is a relationship between actors and structures (Giddens, 1984; Skill, 2008). The decision to establish an eco-village was taken by strongly committed individuals having the capacity to walk the talk for sustainable everyday life, but they were not isolated from society. In this case they were dependent on the municipality for getting land and for acceptance of the planned alternative energy and sanitation systems. When presenting the idea for the municipality of Karlstad the term common housing or resource friendly was used, and not the term eco-housing or eco-village. According to a definition made by some members of the group common housing was: 'common management and a relatively huge portion of common work'.

The head of the analysing unit of the municipality of Karlstad was positive and claimed: 'I find the project of great interest. Since this is also part of a research project within the field of energy evaluation the project surely will be carried out properly. Passive solar energy probably will be used more in the future, and it is positive for the municipality to get such a construction research project.'[3] The municipality gave the necessary support by offering the group municipal land to buy. Thus society at large supported the vision of having a better ecological action space than in ordinary housing (Skill, 2008, p. 43).

However, the small society turned out to be a possible obstacle for the eco-village project. The available land was situated within a well-established middle-class residential area and the neighbourhood came to be a constraining unit. Several villa owners regarded the project to 'have exclusively negative effects' and set up a protest group. At a public meeting they stated that: 'We will do everything in order to stop or postpone the project.'[4] They came up with a mix of arguments against the building plan. One argument was related to the fear of losing the view. Another was the increased transport of private cars and the protest group claimed that traffic security already was bad. Also, arguments came up related to the experimental character of the area, which, they claimed, broke with the established norms about standards in a villa area. The neighbours were afraid of environmental problems due to smell and smoke from the composting toilets and the pellet furnace. Also, the length of the chimney was a problem for the neighbours. However, the strongest arguments against the eco-village were embedded in individualism and prejudices. The protest group claimed that the municipality had promised that the field in question should be open or potentially be developed with more villas, a school and a corner shop. 'One certainly knows what kind of problems it will be with apartment building – housing with vandalism and housebreaking... Do we need to look at their clothes lines? Those terraced houses don't belong to a residential area with villas.'[5]

In the end a protest was sent first to the administrative court of appeal, then to the government, but it was not approved. The arguments against were regarded to be irrelevant and in September 1983 one newspaper announced that 'it is green light for the "future people" who intend to build energy friendly houses in Skåre'.[6]

The first families moved into the eco-village in the autumn of 1984. The ecological basis centered around two issues: alternative energy and sanitation. In the early 1980s there were not many energy alternatives, but two possibilities seemed of interest, which made the energy friendly houses 'twenty years ahead'.[7] One technique was the use of passive solar energy and the other was to use biofuel-like pellets for additional heating and hot water. To use passive solar energy was nothing new in Sweden where simple wooden and well-insulated houses with small windows to the north had been a tradition far back, but this technology had normally not been used on a larger scale. When constructing Tuggelite and in order to get optimal passive solar energy, the architect had to adapt the buildings to natural conditions like wind, sun and shadow. In addition the houses needed thick insulation with tick wind tight walls and a circulation system to circulate the hot air.

Wood pellet was not widespread, but there was available technology to test and there was a local pellet producer close to Tuggelite. This was important in order to save energy for transportation and also for economic reasons. Wood pellets were half the price of oil energy. Since the main heating technology was experimental, additional heating was needed. In order to follow their ecological vision the Tuggelite residents chose wood for the smaller central heating furnace and after a few years also added solar panels to the roof of the common house. However, the wood was later substituted with oil combustion.

Ecological principles also guided the experimentation with an alternative sanitation system. One main argument for doing this was the idea of not wanting to waste potable water on toilets, thus they had to find another system to replace ordinary water closets. After discussing several alternatives they ended up with a Norwegian composting toilet system, often used in cabins and which was normally not used in standard houses. Organic waste was put in the toilet and a compost process took place in a mould room with faeces and urine. All the inhabitants were in favour of the system and from an environmental point of view the system was in principle more environmentally friendly than water closets. Another experiment or unusual everyday routine was to sort waste according to non-organic and organic material and a central recycling trash was located close to the common house.

In Tuggelite the ecological and social dimensions were closely weaved together and constituted an interrelational structure. The ecological experiments could not function without a well-reasoned social organization of the eco-village. In order to take care of the self-imposed extra work all householders were organized in different working teams. For instance one team was in charge of the running of the pellet furnace while other groups took care of outdoor work and the responsibility for maintenance of the buildings. Additional working days were held regularly during the year. The do-it-yourself spirit kept the monthly costs down and strengthened the social network among the householders. A study of eco-villages shows that environmental awareness has a tendency of declining (Norbeck, 2009). The householders in Tuggelite have from the beginning kept up with having house meetings every month and also an ideological meeting once a year where discussions have been held about how to keep up with the original vision of living environmentally friendly in everyday life.

The physical organization of the eco-village also reflected the interrelational structure between ecology and social life, which built on traditional community living. In order to take environmental concern and use passive solar energy the buildings had optimal north–south exposure and the houses were at the same time situated around a common house, which was meant to be a natural meeting point, like the square in an old village. The common house played an important role in strengthening to social relations between households. It was constructed in order to take care of multiple functions related to practicalities like doing the laundry, having meals together, watching TV together, or having a sauna. When entering the eco-village from the main entrance there are letter boxes and an information board, which also constitute a natural meeting point, just outside the common house.

HOUSEHOLDS' BEHAVIOUR WITHIN THE ECO-VILLAGE

The environmental commitment was strong among the residents in Tuggelite in 1984 and a general comment was that to live in Tuggelite was environmental activism in practice (Tidäng, 1992, p. 48). The inhabitants felt that they were empowered by having strong influence over their own life and by deliberately taking on extra work due to alternative and experimental solutions in everyday life routines. The eco-village as a system structured the ecological action space for its residents' everyday life, and we can expect that citizens living in an eco-village continued to promote pro-environmental behaviour, also at household level. We seek to explore how environmentally friendly activities within different households have developed over time and to discuss continuity and change in attitudes and habits. To what degree does pro-environmental behaviour differ within and between households? Our empirical examples are drawn from three sectors that involve citizens' environmental responsibility in everyday life: energy, transportation and consumption.

When planning Tuggelite, energy saving and use of renewable energy were top priority, but also in the Swedish society at large energy issues were, as we have seen, highly debated. The houses as such are energy friendly, but has the energy saving attitude trickled down to the households? When asked about energy use there is little difference between them. All households stated that their attitude towards energy saving is the same, but habits have changed in tandem with the technological development in society at large. First of all this is due to more or less extensive use of computers. But all households expressed pro-environmental behaviour, which included the use of energy light bulbs when possible, they switched off the light when leaving the room and one household has also installed cells that automatically switch off the light when people go out of the room. Other householders have chosen to keep down consumption of electrical goods, like kitchen machines, and for instance also bought a chest freezer instead of an upright cabinet freezer, which uses more energy.

Transportation has in the last decade become a prominent issue in the global environmental debate about climate change. In the early 1980s, however, transportation was not an important issue, neither in society nor among the eco-village group. On the other hand one argument for accepting the land offered by the municipality eight kilometres from downtown was that one of the bus lines passed close to the area. After a few years' discussions the use of private cars did come up, and the eco-village householders discussed the possibilities for a car pool, but they never managed to establish one. However, for some years they leased an electric car, which was available for booking by all householders, but this arrangement ended after a few years.

Research has approached the environmental problems caused by consumers' attitudes and behaviours towards the automobile and pointed at the fact that there is a gap between awareness about the problems and practice (McCarty, 2007). This is also the case with eco-village householders. When it comes to the use of everyday transport with private cars there are differences in both attitudes and behaviour between the households. Three out of the five households, however, claimed that they as a general attitude have used the car as little as possible. All householders stated, however, that they often chose alternatives like riding the bicycle as the first priority or going by public transport for instance in winter time. One householder stated that she 'always' took her bicycle to work, and another also has the habit of skiing to work when there is sufficient snow. In one household their habit of using the car had increased over the past years due to changes in the family situation, even if the attitude had remained the same. They had elderly relatives that could not be visited by public transport. Another householder pointed at some exceptions when using the car, for instance when travelling to her summer house, and all householders often use the car when buying food at the supermarket. Some parents have also restricted the amount they drive their children around and have as a principle filled up the car with people before driving any place.

In one of the households both householders stated that transportation was their worst unsustainable habit and this has not changed. The male member of the household normally took the bicycle when he worked close to Tuggelite, but after having changed work he used the car because of the longer distance. The female, however, works in the town centre and as a basic principle she rides her bike or runs to work. But sometimes she has to use a car because of her work situation. Due to a high level of leisure activities the household has used the car much, but their habit has always been to bring friends and fill up the car. They have never deliberately been very restrictive when it comes to driving, but they are thinking about the environmental effects and about buying an environmentally friendly car the next time. On the other hand there are situations when they never go by car. Instead of driving to, for instance, a fitness centre, the everyday exercise takes place in the nearby forest.

One of the five households admitted that the everyday transportation habits have changed. The female householder used to ride a bicycle or frequently went by bus into town, but she now uses the car more often. Still, she claimed that she thinks about transportation, but that there is a gap between thinking and doing. The male householder has always used the car for different activities and also because of his work situation and he is less concerned about the environmental consequences of the use of the car than his partner.

In the late 1980s Swedish politicians started to talk about consumption in everyday life as an environmental problem, and since then consumption has got much attention in politics and research. We have also seen that the residents in Tuggelite were concerned about the 'waste-and-throw' society and several families had been members of a food organization that provided organic food in Karlstad, even before they moved to the eco-village. For many years households at Tuggelite bought organic vegetables from alternative farmers in the county, which was facilitated by the county being in the forefront as regards organic farming. Since 1984 the consumer society has developed as a dominant phenomenon and structures a great part of everyday life activities (Bauman, 2004). To what extend has living in a consumers' society influenced the eco-village households and their attitudes towards consumption? Have their consumption habits changed?

There is a general trend among all households that they believe themselves to be anti-materialistic and some householders talked about the importance of limiting consumption. They explained this with reference to their childhood in the 1950s when they learnt that 'you do not need everything'. The general attitude towards the 'waste-and-throw' society has not changed, and the householders reported little or slight changes in consumption habits.

All households have historically bought organic food and one householder claimed: 'Consumption of organic food has always been and is a priority.' Another stated: 'I have always gone green and buy a lot of' organic food, both basic items like milk, egg, flavor, vegetables and some meat. I am a small household and can afford to buy organic products even if they have higher prices.' The price argument is often used as a counter-argument for buying organic food.

When there were few organic products available in the ordinary supermarkets several householders made efforts vis-à-vis the local supermarket by asking them to take in more organic food. Several householders stated that they were sure that members of their household had influenced the supermarket and contributed to the increased selection of organic products. Today they have extended the pressure towards Fair Trade products. None of the householders is vegetarian, but in some households they actively seek to keep down meat consumption. When they buy meat, they look for ecological products. Members of one of the households buy a moose every year, arguing that this is for health and environmental reasons. Choices about food, however, cause dilemmas of sustainability and this is also the case within some households. One male householder said: 'When I want to eat sausages, I do not buy eco-labelled meat. Sausages are one of my vices.' When it comes to fish, the same male householder and also the female said they avoided cod, but also that it was difficult to be updated about which fish are threatened. In the case of fruit the female household member buys Swedish apples, which are not eco-labelled, instead of buying eco-apples, which have been transported from abroad. They seek to adapt their eating habits to seasons, like not buying tomatoes during the winter, but they find it difficult to follow strict principles. Also, other householders pointed to the difficulty of 'always' buying ecological food and said: 'We have always bought eco-labelled products, but sometimes we choose not to. In general there have been some changes as regards our everyday consumption habits and we have been more easy-going or lazy.'

Another common characteristic of eco-village householders is their general concern about consumption issues. One female householder said: 'I both think about environmental friendly goods and I buy eco-labelled products. I am more concerned about this than my husband and I actively seek information or knowledge about environmental friendly consumption by reading different publications on the topic.' One household explicitly stressed that they had priorities other than consumption of goods and services and favoured time instead of money, both for ecological and economic reasons. Even though all householders expressed concern about consumption, one also admitted that consumption habits had changed since the early 1980s, due to her present life situation. She has spent some more time on 'luxury' activities with her daughter after being widowed and she consumes more wellness services, for instance massage and yoga. She and her daughter also do some more shopping trips and eat out more, but, she said: 'I am not concerned about getting the latest products.'

The analysis of habits and attitudes related to energy, transportation and consumption revealed that there are most differences among the householders as regards transportation habits, even if their basic pro-environmental attitude is still strong. There are different explanations. Some householders had no other option than going by car to the workplace, some had elderly relatives that could not be visited without the car and some claimed that they had become lazy now because they had grown older. Others stressed that their leisure preference structured their transportation habits. One household explicitly said: 'We are not very adventurous.' The female had been in a plane only 3–4 times in her lifetime. They preferred to visit their local surroundings. Another household claimed the opposite. They liked to travel and had always travelled a lot by plane, and after they bought a summer house, they had to use the car in order to get there.

GROWING UP IN TUGGELITE

All the adults who settled in Tuggelite deliberately choose alternative or experimental housing, and by doing this they created specific routines and habits in everyday life that were more sustainable than was the case in society at large and in ordinary dwellings. One reason was the lack of governmental policies in the early 1980s, stimulating environmentally friendly activities at the household level. In addition to gaining detailed knowledge about householders' everyday life activities, our aim has also been to study the transfer of intergenerational attitudes and behaviour. The children were from part of a specific household behaviour, which was structured by the eco-village as such. Both eco-village living and parents influenced the children's everyday life by 'imposing' on them certain social and environmental practices. To what extent have the children experienced eco-village living positively or negatively? In what way has eco-village childhood influenced the environmental actions of the interviewed?

All the children started with commenting about the positive social gains from growing up in Tuggelite. The positive social experiences were captured in a bundle of keywords. First, it was 'safe' and encouraged 'solidarity'. There were always many children to play with and for instance one could 'walk into the fridge' in a friend's house without a problem. And it was safe to know all the neighbours. Spontaneous visits were always possible and compared to friends outside of Tuggelite they 'could run in and out in the friends' houses in a natural way'. One child said that he characterized several of his friends as 'siblings'. Another stressed that she belonged to a generation of many girls and they always had each other and 'lots of fun'. Another important factor that underlined the safety was the close connection with the friends' parents and that there always were some adults available. Second, the children had experienced 'trust', 'a sense of coherence' and 'solidarity'. One pointed at the fact that children and adults had done things together, like travelling and arranging parties and another that they were used to socializing across generations.

As regards the social experience, however, two of the children discussed also negative aspects, even if they said that the positive out-weighed the negative. One reported that she had felt some kind of control, like 'everybody knows'. She felt 'observed' and it could be 'too much with people all over the place'. Another result of the high degree of collectivism was that she 'took on responsibility' for other people in the area and thought much about not doing something that could give her a 'bad reputation'. The other one pointed at social changes and said that the degree of solidarity had become weaker. One reason, she believed, was that many householders seemed to be more occupied with activities outside of the area than they had been some years ago.

With reference to the positive social experiences we will argue that there is a high degree of transfer of the parents' attitudes and behaviour. All the five children grew into the social vision guiding their parents' eco-village project, and they all stressed that they had taken collectivism with them as an ideal.

One stated explicitly that 'the social dimension has influenced me as a human being more than the environmental'. Most of them also claimed that they were attracted by collective living in the future and again for social reasons.

When discussing the environmental aspects of growing up in Tuggelite there are differences among the children as to what degree the influence has become manifest in everyday life. A majority said that they had been influenced by their parents and even 'appreciate that the parents have encouraged environmental friendly activities', even if environmentally friendly activities might have been 'nagging' and sometimes 'tiresome'. There were also statements about the abolishment of the composting toilets and some of the children felt sorry when they disappeared. The composting toilets had made Tuggelite special and they felt some of the ecological legitimacy had faded. Further, we will describe in detail the transfer of attitudes and behaviour within the fields of energy, transportation, waste and organic products.

In all the five households the parents had stressed the importance of switching off the light when leaving a room and when leaving the house. This habit has been transferred to the children, even if one admitted that she sometimes did not switch off when leaving a room, as a kind of protest. On the other hand she would never leave the house with lights on. One interviewed said he is bothered about unnecessary lighting, but that he normally has his computer on all the time, and his concern is primarily related to the fire aspect. Transportation attitudes and behaviour differs, as we have seen, among the adult householders and the differences are also reflected in the degree of transfer of transportation habits. Three households claimed to be restrictive about using the private car in ordinary everyday life activities. The children in these households also stressed that they normally would go by bicycle, walk or in some cases go by bus. In these cases the parents in general refused to drive the children and one said she had to work hard for finding arguments if she wanted a lift. Two of the households were not particularly restrictive, but the transfer of transportation habits turned out differently. In one case the child said he preferred to use his bicycle, and go by bus during winter, while the other one did not see the private car as an environmental issue. 'It is natural to use the car.' If he now chose not to go by car it is for economic reasons or because public transport is more convenient. His argument for using the car is that it does not matter in a global context if he as an individual refuses to use it. Emissions in the US or China are of much greater importance. The environmental responsibility, as he sees it, must be global and collective.

Recycling did not represent an active choice taken by the individual householder, but was from the start integrated in everyday routines and in the eco-village structure. We might say that the children growing up had few other options than following the eco-village practice. The issue of waste and recycling occupied all the five interviewed and they all found this positive when they grew up. It was natural and not an issue of discussion. One child said she was very surprised when she realized that her classmates did not recycle their waste. Four of the children have kept up with recycling, when this is possible. For instance, one child was frustrated when he was living in Oslo in Norway, and there was no proper municipal system for sorting waste. Only in one case the interviewed has become critical of recycling. He said he could see no reason to separate organic and solid waste, except glass and batteries. One reason for being sceptical is that he is not really sure what happens in the end. He distrusts the municipal system, and believes that everything is burnt anyway, but he has not bothered to check it out. Part of the waste discussion also circled around 'waste and throw' issues, which was also an important issue among the parents when choosing eco-village living. In this case most of the children have been influenced by their parents and are concerned about not wasting food or other things. One way of transferring concern to practice has been to buy second-hand clothes and never throwing away things that might be used.

A last issue to be discussed was organic products. For some years households in Tuggelite collectively bought organic food, and they also had some ambitions of growing their own vegetables. In tandem with changes in society at large and more organic products in supermarkets the collective purchases ended. But the studied households stuck to their organic food preference and have expanded the individual purchase of organic products. This attitude has to a large extent been transferred to the children who seek to buy organic food when possible. One of them stressed that she never, as a principle, buys Chiquita bananas and when having meat she most of the time buys eco-labelled meat or meat from game. Sometimes, however, she cheats by secretly eating salami. Another girl stressed that the household as such buys organic food, and that she, when she goes to the supermarket alone, at least buys organic standard food like milk and vegetables.

From the description of environmental attitudes and behaviour among the five children we conclude that there is a high degree of transfer. Four of the five children think a lot about the environment, they are convinced that it matters to behave in an environmentally friendly and for them environmentally friendly activities have become habits. They think that they know more about the environment than children who did not grow up in an eco-village. Sometimes there is a gap between how they normally act and feel they should act, and what they do in practice. 'Out of convenience I accept a lift with a private car if possible.' There are also other inconsequences in behaviour patterns. One regarded himself to be restrictive as regards consumption, but with technical equipment as an exception.

Only one of the interviewed, however, very clearly stated that 'acting environmental friendly in everyday life has never really become part of my conviction or vision for how to live my life.' He found some of the practices negative, for instance that they kept up with the composting toilets for many years, even if the system did not function properly. In his opinion this was a sign of being incapable of moving on from old ideological arguments. When he moved from Tuggelite he revolted against the ecological principles – he didn't care – he said. He deliberately bought detergents that were not environmentally friendly and saw this also as an anti-ideological action.

CONCLUDING REMARKS

The first aim of this article was to discuss how it was possible for a group of citizens to set up an eco-village by taking the initiative on their own. As suggested by Berglund and Matti there are often both external and internal motives for environmental activities in everyday life. In this case there are external factors which explain how Tuggelite became more than a vision on paper. First, the eco-village project was rooted in alternative development ideologies characteristic of the 1970s among the establishment and grass root people. There was political talk about citizens' responsibility for the environment, scientific efforts to set up a resource friendly housing area as an alternative to the 'million programme', and by the end of the decade came the campaign against nuclear power. These external, or structural factors, are crucial, but according to Anthony Giddens' structuration theory there is a relationship between structures and actors (Giddens, 1984, 1991). Thus we also have to look at internal factors as citizens' motivations for choosing pro-environmental social practices. Many people did not want to support the energy regime provided by the Swedish authorities and among them also the enthusiasts driving the eco-village project. The alternative living they wanted could not be provided by society at large. According to Paul C. Stern's models for explaining environmental behaviour, we have to take into account 'personal capabilities, context, and habits' (Stern, 2000). This model fits well when explaining the internal factors crucial for setting up Tuggelite. The group of people had competence, vision and a strong wish to live environmentally friendly in their everyday life, and they had much energy. There was a strong relationship between environmental concern and behaviour. The context was favourable since energy was a core issue in society at large. The municipality of Karlstad was highly interested in supporting energy saving houses and showed this by selling land.

Our second aim has been to see if there have been changes in attitudes and behaviour among the residents in Tuggelite. When looking at the eco-village as a structure there have not been substantial changes in attitudes about how to keep up with environmentally friendly activities. But we have identified some changes in structural behaviour, which illustrates how the eco-village households have interacted with changes in society at large. The use of pellets has remained, but some years ago the residents decided to abandon the composting toilets. Thus, their sanitation practice has changed, but this was done deliberately since the municipal waste plant had improved considerably since 1984. Also, their compost system has been abandoned. When the municipality started to collect household waste in 2007, all residents decided that they should participate. However, their environmentally friendly attitude has not altered. The behavioural changes are motivated by the fact that they are more environmentally friendly than the original solutions within the eco-village. The municipal waste water plant has improved significantly since 1984 and the composting toilets caused in the end, much nuisance. Also the compost system did not function properly, thus it was better to support the municipal model.

144

After exploring changes at household level our conclusion is that there are not many changes as regards attitudes. All householders claimed that they regard themselves to take environmental concern and that they 'think' much about the environment. They are in general focused on saving energy, on buying organic products and several householders claim that they are still anti-materialistic. But some admit that they end up in dilemma situations and sometimes break with their basic attitude, by for instance driving their private car more than they like. Behavioural changes have been most prominent as regards transportation, i.e. the use of the car. One reason is change in life situation, for instance having elderly relatives that cannot be reached by public transport or bicycle, and some also stressed that they have become more 'lazy' when getting older. Also more travelling has influenced changes in transportation patterns.

To what extent then have children that grew up in Tuggelite adopted environmentally friendly attitudes and behaviour? This has been the third aim to explore. There are differences among them. As regards three of the children we might conclude that the 'apple did not fall far from the tree'. They also claimed that their parents have been models and that their lifestyle is pro-environmental. They both think about the environment and they do a lot. One child was somewhat more hesitatant, but believed that she at least knew more about the environment than her classmates, and that she probably will bring with her environmentally friendly attitudes and behaviour 'to a certain extent'. Only one was quite clear about having been influenced negatively. Even if he believed that he often did more than 'ordinary people', he was not much concerned about environmental issues. He found the environment something 'abstract' and he was persuaded ideologically that changes towards environmentally friendly everyday life had to be implemented from top to bottom.

The case of Tuggelite has shown that it was possible to walk the talk for sustainable everyday life and we have pointed at different explanations. At a theoretical level the case illustrates a shift from governmental to individual responsibility. This shift has been discussed by social scientists and historians. (Öst, 2007). There has been an individual turn focusing on the role of citizens as environmental political agents taking responsibility for harmful environmental actions (Skill, 2008). This turn emerged as a consequence of privatization and deregulation following from neoliberalism in the 1980s and the individual consumer was ascribed with environmental responsibility (Hobson, 2004). Socio-moral obligations were assumed to push citizens to behave environmentally friendly while the state or governments retreated from previous duties characterized by 'top-down configuration of authority' (Shamir, 2008). The shift from government to governance left 'creative, flexible and efficient 'best practice' solutions that leave 'the greatest possible amount of control in the hands of those closest to the problems (Shamir, 2008). Tuggelite was set up in an early phase of this shift and represented both collective ideologies from the 1970s, but also elements of the turn towards citizens' responsibility. The residents saw themselves to be close to environmental problems caused by the consumer society and took control over their own life. They transformed attitudes and behaviour into habits and influenced to a large extent their children. Environmental friendly everyday activities among households in the eco-village became as normal as brushing their teeth.

NOTES

1 The quotation is from a copy of an undated article in the municipal archive in Karlstad. The full reference is: Kommunearkivet i Karlstad. Mapp Stadsplanekontoret, Ritningar med handlingar 1982–1983 JI: 241.
2 Asplin et al. (1981), Hus för bogemenskap i Karlstad. The paper belongs to the municipal archive in Karlstad (Kommunarkivet i Karlstad. Mapp Stadsplanekontoret, Ritningar med handlingar 1982–1983 JI: 241
3 Ibid.
4 This is a quotation from a note by the head of the development unit in Karlstad 13 October 1981. See Kommunarkivet i Karlstad. Mapp Stadsplanekontoret, Ritningar med handlingar 1982–1983 JI: 241.
5 This is a quotation from the protest group referred in a note dated 8 December 1981. See Kommunarkivet i Karlstad. Mapp Stadsplanekontoret, Ritningar med handlingar 1982–1983 JI: 241.
6 Ibid.
7 Undated article which is found in the private collection of articles about Tuggelite. The collection is held by Lars Nilsson at Tuggelite.

REFERENCES

Andersson, Jenny (2002) *Alva's Futures Ideas in the Construction of Swedish Futures Studies*. Arbetsrapport/Institutet för Framtidsstudier; 2002:5
Bäckstrand, Göran and Lars Ingelstam (1975) 'How much is enough? – another Sweden', in *Development Dialogue 1975*, no 1/2, Hammarskiöldfonden, Uppsala
Bauman, Zygmunt (2004) *Work, Consumerism and the New Poor*. Buckingham: Open University Press
Beck, Ulrich (1997) *The Reinvention of Politics: Rethinking Modernity in the Global Social Order*, Wiley, London
Berlund, Christer and Simon Matti (2006) 'Citizen and Consumer: The Dual Role of Individuals in Environmental Policy', *Environmental Politics*, vol 15, No. 4, pp550–571
Eckerberg, Katarina (2000) 'Sweden: Progression Despite Recession, in Implementing Sustainable Development. Strategies and Initiatives', in *High Consumption societies* (eds William M. Lafferty and James Meadowcroft). Oxford University Press: Oxford
Giddens, Anthony (1984) *The Constitution of Society*. Cambridge: Polity Press
Giddens, Anthony (1991) *Modernity and Self-identity*. Cambridge: Polity Press
Hobson, Kersty (2004) 'Sustainable Consumption in the United Kingdom: The "Responsible" Consumer and Government at "Arm's Length"', *Journal of Environment and Development*, vol 13, No. 2, pp121–139.
Lundgren, L. J. (1992) 'Den miljövänlige konsumenten', *Livsstil och miljö. På väg mot ett miljövänligt beteende?* Naturvårdsverket: Lund
Lundgren, Lars J (2005) 'Miljöproblem och miljövård i Sverige', in *Konflikter, samarbete, resultat. Perspektiv på svensk mijöpolitik.* (ed Lars J. Lundgren). Kassandra: Brottby

McCarty, T. (2007) *Auto Mania. Cars, Consumers, and the Environment.* Yale University Press: New Haven and London

Norbeck, Martha 'Individual, community, environment. Lessons from nine Swedish ecovillages', www.ekoby.org 2009-07-22

Olsson, Kåre and Emin Tengström (eds) (1976) *Välsviken: om resurshushållning och demokrati vid planering och förvaltning av begyggelse.* Göteborg: Centrum för tvärvetenskapliga studier av människans vilkor

Öst, Thomas (2007) *Livsstilsförändringar och "grön" teknik. Om relationen mellan ekonomisk och ekologisk rationalitet i miljöpolitiken.* PhD Dissertation Uppsala: Uppsala University

Shamir, Ronen (2008) 'The Age of Responsibilization: On Market-embedded Morality', *Economy and Society*, vol 37, No. 1, pp1–19

Skill, Karin (2008) *(Re)creating Ecological Action Space: Householders' Activities for Sustainable Development in Sweden.* PhD Dissertation, Linköping: Linköping University

Söderholm, Kristina (2009) 'Sustainability and Swedish Household Consumption since the 1950s: The role of Policy-driven Socio-technical Systems', paper presented at the World Congress of Environmental History 'Local Livelihoods And Global Challenges: Under-standing Human Interaction With The Environment', Copenhagen, August 4–8, 2009

SOU 1972: 19 *Att välja framtid.* Stockholm

SOU 1987: 32 *För en bättre miljö.* Stockholm

Spaargaren, Gert (2003) 'Sustainable Consumption: A Theoretical and Environmental Policy Perspective', *Society and Natural Resources*, pp687–701.

Spaargaren, Gert and Bas van Vliet (2000) 'Lifestyles, Consumption and the Environment: The Ecological Modernisation of Domestic Consumption', *Environmental Politics*, vol 9, No 1, pp50–77

Stern, Paul, C (2000) 'Toward a Coherent Theory of Environmentally Significant Behaviour', *Journal of Social Issues*, vol 56, No. 3, pp407–424

Tidäng, Kristina (1992) *Att bo i Tuggelite.* Göteborg

Policy-driven socio-technical structures and Swedish households' consumption of housing and transport since the 1950s

Kristina Söderholm

INTRODUCTION

Swedish households generate, through the goods and services they consume (and considering the whole chain of production), almost 90 per cent out of Sweden's total carbon dioxide emissions (Carlsson-Kanyama et al, 2007). According to a Public Investigation Report from 2004 (SOU, 2004:119), a major part of these emissions are in turn caused by housing- and transport-related consumption.[1] The consumption of transport- and housing-related products and services have historically constituted significant shares of total household expenses in Sweden, and these shares have also increased over time (Söderholm, 2007). This can be compared to household consumption patterns in England where a number of other expense categories have increased more in relative terms, e.g. recreation and entertainment,[2] communication[3] and domestic appliances (Jackson and Marks, 1999). This chapter aims to contribute a more in-depth understanding of the historical development of Swedish household consumption of housing and transport during the second half of the 20th century. The analysis focuses on the socio-technical context of household consumption behaviour, and illustrates in particular how the Swedish government during this period has (directly and indirectly) intervened in household consumption with significant complications for the environment.

There exists a rather extensive contemporary research on consumption, a lot of it conducted by sociologists and psychologists.[4] A major part of this research focuses on different socio-psychological aspects of consumer behaviour, the socio-economic prerequisites for changes in consumption levels, and on the consumption of positional, luxurious and conspicuous goods. In recent years, though, a number of researchers have been shifting the focus away from individual consumers and the conspicuous aspects of modern consumer lifestyles, to the inconspicuous aspects where consumption is about convenience, habits, routines, social norms and institutions over which the individual have little control, and towards the way prevailing systems of provision constrain the way consumers act (e.g. Shove and Warde, 2002; Southerton et al, 2004; Jackson, 2006). It has been suggested that such an approach needs to be socio-technical in its character whereas these consumption patterns: 'so often require the use of technologies and appliances [...] frequently implicated in the invention and reproduction of practice' (Shove, 2006, p. 294), and often are embedded in socio-technical systems with infrastructural character, and have to do with how collective services are managed and handled (e.g. Røpke, 1999; Shove and Warde, 2002; Southerton et al, 2004; van Vliet et al, 2005; Shove, 2006). The socio-technical systems influence household consumption while providing collectively imposed and basic everyday services, such as transport, communication, energy and water provision, and, in a wider sense, the structures of the town/town plan and its different parts, like public residential areas and external shopping areas. These systems have dramatically contributed to social development, but have also limited our possibilities to choose, not least when it comes to consumption patterns with less environmental impacts.

The Swedish ethnographer Karin Book (e.g. Book and Eskilsson, 2001) uses the 'structures-matters-for-everyday-activities-approach' (thus not explicitly related to consumption) as a point of departure in studying the changing structures of cities in the Western world from early industrial society until today's information society. Book discusses 'the structures' in a context of general trends in the Western society, and concludes that the 20th century society in the Western world has changed from concentration, centralization, integration and public transport to scattering, decentralizations (however, presently to a certain degree back toward recentralization), separation and private transport. At first the autobus, but in time the passenger car, made large-scale decentralization of activities and housing possible in 20th century cities in the Western world. In parallel, new economic and social conditions, such as increased standards of living, equality and eventually welfare programmes, expanded our everyday room, and many moved to the suburbs where the technology of premanufacture made mass-produced houses possible. The assembly-line technology and the lorry in turn contributed to the decentralization of industry as it often required space-demanding, one-flat buildings (Book and Eskilsson,

2001). Book further finds the service society (1945 to the 1970s) to have experienced not only an increase in welfare, equality, middle class, leisure time and number of women in workforce, but also social development in the sense of increased importance of the core family alongside incipient individualism.

The socio-technical structures and systems embedding our everyday practices, and thus not least consumption, mean that policy already intervenes in people's behaviour, which in turn 'opens out a range of vital avenues for policy intervention in pursuit of behavioral change' (Jackson, 2006, p. 119). Socio-technical transformations can, however, be very difficult to achieve, whereas prevailing socio-technical systems tend to act as barriers to the creation of new systems (e.g. Meijer et al, 2006). This path dependency and irreversibility characterizing established socio-technical systems partly stems from increasing returns to adoption caused by learning and by using network externalities, scale economies in production, informational increasing returns and technological interrelatedness (Arthur, 1988; Meijer et al, 2006). Meijer et al (2006) also point to the socio-institutional framework of the system to be:

> *aligned to the existing technology by a process of technological and institutional co-evolution [...] [which] can lead to a lock-in of the prevailing system: the prevailing system has gained an advantage on the basis of its history, not on the basis of technical superiority.* (Meijer et al, 2006, p. 215).[5]

When it comes to scholarly work on consumption by historians, it has so far tended to focus more on consumerism and consumer society, and on social, cultural and psychological aspects of consumer behaviour, rather than on the consumption of everyday goods and on structures explaining consumption patterns.[6] Oldenziel et al (2005) review extensive historical writing on the relationship between consumption and technology; however, this in general has less to do with explaining consumption patterns and more with how both producers and consumers have mattered in the making of the technology consumed. These authors also establish that scholars rarely consider consumption as the outcome of collective political choices, but as it is a matter of individual choice and 'excessive expression of materialism' (Oldenziel et al, 2005, p. 120). Trentmann (2004) in turn points out how this view of consumerism contributes to a 'diminishing analytical and conceptual usefulness' of concepts such as 'consumerism' and 'modern consumer society' in historical research on consumption (Trentmann, 2004, p. 376f):

> *It is problematic to read back from increased consumer spending the dominance of consumerist mentalities. For many people, it might be very 'necessary' for subsistence to purchase a car in suburban America, because of the lack of public transport and a dispersed socio-economic and cultural infrastructure, not because of a consumerist definition of one's goals in life.* (Trentmann, 2004, p. 377)

Jackson and Papathanasopoulou (2008) argue in line with this while ascribing a 'major part' of the increase in consumption of resources associated to commuting and business travel of UK households since the late 1960s to structural and institutional factors partly outside the influence of individual choice, like increased emphasis on economic mobility and increased participation in the workforce by two partners.[7] They thus ascribe the overall trend in consumption both to changes in lifestyles as well as to changes in 'systems of provisions'[8] where rising economic mobility, out-of-town superstores, etc., have shifted 'the burden of resource consumption' from production to consumption. Jackson and Papathanasopoulou (2008) as well as Jackson and Marks (1999) complement their qualitative analysis by using real consumption data, i.e. UK household consumption expenditures from the 1950s and onwards. Apart from these two examples, though, there is generally very limited previous empirical consumption research based on data from an additional number of countries as well as using longer time series.

In this chapter we address the consumption patterns of Swedish post-war households with particular reference to housing and transport, and we emphasize a number of socio-technical structures of central importance for understanding these patterns as well as trace how the structures have been influenced by public policy in different areas. Only to a limited extent we also discuss the different socio-economic, socio-psychological and individualized driving forces behind consumption, which clearly also play a role in the present context. The chapter begins by exploring the actual consumption patterns of Swedish post-war households in the cases of housing and transport, and we then revert to a discussion of how government influence may be regarded as the more or less deliberate construction of systems that impinged on households' daily lives and consumption patterns. The socio-technical systems addressed are primarily: (a) Swedish post-war housing policy; (b) the motorization of society; and (c) the post-war rationalization of retail distribution.

EXPLORING SWEDISH HOUSEHOLDS' CONSUMPTION OF HOUSING AND TRANSPORT FROM THE 1950S AND ONWARDS

By studying data compiled by Statistics Sweden, mainly from the examination and documenttation of the consumption patterns of 2000–4000 individual Swedish households since 1958 at about a decade's interval,[9] we learn that the average Swedish household more than doubled its expenses (in the money value of 2005) between 1958 and 2005 (see Figure 7.1).[10] The increasing disposable incomes of Swedish households can in large be explained by increased real wages and by a raised proportion of women with paid employment. In the remainder of this section we pay particular attention to the housing and transport components of this total picture.

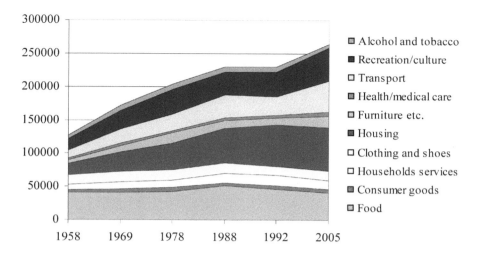

Figure 7.1 *Swedish households' consumption 1958–2005 by category (SEK 2005)*

Sources: Statistics Sweden

Housing

Household consumption of housing-related goods and services (rent/fees, reparations, energy, interests, insurance, tax, etc.) increased by as much as 277 per cent in real terms between 1958 and 2005. Housing thus took over from 'food' as the most significant expense category for the average Swedish household over this time period (Figure 7.1). This can be explained by both increased prices for housing-related consumption,[11] altered preferences towards, and changed socio-technical prerequisites for, housing consumption over the period (see also below).

Looking closer into the components of housing expenses (Figure 7.2) we find that the expenses for interests, electricity and rents/fees multiplied for the average Swedish household between 1958 and 2005 (in the money value of 2005), whereas expenses for housing energy in total 'only' doubled (expenses for electricity trebled). Interests started from a very low level in the 1950s (the second smallest expense category within housing) and increased a remarkable 800 per cent in real terms up to the 1970s, whereas the increase in housing-related expenses on interests 'only' was about 80 per cent for the average Swedish household between the 1970s and the 1990s. Rents/fees started from a relatively high level in the 1950s, but increased by as much as 70 per cent for the average Swedish household only between 1958 and 1969. It thereafter took more than 30 years for the average Swedish household to reach the same level of percentage increase in the expenses on rents/fees.

153

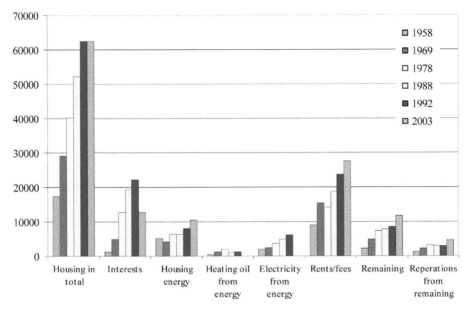

Figure 7.2 *Swedish households' housing expenses by category, 1958–2003 (in the money value of SEK 2005)*

Sources: Statistics Sweden

From other sources we know that the number of apartments in the total Swedish apartment stock doubled between 1945 and 1975, whereas the proportion of apartments with private water closet (WC) and bath-/shower room increased from about 30 to over 90 per cent (Franzén and Sandstedt, 1981, p. 233f).[12] This indicates that a very large part of the apartment stock was modernized/new-built over the period. We also know that the living area per average Swedish household increased from 93 square metres in 1970 to 109 square metres in 2003 (SOU, 2004:119, p. 140), in parallel to a development towards a decreased number of persons per average household, from 2.8 persons in 1960 to 2.1 persons in 1990 and onwards (Folk och Bostadsräkningarna). Moreover, smaller apartments gave way to bigger ones in the second half of the 20th century. Apartments bigger than two rooms (plus kitchen) increased in proportion to the total Swedish apartment stock from one to almost three-quarters (Franzen and Sandstedt, 1981, p. 234).[13] In addition to this, private housing ownership increased dramatically in that the construction number of small houses increased from a little less than 20,000 to a little more than 30,000 houses per year in the 1960s, and to almost 50,000 houses per year in the 1970s (Wigren, 1997). The above provides some added perspective and understanding of the important role of housing in Swedes' overall consumption behaviour.

Transport

Across all groups of goods and services for the average Swedish household, the percentage increase in the expenses on 'transport' between 1958 and 2005 (284 per cent) is the most striking. 'Transport' expanded from being the fifth biggest expense category for households in 1958 to become the third biggest in 2005 (Figure 7.1). This development occurred in parallel with increasing transport prices,[14] but do indeed also mirror a constantly increasing consumption of transport services over the period. The biggest component of the transport expenses is the operation of the passenger car whereas the second biggest is the purchase of the passenger car. This is the situation for all of the investigated years, although the relative share of the two expense categories differs over the years, from about two to one in 1978 (during the second oil crisis) to about one to one in 1958 and 1988 (low fuel prices and an economic boom in 1988).

The expenses for 'transport' increased as a share of total consumption for the average Swedish household throughout the entire period, with the exception of the economic recession in 1992. The latter decrease can, however, mainly be attributed to reduced purchases of passenger cars whereas expenses on the operation of passenger cars and on public transportation remained unaltered with the recession; most households thus chose to travel in older passenger cars instead of travelling less. Furthermore, although households overall earned considerably more money in 2005 compared to 1958, the share

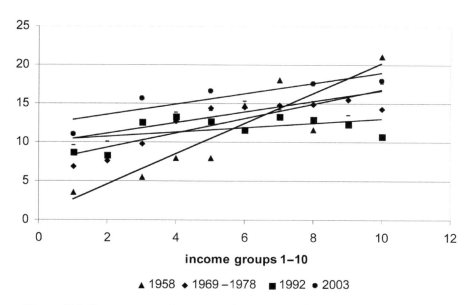

income groups 1–10

▲ 1958 ◆ 1969 – 1978 ■ 1992 ● 2003

Figure 7.3 *Consumption share (%) of transport related to household income group, 1958, 1969, 1978, 1992 and 2003*

Sources: Statistics Sweden

of transport expenses out of total expenses: (a) has increased over all the period (except in 1992) for all income groups; (b) is still increasing with income in the more recent of these years (see Figure 7.3). However, the differences between the lowest and highest income groups tend to even out over the years, i.e. the divergence in transport expenses between the different income groups was bigger in 1958 and 1969, respectively, than in more recent years.

The above development reflects a major increase in the use of the passenger car since the 1950s, and we discern a situation where mobility becomes a structural requirement with ever-increasing distances between family, work and shopping. Passenger cars have become more and more fuel efficient over the period. The average amount of fuel required for a new passenger car was 26 per cent lower in 2005 compared to 1978. On top of that, long-run (real) fuel prices have been fairly stabile. For example, the year average price for 95 octane was a little bit over SEK 9 in both 1981 and 2003 (in the money value of 2007), although this period also witnessed substantial price slumps (e.g. in the late 1980s) and price peaks (e.g. during the first half of the 21st century). The cost of purchasing a new passenger car has increased in real terms since the 1950s in parallel to the advancement of the passenger car. The purchase of a new car in the 1950s claimed roughly about 60 per cent of the total yearly expenses of the average Swedish household, whereas purchasing a new car today claims about as much expenses as the average household have in total over the year.[15] An important difference between the 1950s and today is, however, that it is now much easier to obtain loans.

The passenger car started to diffuse among Swedish households in the 1950s, but it was first in the 1960s and the 1970s that we could witness a significant increase in the consumption of passenger car transport; the number of registered cars in Sweden increased by almost 300 per cent between 1958 and 1978.[16] This in turn expanded the average length travelled per person per day from about 5 kilometres in 1950 to over 30 kilometres in 1975. Moreover, the proportion of public transportation of the average length travelled per day has stayed at unaltered levels since the 1970s, i.e. at about 10 per cent (Krantz, 1999, p. 69ff; SIKA, 2007).

If we take a closer look at the development of passenger car transport we also find that it has become more and more individualized, i.e. Swedes travel more often as drivers than as passengers today compared to a few decades ago. This can partly be explained by the fact that more women use passenger cars as drivers instead of assuming the role of passengers; women's car ownership increased from 20 per cent to more than 30 per cent of the total number of passenger cars in Sweden between 1972 and 2006. At the same time the total number of registered cars increased from 2.4 to 3.3 million. Furthermore, the possession of two cars has increased faster than car possession in general during the last decades (Vilhelmson, 2000, p. 31f; SIKA, 2000, 2007). The increase in the number of registered passenger cars was thus still high in the 1980s and onwards (about 145 per cent between 1978 and 2005), although not as high as in earlier decades.[17] When it comes to the purpose of the travel undertaken by household members, we find that the distances travelled increased for work and shopping travels between 1978 and 1996 and for shopping travel still after that (SIKA, 2000, p. 13; SIKA, 2007, p. 7). Shopping travel has at the same time become more concentrated in the time since the 1970s, i.e. they occur more seldom but at longer distances from home.[18]

In the remainder of this chapter we will try to widen our understanding of the observed consumption patterns by pointing out some important socio-technical structures that have shaped and embedded consumption behaviour in Sweden. We also comment on the underlying political decisions and motives behind these structures.

UNDERSTANDING THE SOCIO-TECHNICAL CONTEXTS OF SWEDISH HOUSEHOLD CONSUMPTION SINCE THE 1950s

We have already established that the socio-technical structures and the associated policies in focus here will only explain the consumption patterns of post-war households (in Western society) in combination with a number of important socio-economic, socio-psychological and individualized factors. For this reason it is useful to start with a brief overview on some general societal development factors, such as the socio-economic development and the general individualization process, that are of relevance in understanding Swedish households' consumption of housing and transport since the 1950s.

Naturally, increased real wages and increased household income due to a massive increase of women in paid work (in turn heavily dependent on a strongly expanded public childcare) ought to have contributed to Swedish households' increased consumption of modernized and bigger homes since the 1950s, as well as to increased private housing ownership and to the massive increase in the consumption of passenger car transport. Furthermore, the general individualization process of modern Western society ought to be included in the understanding of both the increased consumption of passenger car transport (not least those as a driver), the increased private housing ownership and the increased living areas (which in turn have led to increased housing expenses) for the average Swedish household over the period. Both the socio-economic development and the general individualization process have contributed to the high proportion of single-person households in Sweden,[19] which in turn has greatly influenced consumption patterns.[20]

Of relevance in explaining the consumption of households is, however, also the socio-technical structures within which consumption takes place, as well as the policy decisions underlying these structures. These include the ideas and the products of the post-war social housing policy, which to a great extent was realized through increased local planning authority and rationalized construction processes. In the case of Swedish households' increased consumption of transport since the 1950s, examples of relevant socio-technical structures include the rationalized retail distribution, the expansion of the road system and differentiation of the town, all making personal mobility a structural requirement.

Social housing policy, local planning monopoly and rationalized construction processes

In the early post-war period there was a housing shortage in the bigger cities in Sweden, mostly due to structural rationalizations in the Swedish industry with accompanying resettlements and household splitting. This was also a consequence of income increases and of labour immigration (Bladh, 1992, p. 273ff). In parallel, the socio-economic development actualized the question of larger and modernized homes. The Swedish state responded with an extensive social housing policy, especially in the 1940s to the 1960s. The ambition was to generate satisfactory housing with improved housing standards and to counteract crowdedness for all.[21] Several public investigations provide evidence of the post-war housing ambitions, such as 'The Housing-social Investigation I and II' in 1945, and 'Increased Standards of Housing' in 1965. The latter investigation actualized the so-called 'Million programme' with which the goal was to produce more than 100,000 apartments in urban areas per year over a ten-year period (mid-1960s to mid-1970s).[22] This implied 1 million apartments in 10 years in a country with a population of a little less than eight million in total (in the 1960s) and with about 54 per cent of the population living in cities and boroughs (where the apartments of the Million programme were to be erected) in 1965 (Historical statistics for Sweden Part 1. Population, 1720–1967, second edition). Thus, the Million programme was indeed a large-scale plan that, even though the programme never was to be fully completed due to economic downturn in the 1970s, caused large-scale effects on the Swedish apartment stock as well as on the appearance of the average Swedish town, and not least on the consumption patterns of the average Swedish household when it came to housing and transport.

The influence of the social housing policy on the housing consumption of the average Swedish household from the 1950s onwards has been comprehensive. The large-scale influence of the policy on the apartment stock has encompassed increased size and standards of the apartments, which in turn has influenced the general housing norm, but not least the actual housing market. Larger and modernized apartments, i.e. apartments that are more expensive to buy, rent and operate, were now being supplied. The increased number of apartments available together with an extensive housing allowance policy has further empowered household splitting and an increasing number of single-person households. The social housing policy has also influenced housing consumption, especially in the case of tenancy right apartments, by regulations supporting rent control, protected tenancy and local housing authorities (Bladh, 1992, p. 273ff). Swedish post-war social housing policy, to abolish housing shortage, crowdedness and low housing standards, was further realized through the rationalized and industrialized construction of apartments in a societal regime. Within this concept the idea of neighbourhood units played a central role.

The idea of neighbourhood units, which aimed at a distinct division and dissemination of the city with neighbourhood units to live in and city centres and industrial areas to work in, were actualized as town planning reform in Sweden in the 1930s, but still strongly characterized town planning at the time of the Million programme. The neighbourhood unit primarily consisted of apartment houses to reach the necessary density, and a central idea of the neighbourhood unit was that it would strengthen the sense of solidarity among the inhabitants. All should live within walking distance of the community centre where schools, childcare, shops and general assembly halls were situated, although early commerce tended to dominate the public area of the neighbourhood unit at the expense of, for instance, public assembly halls. Although the neighbourhood unit from one perspective contributed to dense housing areas, which usually are regarded as environmentally preferable, the clear borders of the units facilitated an inner and an outer traffic system with a planned web of roads within and between the units as well as from the units to the city centres and to the workplaces.[23] The diffusion of neighbourhood units, in this way, very much worked in favour of the use of passenger cars.[24] This was the situation in most 20th century cities in the Western world due to the improved socio-economic conditions of the working class from the end of the 19th century together with social welfare considerations giving expression to functionalistic ideals of simple and functional housing for everyone. At the same time, the passenger car is the technology with the most profound impacts on this development (earlier in USA than in Europe) (Book and Eskilsson, 2001, p. 166ff).

The realization of neighbourhood units was facilitated by the 'Law of construction', issued in 1947, with which local authorities were given local planning monopoly. Now local authorities had the right to decide when and where construction projects should take place although they most certainly often had to consider other powerful local actors in the planning process (see further below), such as big local companies and their eventual needs for housing for their workers (Strömberg 2001). The overriding responsibility for the housing provision, at least for planning and initiation, was further put in the hands of the municipalities with the 'Law of housing provision' (also issued in 1947).[25] Now responsibility was set and the necessary tools given to municipal entrepreneurship that came to realize the idea of neighbourhood units. The municipal entrepreneurship was, however, strengthened further all the way into the 1970s.[26]

From an international perspective Sweden has a long tradition of a de facto local planning monopoly. The strong local position in physical planning has been strengthened throughout the 20th century through a number of parliamentary resolutions and law redactions. Municipalities gained the right to approve town plans (however, they had to be confirmed by the national government) with the 'Town planning law' of 1907. The responsibility of municipalities for the use of land within towns was further strengthened in connection with the parliamentary settling of the forms for the post-war social housing policy, which resulted in the above-mentioned laws 'of construction' and 'of housing provision' in 1947. An important parliamentary reason for decentralizing even more planning power to the local level was at this stage to maximize the chance for new housing to be built in the most suitable places. The planning power of the municipalities was further strengthened in connection with the 'Building regulation' of 1959, when it was extended to include high density building in rural areas. The former free building right in rural areas was totally abolished in 1972, mostly due to the development of 'National physical planning' from the 1960s, which principally also was to be completed through the physical planning of municipalities (Government Bill, 1976/77:129, p. 7).[27] Municipalities gained even more planning power through the 'Planning and Building Act' of 1987, with which they obtained the final decision over the use of land. This is clearly mirrored in a central formulation of the law wording: 'it is a municipal concern to plan the use of land and water', (1st chapter, 2 §, author's translation). The national government has retained a final influence on planning only concerning national interests, environmental quality norms, health, security and issues relating to more than one municipality. There is thus a fairly well-established tradition of the rather strong position of Swedish municipalities in planning and thus a rather weak position of regional and national planning with the focus on supervision and control rather than on active societal planning.

The social housing policy was further realized through a wide-ranging rationalization and industrialization of the construction process, which to a considerable degree was initiated by state intervention. This was, for example, obtained by economic instruments of control, such as different forms of loans and allowances making it possible for construction and housing companies to initiate large projects production series. One example is the 'machine-loan-fund', established in 1952, from which construction and housing companies could apply for loans financing appliances in factories and building sites (e.g. Bergström et al, 1968). Advantages were also initiated for lager projects of more than 1000 apartments planned and projected with a high degree of standardization, so-called 'thousand-apartments-projects', where applicants could get advanced notice of guarantees for financing (Statens råd för byggnadsforskning, 1975; Hyll and Lessing, 2004).

The rationalization and industrialization of the construction process took off primarily in the 1950s, mostly due to increased wages for and a general shortage of construction workers; with assemblage construction and prefabrication, unskilled labour could be used to a greater extent. Rationalization and industrialization was foremost about the introduction of machines and appliances in the construction process, such as the tower crane, which enabled the use of reusable steel moulds instead of moulds made of wood in the concrete-casting process. The provision of tower cranes was thorough in the 1950s and 1960s in Swedish construction and housing companies; the number of tower cranes increased from 20 to about 5000 from 1950 to 1970 (Björk et al, 1983; Marmstål, 1992). Rationalization and industrialization was also about repetition, standardization and systems thinking. One example of the latter is the development of the total contract reform in connection to the 'Million programme' in the 1960s, with one single producer, i.e. often municipal entre-preneurs, in close cooperation with constructors and town planning authorities in contrast to earlier procedures where town planning preceded construction. The total contract reform, which was supported by the Swedish government, gave room for considerable rationalization of the construction of apartments towards a production steered system construction and prefabrication (Franzen and Sandstedt, 1981).

Another central example of the rationalization of the construction process from the 1950s onwards is the changed handling of construction material, such as the brick. Several years into the 1950s, the brick was handled no less than nine times on its way from the kiln to where it was used, and the brick carriers was a special profession at the construction site. With a new way of bundling-up and packing the bricks, and with the development of special brick carts, bricks handling became considerably rationalized (Cornell, 1979). The effects of the rationalizations are mirrored in the decreasing number of man hours needed for a cubic metre building-volume during the 1950s to the 1970s; in 1950, the average number of needed man hours was 8, in 1961 it was 4.5, and in 1971 it was only 2.5 (Statens råd för byggnads forskning, 1975).[28]

The production of apartments increased dramatically all through the 1960s and reached the first component of the goal of the 'Million programme', more than 100,000 apartments a year, in the late 1960s (Wigren, 1997). The demand for apartments, however, decreased alongside the general economic downturn in the early 1970s (Statens råd för byggnadsforskning, 1975). The market for apartments became weak and construction started to decrease, and did so all through the 1970s and throughout most of the 1980s. The trend was the same in all Nordic countries, with a post-war boom in housing construction at least up to and including the 1960s and thereafter a considerable decline in the 1970s and 1980s. Still, the decline was particularly strong in Sweden (Bostads och byggnadsstatistisk årsbok, 2005, Table 1.1.9). Whereas the market for apart-ments has been rather small since the early 1970s compared to earlier centuries, and thus the production series, much of the industrialization achieved within the construction process in the 1950s and 1960s is lost today (Hyll and Lessing, 2004). Industrialization has, however, remained within the construction process of small houses, not least through the many catalogue houses (see below).

By the end of the 'Million programme', i.e. in the first half of the 1970s, the building of small houses increased markedly, which continued the differen-tiation and dissemination of the Swedish town. This should partly be looked upon as an effect of favourable tax conditions and changed monetary policy, which made it easier to obtain loans, as well as of general socio-economic devel-opment. The boom-like increase could, however, also be looked upon as a reaction to underlying decades of a social housing policy based on the industri-alized and standardized construction of apartments. After years of homogenized production of apartment houses in most mid- to big-sized Swedish towns in parallel to a general individualization process, it is reasonable to assume that housing preferences changed and people began to invest more heavily in small houses. Ironically enough, however, the increase in small house building would not have taken place had it not been for the growing abundance of catalogue houses produced in rationalized and industrialized ways, and thus at reasonable costs.

Sweden experienced an increase in the building of small houses in the first decades of the 20th century, in connection to the 'one's-own-home-movement' where some ten thousand families received national loans, in the first place for homes in the countryside but later on also in the suburbs. At the time, the one's-own-home, i.e. the small house in contrast to the apartment house, was thought to be a good solution to the housing problems of the not so-well-off and it was also believed to contribute to good upbringing, good family life as well as to discipline of the workers. Almqvist (2004) establishes this basic idea of the one's-own-home-policy, i.e. to change the society with the good home as the model, to have been abandoned in the 1930s in favour of the idea of making the home more societal, where the home became 'an object for the regularization and intervention of planners and experts with the aim to create rational housing and habits for social life' (Almqvist, 2004, p. 33, author's translation).

About two thirds of the small houses built at the beginning of the 1970s were catalogue houses constructed in house factories.[29] The customer chose a house-type in a catalogue and house elements were constructed at the house factory for further montage at the building-site. The Swedish government contributed to the industrialization and standardization of the small-house construction process by, in reference to obtaining national loans, claiming 'Swedish standards' in respect to measure, design and quality for doors, windows, cabinet carpentries, etc. (Gabrielson and Ringmar, 1970). The Technical office of the Royal housing committee (established in 1948) further contributed to the standardization of small houses by issuing outlines for type-plans for sale for those applying for house loans. The type plans at an affordable price offered excellent technical solutions and work instructions previously accessible only to consulting building technical expertise. The type-plans even worked as prototypes for the catalogue houses of the 1950s (Engfors, 1987).

Even though a majority of the small houses in the 1970s were constructed in rather industrialized and standardized ways, the consumer could choose his/her house among a growing abundance of different catalogue houses exposed to fashion changes and constructed in ways that appealed to target groups with a high purchasing power. The choice of house did, especially from the 1970s onwards, even become a way of expressing a certain lifestyle and taste of the houseowner. Almqvist (2004) supports this notion and uses a phenomenological interpretation, trying to understand the home in relation to the development of modernity:

> Given the rapid changes in life style and consumption patterns of
> modern society, the need to create has been transformed from being
> an expression of knowledge of building and cultivation into an
> expression of personal style and taste. [...] Today, the design
> of one's house and interiors indicate whether one has kept up

with modernity's constant demands for renewal. (Almqvist, 2004, p. 180)

Rationalization of retail distribution and mobility as a structural requirement

We have seen above that the length of shopping travels increased continuously for Swedish households from at least the 1970s. This can be related to the far-reaching rationalization of retail distribution that has taken place in Sweden since the 1950s. Up to then, a number of small stores were simply scattered around in the community centres whereas a more marked differentiation emerged in the planning of the bigger towns in the 1960s, between smaller district centres, local town centres (large centres) for about 10,000 customers and regional centres for a multiplied number of customers. The centres further came to be characterized by more connected constructions with a dense urbanity and service culture after inspiration from the USA and in an increasing amount of suburban centres as well as in town centres, indoor constructions were erected. The suburban development and increasing private motoring further contributed in making the traffic routes and connected cheap ground areas interesting for new external shore establishments, e.g. discount stores, food stores, department stores, etc. The external establishment calmed down in Sweden in the 1970s, to increase in the 1980s when a large number of regular shopping centres were erected in external locations alongside situations alongside the suburban centres (Bergman, 2003).

In parallel to the differentiation of diverse centres and the external establishments in the 1960s, new department stores with substantial food departments were established in more or less every Swedish town in the 1960s and in the first half of the 1970s. This of course heavily influenced the appearance of the town centres. The department stores in the city centres as well as the supermarkets in the suburban areas took advantage of the increasing use of the passenger car and established larger parking lots, multi-storey parking facilities or widened the streets in order to increase on-street parking capacity. Only with an increase in the amount of car-based customers, could the store capacity increase (Svensson, 1998).

Rationalization thus pushed development away from many small specialized food stores to fewer and bigger food stores and to department stores in the town centres in the 1950s and 1960s, to superstores in the town peripheries in the 1960s and 1970s and thereafter to external shopping centres. This development has caused a constantly growing distance to convenience goods stores for many households. However, as the development simultaneously has brought about a constantly growing assortment and number of articles in the stores, the transaction volumes have increased and the number of necessary contacts between the household and the store has decreased. Rationalization and growing competition in the distribution chain have simultaneously contributed to an increasingly concentrated ownership, from many small independent distribution retailers to oligopolies in large oligopolies (Franzen and Sandstedt, 1981; Svensson, 1998). The number of convenience goods stores decreased by over 80 per cent during the second half of the 20th century in Sweden. The big change occurred in the 1960s when a new system of convenience goods distribution with bigger stores and self-service was introduced at the expense of a large number of small stores (Svensson, 1998).[30] The concept of self-service rapidly gained ground in Swedish convenience goods distribution during the 1950s and the 1960s. At the end of the 1960s, 70 per cent of Swedish food sales were distributed through self-service stores (Svensson, 1998, p. 53). This was the highest share in Europe at the time. The continued structural change of food distribution, with a constant reduction in the number of convenience goods stores, has taken place within this new form of store. Today, Swedish convenience goods distribution is dominated by only three big blocks.

It was in connection with the planning of neighbourhood units from the 1930s onwards that retail distribution became subject for town planning in Sweden. Cooperation was established between the local town planning authorities and local distribution firms where representatives of the distribution firms received expert status and worked out guidelines for establishments, which in turn were broadly accepted by local authorities. Thus, the part of town planning concerned with distribution in practice was in the hands of the distribution firms themselves and/or the trade associations. One important aspect of the distribution lobbyism in Swedish town planning is that whereas the development of the lorry and increasing investments in road infrastructure substantially reduced the costs of transportation and expanded the market after the Second World War, the rationalization of the distribution process in total was delayed due to the high transportation costs of the final component of the distribution chain, i.e. when the goods are transported from the stores to the households. In the 1950s, when the typical Swedish housewife did all the shopping without a car, distribution firms and allied organizations thus had to, and did, influence town planning to ensure that stores were established within walking distance from the consumers (Franzen and Sandstedt, 1981; Svensson, 1998).

Alongside the increasing influence of distribution in town planning, retail distribution was, as we have seen, heavily rationalized. In the 1950s the rationalization consisted of the abolishment of gross pricing (an early link in the supply chain, i.e. a wholesaler sets the sales price for a downstream supplier) and of establishment control (new establishments had to be approved by an establishment committee), and through changed food legislation.[31] The previous food legislation had prevented meat and vegetables from being sold together, or food from being sold together with, for instance, technical household appliances. A building legislation formerly holding back the size of the stores was further repealed in 1959 (Franzen and Sandstedt, 1981). Retail distribution was heavily rationalized through these measures and made possible continuation of the phenomena of self-service shops. The Swedish government emphasized the labour savings for both commerce and society with self-service shops, where purchase over the counter gave way for the self-service system through which the consumer essentially took over the responsibility for some of the distribution work (Svensson, 1998).

Although the innovation of self-service is organizational in its character, it builds upon the introduction of a number of innovations of a technical nature, such as the packaging technology. The packaging exposes and signals information about the goods to the customer, on shelves designed to suit the standardized packages in self-service stores. In line with this development, the goods ceased to be anonymous products with only their function as identification and instead gained names and trademarks, which increased the importance of advertising (Svensson, 1998).

With the self-service innovation and the parallel packaging, shelf and advertisement technologies, the required store areas gradually increased, or as Svensson (1998) puts it 'It was a matter of preparing space for the unpaid stock-room workers, i.e., the customers' (Svensson, 1998, p. 58, author's translation). Cost-effective goods handling required, as far as possible, horizontal goods removal. Hence, the convenience goods store has increasingly come to resemble a wholesale stock (Svensson, 1998). Franzén and Sandstedt (1981) established the neighbourhood unit to be a form very well suited to the expansion of the convenience goods trade as it could both embrace large stores as well as constitute a driving force in the development towards large-scale distribution. However, alongside greater diffusion of the passenger car in the 1960s onwards, rationalization pushed development towards a greater differentiation of retail distribution in town planning – between smaller district centres, local town centres and regional centres – and towards department stores in the town centres, superstores in the town peripheries and, from the 1970s onwards, to external shopping centres. It is, however, as we have seen, too simplistic to explain this development solely by the diffusion of the passenger car. Instead, a number of political decisions within a range of different policy areas have enabled a situation where mobility has become a structural requirement in the Swedish society. These include monetary policy and food and building legislations, the establishment of economic instruments of control and of 'Swedish standards' in construction, and law redactions within housing construction and provision. Some of those policies have more nationally unique content than others, but they have all contributed to enabling a situation that unifies most of the modern world, i.e. that of ever-increasing distances between family, work and shopping, and where increasing consumption of passenger car transport at best corresponds to the attempted satisfaction of a range of basic needs.[32]

The Swedish government has also supported the expansion of motoring in more distinct ways, such as through the standardization of the traffic and town planning, with expanding motoring as one of the main objectives. This has been done through a number of national guidelines, in turn often reproduced in a number of official reports and thus rather difficult to avoid (Hagson, 2004; Lundin, 2008). The SCAFT standards ('Guidelines for town-planning whilst considering traffic safety') were, for example, published by the Swedish National Planning Agency in cooperation with the Swedish National Road Association in 1968. Six years later, in 1974, the same organizations together with the Swedish National Road Safety Office published a report, 'Trafiksanering' ('Traffic decontamination'), on town planning for traffic safety in central and semi-central parts of the town. Furthermore, in 1982 the same organizations together with the Swedish Environmental Protection Agency published the report 'TRÅD: Allmänna råd för planering av stadens trafiknät' ('General advice in planning for the traffic network of the town'). A revised version, TRÅD -92, was published a few years later by the same organizations together with the Swedish Association of Local Governments. Lundin (2008) argues that the large number of involved authorities and organizations in these processes indicates that the guidelines in their different versions, for several decades have affected local, regional and national administration. He further ascribes the fast and extensive adaptation of the Swedish towns to motoring both to the guidelines in traffic planning mentioned above as well as to the ideologies of the traffic planner experts, especially the 1950s and the 1960s, who repeatedly articulated motoring as a massive nature power that society *had* to plan for (Lundin, 2008).[33]

The mobility-as-structural-requirement-standpoint is also supported by the fact that the oil crises of the 1970s (and later the economic crisis of the 1990s) did not decrease the consumption of passenger car transport in the average Swedish household. This consumption was further never a target in the Swedish energy policy of the 1970s and 1980s, otherwise aiming for decreased oil consumption; the consumption of oil had increased extensively in the 1950s and the 1960s, primarily due to the increased use of oil in residential heating and for industrial processes (Kaijser, 2001). All the energy policies of the 1970s and the 1980s did thus focus on residential heating. Both electric heating and district heating/combined power and heating was enthroned as appropriate alternatives in residential heating; however, it was really only electric heating that was to be actuated as an alternative. This can be explained by the small number of very large power companies dominating the Swedish power market in the 1970s and who were in the midst of investing in nuclear power and thus had to secure a continued market for electricity. They kept down prices on electricity and thus worked as brake blocks against an expansion of district heating/combined power and heating. Effectively, consumption of electricity increased considerably more in Sweden compared to other European countries, especially in the 1970s and 1980s (Högselius and Kaijser, 2007). Thus the energy policy of the 1970s and the 1980s contributed to the decreased consumption of heating oil of Swedish households, by about 50 per cent between 1978 and 1988. Instead, the average Swedish household increased its expenses on electricity by a good 30 per cent during the same period of time (and by 200 per cent between the 1950s and the beginning of the 21st century).[34]

CONCLUDING REMARKS AND IMPLICATIONS

The analysis in this chapter has illustrated how public intervention and policy traditions to a considerable extent help explain the socio-technical context within which the average Swedish household has consumed housing- and transport-related goods and services since the 1950s. This opens vital paths for policy aimed at behavioural change, although a fundamental condition is naturally that the government intent on motivating sustainable consumption is cognizant of its own historically determined role in the context. For that reason, the following key policy implications can be cited:

- The socio-technical context in which people live their daily lives has historically had distinct impacts on Swedish households' consumption patterns, which reinforces the need for environmental policy that examines and explains opportunities to influence this context.
- Effective policy for sustainable development should focus attention on how multiple policy areas affect – directly or indirectly – household consumption patterns.

As shown in many other chapters in this book, social and personal norms may play an important role in explaining the prevalence of sustainable activities, but at the same time individual responsibility has its limits as shown in, for instance, Chapter 8. Collective measures, such as investment in infrastructure as well as territorial planning measures, fundamentally embed households' consumption patterns and as long as these path dependent structures are not altered, long-term behavioural change may be difficult to pursue.

NOTES

1   This investigation divides the discharges into 'direct discharges', 'indirect domestic discharges' and 'indirect international discharges'. With the help of data from the national and environmental accounts the investigation finds that the energy consumption of Swedish households in connection to housing and transport made up for the highest direct carbon dioxide emissions from household consumption in the 1990s, whereas the somewhat lower domestic indirect emissions were predominantly caused by the consumption of housing, transport and food. In the case of international carbon dioxide emissions caused by Swedish household consumption, transport/travel and food made up for the most significant shares during the 1990s (SOU, 2004:119).
2   Recreation and entertainment is a significant and increasing expense category also for the Swedish post-war household, however, without such a dramatic increase as in the British case (Jackson and Marks, 1999; Söderholm, 2007).
3   In the Swedish case, communication is included in the recreation and entertainment category (Söderholm, 2007).
4   For surveys of research on consumption and consumerism and the associated impacts on the environment, see Røpke (1999) and Swedish Environmental Protection Agency (2005).

5 This is in turn based on van Lente et al (2003). Rosenberg (1994) argues along the same lines, and points out the historical character of path dependence, which he principally defines as a cumulative 'sequence of events' constituting 'the history' (p. 10).

6 For an overview, see Strasser (2002).

7 Jackson and Marks (1999) arrive at the same conclusions concerning the increased consumption of travel and mobility of UK households since the 1950s, and establish that this consumption pattern has become a structural requirement in modern society.

8 For the 'systems of provision' approach, see Fine (2002) and Fine and Leopold (1993).

9 The Swedish population grew from 7 million in 1958 to about 9 million in 2007.

10 See Statistics Sweden (www.scb.se), HUT 1958, 69, 78, 85, 88, 92, 03 and 05.

11 These include increased relative prices (consumer price index (CPI) for housing-related consumption) and increased value-added tax (VAT) and taxes (e.g. energy taxes). Simultaneously, low interests kept total housing expenses down for long periods.

12 See also Ivre and Lundevall (1978).

13 See also Bostads och byggnadsstatistisk årsbok, 2005, Table 1.1.1.

14 The year average for CPI on transport goods was 362 in 2005, while CPI in total was 280 (index year 1980).

15 For instance, by studying the price development of Volvo's passenger cars from 1957 to 2003, we find that a Volvo Amazon cost about SEK 139,000 in 1957 (money value of 2005), a Volvo 144 about SEK 146,000 in 1967 (money value of 2005), and a V50 about SEK 244,000 in 2005 (www.newsdesk.se).

16 From about 972,000 registered passenger cars in 1958 to about 2,856,000 registered passenger cars in 1978 (www.scb.se, 'Antal registrerade personbilar i trafik 1923-2007', accessed July 7, 2008).

17 From about 2 856 000 registered passenger cars in 1978 to about 4,152,000 cars in 2005 (www.scb.se, 'Antal registrerade personbilar i trafik 1923–2007', accessed July 7, 2008).

18 Shopping travels have, though, together with social/visit travel and leisure travel, decreased as a share of total mobility, whereas business travels and travels related to childcare have increased in relative terms (Krantz, 1999, p. 102f; SIKA, 2000, p. 13; SIKA, 2007, p. 7).

19 Every second Swedish household, 46 per cent, is today a single-person household (single-parent households with children living home not included). This implies an increase from 6 per cent of the adult population in single-person households in 1945 to 29 per cent of the adult population in single-person households in 2006. In 2006 there were 4.4 million households in Sweden in total (Statistics Sweden).

20 Single-person households tend to allocate a higher expenditure share to housing than other households, at least in relative terms. This is consistent with the observation that single-person households are generally less space and energy efficient compared to multi-person households in which coordination of things like cooking and heating can be better utilized (Söderholm, 2008).

21 The Swedish state had in part communicated a social housing policy through the own-one's-own-home policy already in the first decades of the 20th century (Almqvist, 2004). Turner and Vedung (1997) further argue that a paradigm shift in Swedish housing policy (from a general to a selective policy) occurred in the 1990s.

22 For an overview of the government efforts in social housing policy, see for example Strömberg (2001) and Franzén and Sandstedt (1981). While most of the Swedish post-war housing research has a strong positivistic character, aiming for producing foundations for contemporary social housing policy, housing research in more recent years has questioned this focus on a general (as opposed to a selective) policy founded on functionalism where every man and women is thought to have the same needs and where justice, instead of, for example, traditions, is thought to be the best foundation in the creation of a new and modern society (e.g. Almqvist, 2004).

23 For a general overview over the idea of neighbourhood units, see Franzen and Sandstedt (1981).

24 In Sweden, the neighbourhood units except from decentralizing the cities also disfavoured public transportation by encouraging the location of public transport routes further away from the apartments than the parking lots.

25 The government took the main economic responsibility for these efforts (Bladh, 1992, p. 203ff).

26 On the post-war municipal entrepreneurship in Swedish housing construction, see Bladh (1992) and Isaksson (2003).

27 The National physical planning emerged out of an economic boom and industrial expansion in several environmentally sensitive regions in Sweden, such as in the west coast of Sweden, and aimed to make clear what land and water resources that were of national interest and thus to increase the possibilities to govern the administration of the same.

28 For a discusssion on the economic effects of the post-war industrialization of housing construction, see Bladh (1992).

29 This number is even bigger today. Since 2006, more than 75 per cent of the new-built small houses are catalogue houses (www. byggfaktadocu.se).

30 For an overview of the Swedish department store and supermarket developments (e.g. turnover) from the 1960s/70s to the 21st century, see Arnberg (2002).

31 Gross pricing and establishing control were abolished through 'the law of 1953 about countervailing some cases of competition reduction' (1953-års lag om motverkande av vissa fall av konkurrensbegränsning, KBL), (Franzén and Sandstedt, 1981, p. 251).

32 This notion is also put forward by Jackson and Marks (1999) as well as Jackson and Papathanasopoulou (2008).

33 See also Tengström (1991).

34 An important explanation behind the increase in the electricity consumption of households is of course the parallel general increase in the consumption of power-driven household appliances. For an historical overview of changes in household technology and of related socio-economic effects in the 20th century and earlier, see Schwartz Cowan (1983).

REFERENCES

Almqvist, A. (2004) Drömmen om det egna huset: från bostadsförsörjning till livsprojekt, Ph.D dissertation, University of Uppsala

Arnberg, J. (2002) Detaljhandelns struktur och utveckling 2001, AB Handelns Utredningsinstitut (HUI), Stockholm

Arthur, W. B. (1988) "Competing technologies: an overview" in *Technical change and economic theory*, Dosi, G, Freeman, C, Nelson, R, Silverberg, G and Soete, L (eds.), Pinter, London, pp590–607
Bergman, B. (2003) *Handelsplats, shopping, stadsliv: en historik om butiksformer, säljritualer och det moderna stadslivets trivialisering*, Symposium, Stockholm
Bergström, Hans et al (1968) *Bostadspolitiken*, Tiden, Stockholm
Björk, C. et al (1983) *Så byggdes husen 1880-1980. Arkitektur, konstruktion och material i våra flerbostadshus under 100 år*, Statens råd för byggforskning, Stockholms stadsbyggnadskontor
Bladh, M. (1992) *Bostadsförsörjningen 1945-1985: det industriella byggandets uppgång och fall*, School of Economics and Commercial Law, Gothenburg University
Book, K. and Eskilsson, L. (2001) *Stadens struktur: varför och hur?*, Department of Social and Economic Geography, University of Lund
Bostads och byggnadsstatistisk årsbok (2005), Statistics Sweden
Carlsson-Kanyama, A. et al (2007) *Koldioxidutsläpp till följd av Sveriges import och konsumtion: beräkningar med olika metoder*, TRITA-IM: 2007:11, Kth, Stockholm
Cornell, E. (1979) *Byggnadstekniken: Metoder och idéer genom tiderna*, Byggförlaget, Stockholm
Engfors, C. (1987) *Folkhemmets bostäder 1940-1960. Svenskt bostadsbyggande under 1940- och 50-talen*, Museum of Architecture, Stockholm
Fine, B. (2002) *The world of consumption: the material and cultural revisited*, Routledge, London
Fine, B. and Leopold, E. (1993) *The world of consumption*, Routledge, London
Folk och Bostadsräkningarna, FoB, www.scb.se
Franzén, M. and Sandstedt, E. (1981) *Grannskap och stadsplanering: Om stat och byggande i efterkrigstidens Sverige*, Doctoral dissertation, Uppsala University
Gabrielson, I. and Ringmar, C-I. (1970) *40 sätt att bygga småhus: en undersökning av typhusfabrikanternas standardleveranser*, Statens institut för byggnadsforskning, Stockholm
Government Bill. 1976/77 *Med förslag till lag om kommonernas energiplanering m. m.*, Norstedts, Stockholm
Hagson, A. (2004) *Stads och trafikplaneringens paradigm: En studie av SCAFT 1968, dess förebilder och efterföljare*, PhD dissertation, Chalmers University of Technology, Göteborg
Högselius, P. and Kaijser, A. (2007) *När folkhemselen blev international*, SNS Förlag, Stockholm
Hyll, H. and Lessing, J. (2004) *Industrialisering av bostadsbyggandet under 1900-talet*, Report from doctoral student course: Building and installation technology during the 20th century, Lund Institute of Technology
Isaksson, A (2003) *Bostadspolitiken slår knut på sig själv*, Expert report, Byggkommissionen (www.byggkommissionen.se)
Ivre, K. D. and Lundevall, P. (1978) *Samhällsförändring och byggmarknad*, HSB:s riksförbund, Stockholm
Jackson, T. and Marks, N. (1999) "Consumption, sustainable welfare and human needs – with reference to UK expenditure patterns 1954–1994", *Ecological Economics*, 28(3), pp421–442
Jackson, T. (2006) 'Challenges for Sustainable Consumption Policy', in *The Earthscan Reader on Sustainable Consumption*, Tim Jackson (ed), Earthscan, London, pp109–126

Jackson, T. and Papathanasopoulou, E. (2008) "Luxury or 'lock-in'? An exploration of unsustainable consumption in the UK: 1968 to 2000", *Ecological Economics*, 68(1–2), pp80–95

Kaijser, A. (2001) "From tile stoves to nuclear plants: the historical development of Swedish energy systems" in *Building sustainable energy systems: Swedish experiences*, Semida Silveira, (ed), Svensk byggtjänst, Stockholm

Krantz, L-G. (1999) *Rörlighetens mångfald och förändring*, Department of Human and Economic Geography, School of Economics, University of Gothenburg

Lundin, P. (2008) *Bilsamhället. Ideologi, expertis och regelskapande i efterkrigstidens Sverige*, PhD dissertation, Royal Institute of Technology, Sweden

Marmstål, F. (1992) *Byggarna och maskinerna – Folke Marmstål berättar för Nils Nordberg*, Byggförlaget, Stockholm

Meijer, I. S. M. et al (2006) "Perceived uncertainties regarding socio-technological transformations: towards a framework", *International Journal of Foresight and Innovation Policy*, 2(2), pp214–240

Oldenziel, R., A.A. de la Bruhèze and O. de Wit (2005) "Europe's mediation junction: technology and consumer society in the 20th century", *History and Technology* 21, pp107–139

Ropke, I. (1999) "The dynamics of willingness to consume", *Ecological Economics*, 28(3), pp399–420

Rosenberg, N. (1994) *Exploring the black box. Technology, economics, and history*, Cambridge University Press, New York

Schwartz Cowan, R. (1983) *More work for mother: The ironies of household technology from the open hearth to the microwave*, Basic Books, New York

Shove, E. (2006) "Efficiency and consumption: technology and practice" in *The Earthscan Reader on Sustainable Consumption*, T. Jackson (ed), Earthscan Reader Series, London, pp293-304

Shove, E. and Warde, A. (2002) "Inconspicuous consumption: the sociology of consumption, lifestyles, and the environment," in *Sociological theory and the environment: classical foundations, contemporary insights*, Dunlap, R. et al (ed), Rowman and Littlefield, Lanham

SIKA (Statens institut för kommunikationsanalys) (2000) *Res 1999*, Stockholm

SIKA (Statens institut för kommunikationsanalys) (2007) *Res 2005/2006*, Den nationella resevaneundersökningen, 2007:19, Stockholm

Söderholm, K. (2007) *Swedish Household Consumption and the Environment, 1958-2005: The Historical Transformation of Systems Explaining Consumption Patterns with Significant Impacts on the Environment*, SHARP Working Paper No. 12, Division of Social Science, Luleå University of Technology, Sweden

Söderholm, P (ed) (2008) *Hållbara hushåll: Miljöpolitik och ekologisk hållbarhet i vardagen. Slutrapport till Naturvårdsverket från forskningsprogrammet SHARP*, The Swedish Environmental Protection Agency, Report 5899, Stockholm

SOU 2004:119, *Hållbara laster: Konsumtion för en ljusare framtid*, Stockholm

Southerton et al (2004) *Sustainable consumption: the implications of changing infra-structures of provision*, Edward Elgar, Cheltenham

Statens råd för byggnadsforskning (1975) *Monteringsbyggda flerfamiljshus: rapport från Moby-kommittén med förslag till forskningsprojekt*, Stockholm

Statistics Sweden (SCB). *Household budget/expense studies* 1958, 1969, 1978, 1985, 1988, 1992, 2003, and 2005

Statistics Sweden, www.scb.se, repeatedly accessed in the autumn 2007 and spring 2008

Strasser, S. (2002) "Making consumption conspicuous. Transgressive topics go mainstream", *Technology and Culture*, 43 (4), pp755–770

Strömberg, T. (2001) 'Bostadspolitik – en historik parentes', in *Dennya bostadspolitiken*, A. Lidnbom (ed), Borea, Umeå, pp21–48

Svensson, T. (1998) *Daglivarudistributionens strukturomvandling – Drivkrafter och konsekvenser för städers utformning och miljö*, Linköping Studies in Arts and Science No. 179, Linköping University

Swedish Environmental Protection Agency (SEPA) (2005) *Sustainable Consumption – Research and Policies*, Report 5460, Stockholm

Tengström, E (1991) *Bilismen - i kris?. en bok om bilen, människan, samhället och miljön*, Raben & Sjögren, Stockholm

Trentmann, F. (2004) "Beyond Consumerism: New Historical Perspectives on Consumption", *Journal of Contemporary History*, Vol 39 No 3, p376f

Turner, B. and Vedung, E. (eds) (1997) *Bostadspolitik för tjugohundratalet. Återtåg och nya värde*, Meyers Förlag, Gävle

van Lente, H. et al (2003) "Roles of strategic intermediaries in transition processes: the case of energy innovation systems", *International Journal of Technology Management*, 7(3)

Van Vliet et al (2005) *Infrastructures of consumption: environmental innovation in the utility industries*, Earthscan Reader Series, London

Vilhelmson, B. (2000) *Reser man mindre i täta tätorter?*, Department of Human and Economic Geography, School of Economics, University of Gothenburg

Volvo Passenger Cars Sweden Inc. www.newsdesk.se, Newsdesk, "1927 - 2007 - 80 år med Volvo-bilar", July 7, 2008

Wigren, R. (1997) "Bygg och bokostnader – historisk utveckling och framtidsutblick" in *Bostadsmarknaden på 2000-talet*, Andersson, Å E (ed), SNS i samarbete med Sveriges allmännyttiga bostadsföretag och Institutet för framtidsstudier, Stockholm

www.byggfaktadocu.se, July 7, 2008

www.livsmedelssverige.org, June 23, 2008

8

Shared or individual responsibility: Eco-labelling and consumer choice in Sweden

Mats Bladh, Kristina Ek and Patrik Söderholm

INTRODUCTION

So-called eco-labelling of products and services provides an opportunity for consumers to influence market supplies in a more environmentally friendly direction. Still, as was noted by Nordlund et al in Chapter 5 of this volume, understanding pro-environmental behaviour in the green market place is a complex undertaking, and involves the study of personal, contextual as well as attitudinal factors. In some cases concerns for the environment appear to have had profound impacts on consumer behaviour and the purchase of eco-labelled products (e.g. Teisl et al, 2002; Bjorner et al, 2004), but there exist also plenty of examples of very modest household participation rates in eco-labelling schemes (e.g. Ek and Söderholm, 2008; Bladh, 2008). Behaviour in the green market-place is a function of the individual as well as of his/her social, physical and even political environment, and it is important to understand the development of different eco-labels and the associated criteria for labelling in the light of these often complex personal motives. The driving forces of the labellers do not necessarily coincide with the motives expressed by individual consumers and citizens.

In this chapter we review some of the experiences of eco-labelling in Sweden, and highlight a number of important challenges in the future use of eco-labels for promoting sustainable consumption patterns. We note in particular that this type of instrument typically entails a strong individualization, while many environmental issues often may require the collective adoption of attitudes. Green consumerism largely involves the private provision of so-called public goods, i.e. goods characterized by non-rivalry and non-excludability in consumption, and according to conventional economic models of the consumer these are typically underprovided in the market-place (e.g. Bergstrom et al, 1986). For this reason it is important to consider the role of norms – i.e. informal rules requiring that one should act in a given way in a given situation – as well as the distinction between the individual as a consumer and a citizen (see also Lundmark et al this volume). As will be illustrated below, peoples' willingness to take personal responsibility in the green market place can be influenced by their perceptions of others' contributions and the environmental impacts of their choice, but also by the extra costs of the eco-labelled products compared to the conventional products offered. Moreover, we illustrate that peoples' willingness to support market goods with strong public good characteristics is also likely to depend on whether participation builds on shared as opposed to individual responsibility. The former typically entails a stronger focus on public deliberation and a sense of individual preferences as shaped by these deliberations (rather than taken as given).

The Swedish case of eco-labelling is interesting in the sense that three big eco-labels have grown side by side during the 1990s and 2000s. In the next section we review the historical development for each of these labels, and in a subsequent section the market outcomes for eco-labelled products and services in Sweden are reviewed. Based on the above, some important challenges for successful eco-labelling are discussed and analysed, and many of these challenges are addressed in a more in-depth investigation of Swedish households' willingness to support green electricity, either through voluntary purchases of eco-labelled electricity or by voting in favour of a mandatory (collective) price premium on this type of electricity service. A final section provides some concluding remarks and implications.

HISTORICAL CROSSROADS IN THE DEVELOPMENT OF SWEDISH ECO-LABELS

In Sweden eco-labelling appeared primarily in the mid-1980s and at the beginning of the 1990s.[1] Today there are nine ecological labels in Sweden with extensive environmental demands formulated and controlled by organizations independent from producers and sellers (Miljomarkarna, 2009). The three most important ones are KRAV, Good Environmental Choice (GEC) and the Nordic Swan; their development over time and the associated challenges will be briefly reviewed in this section. KRAV labels food items, and shops and restaurants associated with food, while GEC and the Nordic Swan label all other types of products other than food.

KRAV

KRAV, Kontrollföreningen för Alternativ Odling (the Control Association for Alternative Cultivation) was established in 1985. Its background is mainly to be found in the 'green wave' of the early 1970s when, together with already existing anthroposophic organizations, a so-called 'alternative movement' emerged (see also the chapter in this volume by Ibsen). According to KRAV (1999) one of the founders was KF, a large cooperative retail chain. KF wanted a uniform control of ecological products, and therefore established contacts with wholesale and retail businesses. During the 1990s, KRAV experienced a shift in its membership structure, from the original base of small ecological farmers to one of retailers and processing industries (Boström, 2006).

The basic idea for KRAV is to get rid of chemicals in agriculture; there should be no artificial fertilizers and no synthetic biocides. There are more criteria in addition to this, concerning animal treatment etc., but chemicals are the core. KRAV has inspectors making unannounced visits to farmers, and these inspectors have the right to scrutinize bookkeeping, as well as plants and animals. KRAV's criteria are absolute because these demands are high minimum demands, not to be changed. This is a reactionary demand, in the original sense of the word, i.e. going back to older cultivation methods. Since chemicals in farming have allowed productivity per acre to increase, and thus food prices to fall as a result, a reversal of methods means higher costs for the consumers in the end (Bladh, 2008).

The KRAV principles have run into serious trouble in recent years. Since 2006, when global warming came at the forefront in the media debate, it has become obvious that chemicals are not the only environmental problem associated with agriculture. For instance, a KRAV-certified cow emits methane gas when belching, and this is now admitted on KRAV's homepage (e.g. KRAV, 2009). In addition, KRAV's cultivation methods have been criticized by agrarian scientists. Most notably, in July 2009, a group of researchers at the Swedish University of Agricultural Sciences published an article in one of the biggest daily papers where they attacked the 'alleged advantages' of ecological production. Yields are, they argue, much lower in ecological fields, only about half compared to conventional methods, and biocides with negative effects have been removed so that residues now are quite harmless (SVD, 2009; Sundström, 2009). Even though other scientists came out in support for ecological farming, the critique points at a serious weakness in sticking to the old biodynamic ideology; the old methods were directed at problems other than global warming and land use for both biomass and foodstuff.

An important lesson from the KRAV experience is thus that environmental problems – and not least the scope of the environmental debate – change over time. Labelling criteria based on 'alternative cultivation' may have been appropriate for problems associated with discharges of chemical substances into land and water courses, but they are obviously not optimal when climate change problems also need to be taken into account. Moreover, the pros and cons of

KRAV-promoted farming are controversial. Some agricultural scientists argue that conventional farming has shown improvements, and that it has the clear advantage of much higher yields. In a world of large and increasing population rates this is an important point to make.

Good Environmental Choice

Good Environmental Choice (GEC) is a label issued by an old mass organization called the Swedish Society for Nature Conservation (SSNC). It was founded in 1909 and now has about 170,000 members. The label covers about 13 product groups, many of which are chemicals, but also services such as transport, electricity, district heating and shops. GEC was introduced in 1992, but it already had a five-year long pre-history. This started in 1987 with protests against paper products bleached with chlorine. Discharges of chlorine in rivers and lakes threatened fish with sickness and deformities. SSNC and Miljöförbundet (the Environmental Alliance) defined environmental demands on paper products as an aid to consumers who wanted to buy chlorine-free paper. The paper products that met these criteria were listed. More and more people followed the recommendations in this list, and pulp and paper manufacturers gradually switched away from chlorine-bleached paper. From 1990 to 1993 discharges of chlorine from the pulp industry halved. There was also a surge in the recruitment to environmental organizations. SSNC membership grew in number from 85,000 in 1985 to 150,000 in 1987, and reached a peak in 1991 of 206,000 members. Other organizations, like the World Wildlife Fund and Greenpeace, experienced similar growth rates in Sweden, and a new organization was founded (Boström, 2001; Micheletti, 2003; Bladh, 2008).

In this new situation SSNC opened up a new path for its activities – market pressure on production. One important feature was a green shopping guide published in 1988, 'Shop and act green!' When consumers were informed about the environmental impacts from different products, a green choice could be made by thousands of people and in the end influence production through regular market mechanisms. Initially, 15,000 copies of the book were printed but after ten years about 400,000 copies had been sold. Moreover, a number of significant activities were organized around the 'Shop and act green!' concept. Campaigns were concentrated to one week in the autumn, announced as the 'Green week'. Members at the local level picked out the environmentally best store in town, and distributed leaflets and stickers (Boström, 2001; Micheletti, 2003; Anshelm, 2004).

In this way 'Shop and act green!' became a priority for SSNC. In 1990 SSNC together with ICA, Axfood and Coop, all big Swedish retail chains, defined a programme for an eco-labelling system. GEC was implied to be a provisional label in the advent of a state-supported label. At this time the Nordic Swan was underway (see below), but its introduction was slow, not least since the participating partners had difficulties in coming to an agreement. In 1992 SSNC and the retailers launched GEC as an established label.

In 1991, SSNC had conducted a successful campaign against Lever, the manufacturer of Via, a brand of washing powder with the largest market share in Sweden. SSNC demanded that environmentally harmful ingredients should be removed, but the manufacturer claimed that these were essential for the quality of the product. When SSNC launched its boycott Lever was shocked; the management did not expect such a confrontational strategy from SSNC. The president of SSNC later explained that they had been in contact with Lever prior to the boycott in order to persuade them to change Via, but the company did not comply with their requests. This boycott was successful. Lever suddenly reversed its position and in 1992 it launched a new brand called Via Color, without the criticized ingredients. This new brand was Swan-labelled and gained a market share of about eight per cent. Other manufacturers followed, and between 1990 and 1995 eco-labelled detergents increased their market share from 1 to as much as 90 per cent (Plogner, 1996; Micheletti, 2003; Anshelm, 2004).

What is important in these stories is, first, the combination of vote and voice and, second, the combination of positive and negative choices. While a pure market strategy would be limited to positive choices of silent individuals 'voting' for green products through purchases in shops, the combination with campaigns added some 'voice' to the votes, and a boycott of the bad to the support of the good. The strength of the campaign strategy is that resources could be focused on one product. This increases the chances of success, and success means reinforcing feedback to consumers, i.e. a proof that the individual choice was worthwhile. The basic problem with a pure market strategy is the uncoordinated actions of isolated individuals. The label in itself is a kind of coordination, but it relies on given (exogenous) preferences. Public opinion is largely ignored, and thereby the motivation for the individual to make a green choice may decline. On the other hand, everyone does not wish to join campaign activities, but may still be willing to take a personal responsibility as a consumer in the market. Individual and collective actions therefore tend to complement each other.

In conclusion, the GEC history illustrates the efficiency of combining market and extra-market measures. By way of campaigns existing attitudes and preferences are not simply taken as given, but also influenced through public deliberations. In addition, the negative strategy of eliminating harmful substances through boycotts of specific brands showed clear results in environmental advance, albeit limited to one specific ingredient.

The Nordic Swan

In 1989 the Nordic Council of Ministers decided to introduce an official environmental label in the Nordic countries (Norway and Sweden 1989, Finland 1990, Iceland 1991 and Denmark 1996). The government in Sweden assigned the Swedish Standards Institute (SIS) to manage the label, and in this way SIS Miljömärkning was established. SIS Miljömärkning was turned into a limited company in 1998, owned by Sweden's Council for Standardization (90 per cent) and the Swedish state (10 per cent). This company develops criteria and issues licences for the label. The Nordic Swan is financed through grants from the government but primarily through fees paid by the firms that have labelled products (these fees amount to 0.3 per cent of the products' yearly turnover). Labelled products must be tested in test laboratories, and SIS Miljömärkning conducts inspections at firms with labelled products. Moreover, the company has an advisory board with representatives from the business community, environmental organizations and different government authorities, which develop criteria. These criteria are always common for all the Nordic countries and decided upon in a Nordic committee. The label lasts for three years and after this period the environmental requirements became more ambitious and the firm must apply for a new licence (Unge, 2007; Bladh, 2008; Nordic Swan, 2009).

SIS Miljömärkning has a well-prepared procedure for the potential introduction of new products. Several aspects are investigated, such as the environmental impacts, potential for improvement, as well as whether producers can be influenced or not. After that a pilot study is made, including a detailed investigation of the entire product life cycle. The next step involves negotiations in committees, and after that a working group is formed. After about a year the group's report is circulated for comments among experts and interest groups. Then there may be a decision by the Nordic committee, and after that the criteria must be implemented, implying not least contact with concerned companies as well as the dissemination of information. The whole procedure takes at least two years.

The story of the Nordic Swan shows that eco-labels convey a concise message on a complex issue. As Boström and Klintman (2008, p. 73) note: 'This is of course one of the most basic and obvious reason for establishing labels in the first place.' The label helps consumers in their choice of greener alternatives, which is particularly valuable when it comes to what components are harmful, and how much of these are used in a specific brand. The label is of less help when the environmental effects are well known, such as the benefits of going by train instead of by airplane, and cases in which there exists a complex trade-off between different types of environmental impacts.

The Swan label is organized in a highly professional manner, not least the labelling of a new product type is carefully prepared. Nevertheless, the Swan example illustrates two deficiencies that make us conclude that the full potential of eco-labelling has not been met. First, SIS Miljömärkning has no intention of influencing public opinion, other than what the label itself can signal to the consumer. Second, in the absence of consistent sales statistics (see also the next section) it is hard to prove progress for ecological products and services, something which in turn makes it difficult to evaluate eco-labelling and to give encouraging feedback to consumers. As is illustrated below in the green electricity case, perceptions of others' contributions to the green good may have profound impacts on one's own behaviour and thus give rise to a strong positive feedback effect (see also Nyborg et al, 2006).

Regularly revising and raising standards for the label in each product group implies that eco-labelling is not a business in the usual sense of one that wants to make a profit. An organization solely guided by profit-maximization would not voluntarily cut off income-generating sales of licences. It is thus fundamental that the labeller is independent and can fall back on resources other than the incomes gained from licences.

ECO-LABELLED SALES IN SWEDEN: MARKET OUTCOMES AND CRITICAL ISSUES

Is eco-labelled consumption growing?

An important component of the analysis of the development of eco-labelling is statistics on sales. It is, however, hard to find comprehensive, independent and conclusive numerical data on this, and the data presented in this section originates from five different sources. The first source is a special study conducted by a marketing research consultant at the request of the Swedish Consumer Agency (2002). This study made use of bar codes in two of the biggest retail chains in Sweden, and it covered not only the sales of eco-labelled and other products, but also the number of items supplied. While sales indicate what consumers have chosen, supply indicates what consumers can choose from. A second source is Statistics Sweden's (2009a) data on households' purchases of eco-products. These data are collected by phone interviews and cashbook notes from 4000 households. The definition of 'ecological' is thus dependent on the awareness of the product's green character among respondents. For this reason a third source, also from Statistics Sweden, has been used, namely sales based on cash registers from all big retail chains and petrol stations (Statistics Sweden, 2009b). A fourth source is the Swedish Dairy Association (SDA, 2009), a national industry organization for dairy farmers and the dairy industry. It collects data on milk and milk products, including separate entries for ecological products. This source provides data over a longer period, but only for a specific group of food items, albeit the group with the highest eco-share. The fifth and final source is the organization responsible for one of the three labels studied here, SSNC, and we here report the sales of GEC-labelled electricity (SSNC, 2009).

The results from the Swedish Consumer Agency (2002) indicate that the market share for eco-labelled food items was low in 2002, close to two per cent, and this more or less equals the share of eco-labelled products offered to consumers at the time. In the case of other everyday commodities, such as toilet paper, detergents and other usables, the market shares were bigger, overall at about 20 per cent. It is interesting to note that the sales share was more than twice as big as the share of the total number of products offered (eight per cent), indicating a high willingness to choose green alternatives in this product group. The high market share for eco-labelled everyday commodities is partly explained by the corresponding high market share for the sub-group 'cleansers and other chemicals'. This sub-group constituted 12 per cent of the supply, and

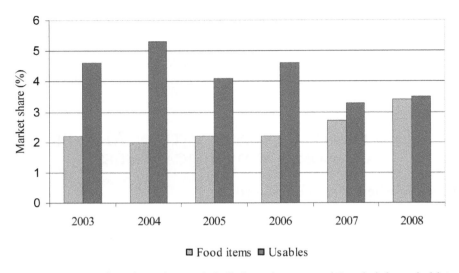

Figure 8.1 *Market share for eco-labelled products out of Swedish households'*
expenses on everyday products, 2003–2008 (percentage share)

Source: Statistics Sweden (2009a)

44 per cent of total sales, and the reported difference between the items' share
and sales share cannot overall be explained by price differentials (on prices and
eco-labelled products see Bjørner et al 2002, and Jørgensen, 2001).

Figure 8.1 shows the share of eco-labelled products out of Swedish households' expenses of everyday products. The sales of eco-labelled usables have
tended to decrease over this short time period. The two per cent market share
for eco-labelled food items reported above has been fairly constant over time,
but during recent years this market segment has witnessed a slight increase (the
change from 2003 to 2008 is statistically significant).

The market shares reported in Figure 8.1 are based on information from
households; they have been asked to mark in their diaries whether the product
bought was labelled or ecological. Nevertheless, this self-reported data comes
pretty close to other data presented by Statistics Sweden, this time based on
cash registers. This information shows a 2007 market share for eco-products at
about three per cent in the food item category (Statistics Sweden, 2009b).
Looking at sub-groups, 'milk, cheese, eggs' has the biggest share for eco-labelled
products in households' expenses – about seven per cent. In terms of specific
items one may note that the top three in 2008 were eggs with a share for ecological brands at 18 per cent, followed by bananas at 17 per cent, and middle milk
(a milk category between high-fat and low-fat milk) at 16 per cent.

Ecological milk products is in fact one of the oldest eco-labelled product
groups in Sweden, and Figure 8.2 shows the sales volumes of ordinary and eco-
labelled milk products, respectively, over the time period 1990 to 2008. The
total in Figure 8.2 refers to raw milk used in the production of consumption

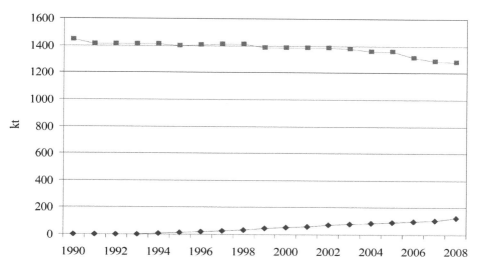

Figure 8.2 *Milk for drinking, cream and sour milk/yoghurt, 1990–2008 (thousands of tonnes)*

Source: SDA (2009)

milk, cream, sour milk and yoghurt. For all these items ecological alternatives exist. The market share for ecological products has increased steadily; it reached one per cent in 1995 and almost ten per cent in 2008. The ecological milk products have also increased steadily in absolute numbers, despite a decrease in the total sales of conventional milk products, especially after 2002.

Overall the sales of eco-labelled products have been relatively low, but this should, however, not be interpreted as a failure. As was noted above, the labelling organizations selling licences for ecologically sound products other than food items introduce more demanding criteria after a few years. This means that the licensees must raise their ecological standards, or else they lose the right to label their products. For this reason ecological progress may have occurred, thus without appearing in the sales statistics. But it is hard to take this progression for granted because new brands and new products are introduced continuously in the market. We cannot know for certain that new brands and products, often offering lower prices, always are environmentally friendly to the degree that they would qualify under the old criteria.

One illustrative example of when a change in the criteria for an eco-label has led to a radically reduced market share is that of eco-labelled, or green, electricity. The label in question, 'Good Environmental Choice', had its criteria set in 1995, but a change in these occurred in the summer of 2002. The volume of sales, reaching a peak of ten per cent of total electricity consumption in 2001, dropped by two thirds from 2001 to 2003 and has since not reached the previously high level (see Figure 8.3). Another reason for the drop is that the Swedish government introduced a so-called green certificate system to support

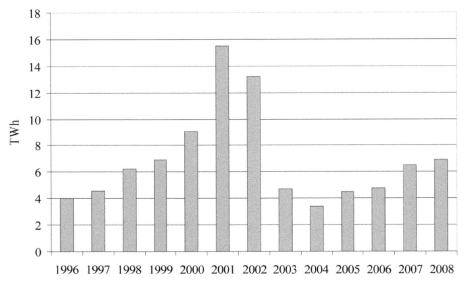

Figure 8.3 *Electricity consumption labelled 'Good Environmental Choice',*
1996–2008 (TWh)

Source: SSNC (2009)

the diffusion of renewable electricity, meaning that a majority of all electricity consumers in the country had to pay a price premium on their electricity bills to finance this additional support. This may have crowded out the willingness to contribute to the voluntary GEC label (see also below).

Below in this paper we provide a more in-depth analysis of households' willingness to support green electricity, either individually by choosing GEC-labelled services or collectively by expressing support for a mandatory support system. A study conducted by Swedenergy (1999) showed that 75 per cent of the Swedish households surveyed would seriously consider buying green electricity, and about 40 per cent of them would also consider paying more for green electricity than for conventional electricity services. In spite of these positive responses and the fairly modest price premiums (generally not more than 0.5 euro cents) in the Swedish market only one per cent of the households stated in 1999 that they actually did purchase green electricity. Since then the household participation rate has only increased slightly, and the major contribution to GEC labelled has come from private and state-owned enterprises.

Critical issues for the success – and failure – of eco-labelling

A central aspect of eco-labelling in Sweden in the recent past is the strong reliance on market forces, and less on public campaigns. This mirrors the observation about Swedish environmental policy documents made by Lundmark et al in

Chapter 2 of this volume: environmental responsibility is primarily placed on individuals in their roles as consumers in the marketplace rather than on their roles as democratic citizens. When representatives from the three major labels were interviewed, they expressed a lot of faith in the market-oriented view on labelling, despite successful experiences from earlier campaigns (Eiderström, 2007). The managing director formulated KRAV's guiding idea as the role of the broker: 'Connecting consumers who want to do something with producers who want to do something' (Söderberg, 2007). What consumers 'want', however, is something that is left more or less untouched, i.e. it is taken as given. The changing of attitudes is left to other parties or organizations, and is essentially assumed to be 'external' to the market. The strong focus on pure market activities will leave eco-labelling in a market game with identity formation strategies on the consumer side and product differentiation strategies on the producer side. Extending eco-labelling with campaigns could add a dynamic component to this game.

This does not necessarily mean that 'ordinary' labelling is of little value. Market-oriented labelling exploits producers' and sellers' need for 'product differentiation'. A firm competing with other firms in the same product group needs to present a product with some premium value, and environmental benefits may obviously play a role here. By selling eco-labelled products, firms can buy themselves a unique supply mix that may attract a significant share of consumer spending. This competitive mechanism can in turn drive up minimum standards in the industry (with potential spillovers to other industries). This may work well as long as green attitudes among buyers are sufficient. Still, these attitudes are typically not given or are private in origin; they originate in public discourse and are thus shaped, for instance, through social interactions with other people.[2] There exists thus a strong interdependence between product differentiation among sellers on the one hand and green consciousness among buyers on the other. Campaigns may play a critical role here.

The lack of data to monitor the progress (or failure) of ecological consumption, also plays a role in this dialectic. Specifically, each individual's perceived responsibility to buy 'green' tends to be affected by the beliefs about others' behaviour in the sense that this provides a 'moral compass' as to whether s/he should take personal responsibility for the issue (Ek and Söderholm, 2008). This notion is also consistent with the presence of market outcomes in which very few actually contribute to eco-labelling schemes, but where policies affecting (directly or indirectly) beliefs about others' behaviour may significantly increase participation rates (Nyborg et al, 2006). However, in the absence of reliable market data such measures will be more difficult to undertake. Thus the lack of statistics on ecological consumption – not to be confused with an increasing number of eco-labelled products, or how many consumers recognize ecological labels – means that the individual is left in limbo. S/he is left with any (self-imposed) personal norms, or the values supported by family and friends, but without knowledge of the overall change in green consumption (see also below). Information about the developments at the aggregate level may – if made available – feed back to the household level. If progress is made at the former levels, the pessimist will find it harder to win the debate at the kitchen table. Eco-labellers see themselves as brokers between consumers and producers, but not as brokers between the individual and the collective levels on the consumer side. In this way the full potential of eco-labelling has not yet been tested. Campaigns and negative choices were there when eco-labelling was born, and can be added to the existing strategy today.

The lack of data on aggregate ecological consumption also makes it difficult to evaluate the impacts of eco-labelling. If ecological consumption is not gaining ground, or even losing out, this calls for critical reflection and probably a change of strategy. Most notably, the more or less regular increases in minimum standards for products to be labelled are an integral part of the strategy of putting the environment into the competitive mechanism. Successive steps toward higher environmental goals will, it is argued, in the end make consumption patterns sustainable. Paradoxically we do not know whether this is so, because sales statistics fail us when standards are raised, and environmental impact assessments may be highly context-specific and hard to interpret.

When the 'environment' was discovered in the 1960s, discharges of poisonous substances were in focus. In later years the emissions of greenhouse gases have been given prominent attention. A shift in focus among environmental problems also alters the perceptions of what is considered ecologically sound. Greenhouse gases were not considered when KRAV was founded. KRAV criteria were based on a ban on artificial fertilizers and synthetic biocides, but also that animals must be treated well. It was unthinkable for KRAV that cows could be a source of environmental problems, but now attention is being directed to the methane gases that cows produce when ruminating. In addition, in many instances there exist intricate trade-offs between different types of environmental impacts, and it becomes difficult to provide a definite definition of sustainable consumption. The reason for this flux in the definition of the ecological can in part be explained by Bhaskar's (1975) theory of the stratified nature of reality. Reality is not limited to experiences or events, but includes mechanisms that produce events, which, if not counteracted, will be experienced. In complex and open systems, such as the climate, scientists may have differing views on causes and how they relate to events and experiences. Differing views are thus not proof of relativism and that resignation is justified, but that knowledge still is limited. This means that even in the case where labellers are perfectly independent and the criteria are based on scientific findings, there is need for readiness for change of these criteria. Consequently, labellers must combine the simplified message with transparency of how criteria are worked out and be prepared to defend their position in open debate (Boström and Klintman, 2008).

THE CASE OF ECO-LABELLED ELECTRICITY IN SWEDEN

Households have been able to choose suppliers who offer eco-labelled electricity since the deregulation of the Swedish electricity market in 1996, and a majority of the power traders offer electricity deliveries with the 'Good Environmental Choice' label administered by SSNC. If a household chooses such a contract, they reject energy sources like oil, coal and nuclear power, and instead contribute to greater use of, for instance, hydropower, wind power and biofuels. Green electricity costs more than conventional electricity, but the mark-up has generally been relatively low, in many cases only a few öre per kWh (i.e. less than 0.5 euro cents per kWh). In spite of this, only a very small percentage, about 1–2 per cent, of Swedish households has chosen to buy green electricity. In this section we illustrate that many of the above challenges facing eco-labelling in general tend to be prevalent in the green electricity case.

The analysis and the results presented in this section build on research conducted within the SHARP programme and presented in, first and foremost, Ek (2005) and Ek and Söderholm (2008, 2009). We first present the results from a simple choice experiment in which a large sample of households were asked to state (in a postal survey) their willingness to purchase GEC-labelled electricity, given the presence of different price premiums. Particular attention is paid to the determinants of green choices in this hypothetical setting (rather than on overall market potential). Secondly, we ask the question of whether these motivational factors remain the same if the participation mechanism is altered to one in which individuals are asked to vote yes or no to an overall policy where all households need to pay a mandatory mark-up on their electricity to support the diffusion of green electricity.

Theoretically the analysis draws on recent developments in the literature on integrating norm-motivated behaviour into neoclassical consumer theory (Nyborg et al, 2006), which addresses the complex interdependencies between norms – informal rules requiring that one should act in a given way in a given situation – and economic motivation. However, different norms may be activated in the two participation mechanisms. Essential for the individual's choice to buy eco-labelled electricity is the presence of an internalized personal norm among individuals, and this may in turn be influenced by others' behaviour as well as by the positive environmental externalities arising from the individual's choice.[3] However, in the collective choice situation we hypothesize that another type of norm is activated instead, a so-called fairness norm implying that people sense a responsibility to contribute as long as others do that too. The extent to which different types of norms are activated in these choice experiments may have important implications for the implementation of measures to increase green consumerism in the electricity market.

Individual responsibility and personal norms in the market for eco-labelled electricity

In this subsection we focus on the results of the choice experiment in which the respondents could choose between two alternatives of a perfectly homogenous electricity good in terms of kWh supplied, although differentiated with respect to eco-labelling and price premiums. Overall, the results show that almost half of all respondents were willing to pay a price premium for green electricity, but they also show that households are price-sensitive. While 49 per cent accepted a price increase of 2 öre (about 0.2 euro cents) per kWh, only 8 per cent said they were willing to buy green electricity if the price increase was 10 öre (1 euro cent) per kWh. Households with electric heating expressed (*ceteris paribus*) a significantly lower willingness to buy green electricity.

Figure 8.4 summarizes the main determinants of the (hypothetical) decision to purchase green electricity in this individual setting. The prevalence of norms plays a key role in understanding why certain households express a willingness to buy green electricity. The stronger the personal norm households express with regard to green purchases in the electricity market, the more likely they are to accept the price premiums offered in the experiment. However, this effect is weakened by the widespread belief that choosing the green alternative has no positive impact. A full 48 per cent of the respondents agreed wholly or partially with the statement: 'If I choose to buy green electricity, it is by no means certain that it will stimulate increased production of green electricity.' This shows evidence of a general scepticism, not necessarily about the product concept as such, but perhaps more directed towards other groups in society and what they are doing to promote the production of green electricity. Although about one third of respondents stated that they (at least partially) felt a personal responsibility for promoting green electricity, most believed the burden of responsibility fell even more heavily on the government and not least on the energy companies. Many also expressed little confidence that these actors are currently meeting their responsibilities. In light of this, it is easy to understand the uncertainty about the ability to influence electricity production in a more sustainable direction by making personal choices as long as other groups in society (presumably) shirk their responsibility. Put bluntly, even though the possibility to purchase green electricity for a relatively small amount of money exists, many households are unwilling to 'give away' money to something that does not achieve any good purpose and for which others have the main responsibility anyway.

Information about how other households act in the electricity market played no meaningful role with regard to the stated willingness to buy green electricity. One possible explanation is that households' purchases of electricity are difficult for outsiders to observe. One interesting finding, however, was that respondents who believed family members and close friends thought they should buy green electricity (the presence of a so-called prescriptive social norm) also expressed greater willingness to do just that. In this case, pressure

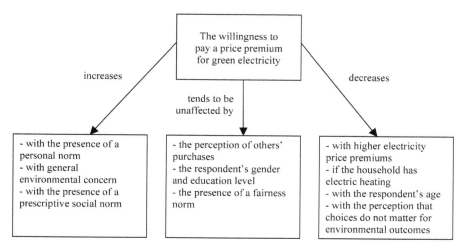

Figure 8.4 *Determinants of the stated willingness to voluntarily purchase eco-labelled electricity*

Source: Based on results presented in Ek and Söderholm (2008)

from others was thus most effective if it came from close quarters. To an extent, this latter result limits opportunities to refer to the positive behaviours of others in public information campaigns. Still, since green purchasing behaviour in the electricity market cannot be easily observed, individuals must in various ways make an assessment of others' behaviour, and in this assessment family members and friends may profoundly influence the individual's perception of others' behaviour.[4] If this is the case it becomes very difficult to make a clear distinction between social and personal norms, and the impact of general information campaigns will be ambiguous. This differs notably from the case of household recycling (not least curbside recycling) where others' behaviour is much more easily observed (Nyborg et al, 2006), and where overall household participation in Sweden (and elsewhere) is much more common.

Shared responsibility and fairness norms in public support for green electricity

The investigation presented above is based on households taking personal responsibility for (voluntarily) paying a price premium for green electricity, but one alternative would be for public agencies to decide that the consumer collective as a whole must pay a (mandatory) price premium. As was noted above, Sweden currently has a so-called green certificate system based on precisely these principles. In one SHARP investigation we therefore studied whether the factors that affect household support for green electricity vary depending on whether the choice to support this product is based on individual as opposed to

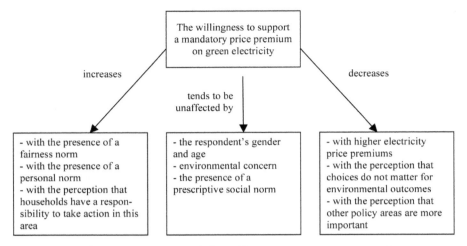

Figure 8.5 *Determinants of the willingness to support a mandatory green electricity scheme*

Source: Based on results presented in Ek and Söderholm (2009)

shared responsibility. Figure 8.5 summarizes the results from this alternative experiment.

The results indicate that different types of factors tend to influence choices depending on the type of participation mechanism considered; this may suggest some important implications for measures undertaken (either by policy-makers or electricity companies) to increase households' support for green electricity. As was noted above, in the green market case it is particularly important that consumers feel confident that the purchases they make imply significant positive outcomes, and personal norms to take action seems to have a decisive impact on the willingness to purchase green electricity. Overall, the impacts of the above factors are – although far from unimportant – significantly less pronounced when choices are assumed to depend on conditional cooperation.[5] In this latter case it becomes less important to appeal to personal obligations as well as to stress the environmental importance of green electricity. Moreover, as households are asked to support a collective undertaking to increase the production of green electricity, the activation of a fairness norm is essential ('I have a responsibility to contribute as long as others do too'). This shows that the design of policy measures aimed at increasing the public's acceptance of green electricity must vary depending on whether the support is meant to be based on individual or shared responsibility. In the former case, activation of a personal norm is the key and moral policy instruments such as environmental information take on added importance. Instead references to the mandatory certificate scheme as a 'collective' undertaking in which all consumers do their share, can be more effective in spurring the public's support for this type of participation mechanism.

Since 2003 the green certificate system has largely taken over the role of the 'green' electricity market as the main vehicle through which individuals contribute to the public goods associated with green (i.e. renewable) electricity sources. While previous studies suggest that such a 'policy takeover' can crowd out moral-based motivations to contribute (e.g. see Chapter 4 by Matti in this volume), one should note that in the case of green electricity in Sweden there is not much household demand to crowd out and a shift to a mandatory system may be necessary to reach the desired policy goals. Our results suggest that one of the policy costs of relying more heavily on mandatory certificate schemes (rather than strengthening the voluntary market) is that individuals are less likely to deliberate on the environmental benefits of renewable power as well as to seriously consider one's own personal responsibility to contribute to these benefits. In a democratic society such deliberations are important, not least in environmental policy. Environmental issues often have a broad ethical content, and since ethics are a matter for argument, public discourse over what is worth promoting and why becomes important. If people routinely contribute to renewable power by paying the certificate fee without thinking much about the impacts of their efforts, the long-run legitimacy of the system may quickly deteriorate in the case of, say, substantial electricity price increases. This suggests that it may be appropriate to promote voluntary and mandatory approaches towards renewable energy support in parallel. However, this also requires that the organizations in charge of the relevant labels promote such deliberations to a greater extent than is the case today.

Concluding remarks

Eco-labelling can be seen as a novel way of organizing consumers as a market force. Still, a basic problem is the uncoordinated, individual choices made by consumers, and the analysis shows that there are limits to the progress that can be achieved with eco-labelling. This type of instrument often entails a strong individualization, while many environmental issues typically require the collective adoption of attitudes. Lessons from the early history of labelling in Sweden show a remedy to this, namely campaigns. The stories of how the Swedish Society for Nature Conservation forced chlorine-bleached paper and harmful in ingredients off detergents in the late 1980s and early 1990s, appear to teach us that 'voice' can be added to the individual 'vote' in the market. Furthermore, these campaigns were not limited to the positive choice in the market, but added the negative choice of raising concerns about harmful substances. During the most recent decades, however, labelling organizations have emphasized the power of the individual consumer rather than that of the collective.

Eco-labels convey a simplified message on an often complex environmental issue, and the perception of the importance of different types of environmental threats tends also to change over time. It is essential that households are convinced their choices actually matter in the context, both that they influence decisions by relevant actors (such as energy companies) and that these decisions lead to environmental improvements. Due to the cognitive demands that surround such considerations, it is unreasonable to expect the individual to be able to actively 'force' eco-labelled products onto the market. The supply of products – and initiatives from responsible companies – is at least equally significant to increasing the market share of eco-labelled products. Moreover, changing and differing views on the ecological impacts remains a challenge to eco-labelling with the risk of disappointment and/or confusion among consumers. Labellers must be prepared to adjust to changing environmental concerns, and be open and transparent about what criteria are used.

In certain cases, it may be possible to create a positive loop of increased participation by referring to other households that are active consumers of eco-labelled products. However, these opportunities are constrained by the fact that such purchases are often made privately and are not always visible to other households and consumers. It may well be more effective to make consumption more sustainable by relying on collective and shared, rather than individual, responsibility. It is often less complicated to build acceptance for such systems (as long as everyone is expected to contribute) than to rely on individual, voluntary choice. Households largely accept that the environmental issue is a matter of collective choice, which to a certain extent constrains individual latitude for free choice.

NOTES

1   It may be noted, however, that since the 1950s the anthroposophic movement in Sweden, for which 'biodynamic agriculture' is a key phrase, has issued the so-called Demeter label.
2   The labellers behind KRAV, GEC and the Nordic Swan may often have an incentive to focus efforts on big customers, such as municipalities who buy food and restaurant services for meals in schools etc., since volumes are larger for these. Still, in the end ecological food, usables, furniture and modes of transportation bought or subsidized by organizations are used by pupils, patients, employees, etc. Persuading the purchasing manager of a collective buyer can be easier and the efforts pay off quickly, but the battle over the large mass of consumers may only be postponed.
3   In the literature on environmentally benign consumer behaviour the latter impact is often summarized in the concept *perceived consumer effectiveness* (PCE) (Ellen et al, 1991), e.g. the extent to which the individual perceives that green electricity is actually more environmentally benign than other power sources and that his/her choice to purchase the green alternative will help increase production of 'green' electric power.
4   Social psychology research shows that individuals tend to overestimate the frequency of events that they encounter frequently (e.g. Ajzen, 1996); thus if people close to the individual often stress the importance of purchasing 'green' electricity s/he may overestimate the importance that others assign to this task.
5   Technically, the responses in the choice experiment were analysed statistically in a random effects binary probit model framework, and the results indicated that the marginal effect of a change in the strength of the personal norm variable had a (statistically significant) smaller impact on the probability to choose green in the

shared responsibility case compared to the voluntary market case. The opposite finding is reported for the marginal impact of the fairness norm.

REFERENCES

Ajzen, I. (1996) "The Social Psychology of Decision Making", In E. T. Higgins and A. W. Kruglanski (eds.), *Social Psychology. Handbook of Principles*, The Guilford Press, New York and London

Anshelm, J. (2004) *Det vilda, det vackra och det ekologiskt hållbara. Om opinionsbildningen i Svenska Naturskyddsföreningens tidskrift Sveriges Natur 1943–2002*, Landskapet som arena, Umeå

Bergstrom, T., Blume, L. and Clotfelter, C. T. (1986) "On the Private Provision of Public Goods", *Journal of Public Economics*, Vol. 87, pp25–49

Bhaskar, R. (1975) *A Realist Theory of Science*, Verso, London

Bjorner, T. B., Hansen, L. G. and Russell, C. S. (2004) "Environmental Labelling and Consumers' Choice – An Empirical Analysis of the Effect of the Nordic Swan", *Journal of Environmental Economics and Management*, Vol. 47, pp411–434

Bjørner, T. B., Hansen, L. G., Russell, C. S. and Olsen, T. (2002) *The Effect of the Nordic Swan Label on Consumers' Choice*, Internet: www.akf.dk/udgivelser/2002/Swan, downloaded 8 March 2007

Bladh, M. (2008) "Shaping the Market? Eco-labelling in Sweden", In B. Frostell, Å. Danielsson, L. Hagberg, B.-O. Linnér and E. Lisberg Jensen (eds.), *Science for Sustainable Development. The Social Challenge with Emphasis on the Conditions for Change*, Proceedings of the 2nd VHU Conference on Science for Sustainable Development, Linköping, Sweden, 6–7 September 2007, VHU, Uppsala

Boström, M. (2001) *Miljörörelsens mångfald*, Arkiv, Lund

Boström, M. (2006) "Regulatory Credibility and Authority through Inclusiveness: Standardization Organizations in Cases of Eco-labelling", *Organization*, Vol. 13, No. 3, pp345–367

Boström, M. and Klintman, M. (2008) *Eco-standards, Product Labelling and Green Consumerism*, Palgrave Macmillan, Basingstoke, England

Eiderström, E. (2007) Managing director of Good Environmental Choice, Swedish Society of Nature Conservation, Interview, October 26, 2007

Ek, K. (2005) *The Economics of Renewable Energy Support*, Doctoral Thesis 2005:40, Luleå University of Technology, Sweden

Ek, K. and P. Söderholm (2008) "Norms and Economic Motivation in the Green Electricity Market", *Ecological Economics*, Vol. 68, pp169–182

Ek, K. and P. Söderholm (2009) "Shared or Individual Responsibility: Framing Effects in the Case of Public Support for Green Electricity", unpublished manuscript, Economics Unit, Luleå University of Technology, Sweden

Ellen, P. S., Wiener, J. L. and Cobb-Walgren, C. (1991) "The Role of Perceived Consumer Effectiveness in Motivating Environmentally Conscious Behaviors", *Journal of Public Policy and Marketing*, Vol. 10, pp102–117

Jörgensen, C. (2001) *Prisbildning och efterfrågan på ekologiska livsmedel*, Rapport 2001:1, Livsmedelsekonomiska institutet, Lund

KRAV (1999) *Femton goda år med KRAV*, Stockholm

KRAV (2009) "KRAV och klimat", Internet: www.krav.se/Konsument/Om-KRAV-markningen/Fordjupande-lasning-/Miljo/KRAV-och-klimat/, downloaded 9 September 2009

Micheletti, M. (2003) *Political Virtue and Shopping: Individuals, Consumerism, and Collective Action*, Palgrave MacMillan, Gordonsville, USA

Miljomarkarna (2009) Internet: www.miljomarkarna.se/miljomarken/tabell.asp, downloaded 11 September 2009

Nordic Swan (2009) *The Nordic Swan – From Past Experiences to Future Possibilities. The Third Evaluation of the Nordic Ecolabelling Scheme*, Internet: www.svanen.nu/-SISMABDocs/TN2008529.pdf, downloaded 11 September 2009

Nyborg, K., Howarth, R. B. and Brekke, K. A. (2006) "Green Consumers and Public Policy: on Socially Contingent Moral Motivation" , *Resource and Energy Economics*, Vol. 28, pp351–366

Plogner, A. (1996) *Miljöanpassning och strategisk förändring*, AFR-report 132, Stockholm School of Economics, Sweden

Söderberg, L. (2007) Managing director of KRAV, Interview, 18 October 2007

Statistics Sweden (2009a) "Hushållens utgifter. Andelen köpta ekologiska och miljömärkta varor per utgiftsgrupp och hushåll" , 2003–2008, Internet: www.scb.se, downloaded 4 September 2009

Statistics Sweden (2009b) "Försäljning (inkl moms) av ekologiska livsmedel och alkoholfria drycker inom handeln (enligt COICOP), löpande priser, mnkr efter varugrupp och tid", 2004–2007 and "Försäljning (inkl moms) av livsmedel och drycker inom handeln (enligt COICOP), löpande priser, mnkr efter varugrupp och tid", 2004–2007, Internet: www.ssd.scb.se/-databaser, downloaded 8 September 2009

Sundström, J. (2009) "Vad ska vi göra åt alla tistlar?" ("What to do about all the thistles?") Internet: http://forskarbloggen.typepad.com/forskarbloggen/2009/07/vad-ska-man-göra-åt-alla-tistlar.html, downloaded 5 September 2009

Svenska Dagbladet (SVD) (2009). "Tveksam vinst med ekolantbruk" ("Doubtful advantages with ecological farming"), Internet: www.svd.se/opinion/brannpunkt/artikel_3193265.svd, downloaded 5 September 2009

Swedenergy (1999) *Vad tycker elkunderna om grön el*, Sveriges Elleverantörer, Stockholm.

Swedish Consumer Agency (2002). *Omsättning av miljömärkta dagligvaror. Utveckling 2001-2002*, Internet: www.svanen.nu/info/rapporter.aspx?material=true, downloaded 8 March 2007

Swedish Dairy Association (SDA) (2009) "Statistics on milk and milk products", Internet: www.svenskmjölk.se/Branchfakta/Mjolkens-anvandning/, downloaded 7 September 2009. Additional information from Lennart Holmström, Svensk Mjölk, email communication 7 September 2009

Swedish Society for Nature Conservation (SSNC) (2009) Sales Volumes on Good Environmental Choice Electricity, email from Mathias Gustavsson, Bra Miljöval, 8 September 2009

Teisl, M. F., Roe, B. and Hicks, R. L. (2002) "Can Eco-labels Tune a Market? Evidence from Dolphin-safe Labelling", *Journal of Environmental Economics and Management*, Vol. 43, No. 3, pp339–359

Unge, R. (2007) Managing director at the Swan, Interview, 12 October 2007

9

Household recycling and the influence of norms and convenience

Christer Berglund, Olle Hage
and Patrik Söderholm

INTRODUCTION

As has been stressed throughout this book, environmental policy requires people's active involvement, and many obligations are therefore expressed in household-related activities. The most commonly cited example of such an activity is the sorting of household waste. Recycling rates have increased consistently over time in most industrialized countries, and people are generally very willing to increase their recycling efforts even further. Even though it is often stressed that the sacrifices households make – not least in terms of time – may be substantial (e.g. Bruvoll et al, 2002), Skill and Wihlborg (Chapter 3 in this volume) note that household recycling may often be an excuse for household members not to undertake other pro-environmental activities. Moreover, recycling is typically a well-integrated activity in various 'household projects' (such as family meals), and it is often easy to perform recycling activities in daily life (e.g. if drop-off recycling stations are located close to large shopping centres). In this sense recycling takes a prominent role in the environmental consciousness of many households (see also Skill, 2008), and the separation of household waste appears to be a cost-effective way to take environmental responsibility.

In this chapter we investigate why households generally are keen to participate in recycling schemes, and the role of different types of policy instruments in promoting and maintaining high overall recycling rates. However, we also address the issue of why some households – in spite of their current sacrifices in terms of effort and time – may be reluctant to be relieved from these responsibilities. Responsibility relief situations may become more prevalent in future environmental policy, not least as a result of technical development and institutional innovations. For instance, if technical progress permits mechanical sorting of household waste (something that is essentially a reality already today), individual efforts could be deemed ineffective and there would exist a case for the government to take over the responsibility for recycling activities. As shown in the chapter, however, this new situation may remove from the individual the possibility to provide a public good that she feels pleased to provide on her own, in spite of the fact that her voluntary efforts would be better focused on other urgent environmental activities.

Empirically we pay attention to the Swedish case. In 1994 a producer responsibility ordinance for packaging was introduced in Sweden; this mandates households to sort out packaging waste from other waste, clean the waste, make use of the collection systems that packaging producers provide, and finally sort different packaging materials – paper, plastic, glass and metal – in assigned recycling bins. Households' participation is mandatory but in practice it is rarely controlled and enforced, and it is easy to defect and free-ride on others' contributions. Nevertheless, official statistics show that households in Sweden recycle substantial amounts of packaging materials (SEPA, 2006). In Sweden the ordinance requires that the producers of packaging materials provide a collection system, and they have chosen to establish about 6000 drop-off stations where households can leave their packaging waste. Still, since Sweden is a sparsely populated country some households may be located far away from their nearest drop-off station.

Local authorities have introduced new waste management policies providing economic incentives for households to increase recycling rates. For instance, almost all Swedish municipalities have abandoned the flat fee pricing policy for waste collection and introduced either volume- or weight-based waste fees for single-family dwellings (Hage et al, 2008). Infrastructural measures have also been undertaken to facilitate households' recycling efforts. Some municipalities offer *curbside recycling* of packaging waste to single-family dwellings, and many of the multi-family dwelling houses buy a similar service, *property-close collection*, from recycling entrepreneurs. In spite of these new measures, though, the producer responsibility ordinance imposes burdens on Swedish households, who are not economically compensated for their efforts.

An important starting point of this chapter is the fact that waste management policies typically rely on a combination of economic and norm-based policy instruments, thus adhering both to personal moral responsibilities while at the same time providing the incentives that induce people to translate any felt obligation into recycling action. In the next section we outline a broad theoretical framework, which integrates norm-based motives into a simple economic model of household behaviour (building on the work by Nyborg et al, 2006). The chapter then proceeds by presenting the results from a number of empirical investigations on household recycling conducted within the SHARP programme. These address: (a) the presence of inter-household participation rates in packaging recycling schemes, and the role of public policy in stimulating additional recycling efforts; as well as (b) the determinants of household preferences towards a policy change implying that households are relieved from the responsibility for transporting the waste to assigned drop-off stations. A final section provides some concluding remarks and implications.

NORMS AND ECONOMIC MOTIVATION IN HOUSEHOLD WASTE MANAGEMENT

The role of norms in understanding recycling behaviour

Economically household recycling activities contribute to the production of public goods such as improved environmental quality, i.e. goods characterized by non-rivalry and non-excludability in consumption. Economic theory predicts that such voluntary contributions will be limited in a non-cooperative setting (Bergstrom et al, 1986). This is the typical situation in a so-called social dilemma, i.e. the pay-off to each individual of not contributing to the public good is higher than the pay-off for voluntary public good provision, but yet overall, all individuals receive a lower pay-off if all choose to defect than if all contribute. Andreoni (1988) also showed that even in the presence of pure altruism, the contribution to public goods, and hence recycling, would be insignificant in large economies.

In the social psychology literature it is, however, suggested that the presence of norms – informal rules requiring that one should act in a given way in a given situation – may provide an important reason for a departure from a social dilemma outcome (e.g. Biel and Thogersen, 2007). It is useful to distinguish between *moral* and *social* norms. A moral norm implies that the individual sanction him-/herself, while a social norm is enforced by explicit approval or disapproval from others. In practice, however, it can be hard to make a clear empirical distinction between these two types of norms, especially since it may be asserted that any influence of social norms is mediated through internalized norms (e.g. Schwartz, 1977). In other words, moral norms are activated through social interaction. Numerous studies find that norms are important for explaining household recycling behaviour. Hornik et al (1995), Schultz et al (1995) and Thogersen (1996) review this research, and the more recent research efforts by Chan (1998), Barr et al (2003) and Tonglet et al (2004) confirm this conclusion. The bulk of the recycling literature concludes that moral norms and attitudes are more important than social norms. However, Tucker (1999) and Barr et al (2003) stress that social norms are important in cases where the visibility of recycling behaviour is high. Derksen and Gartrell (1993), Guagnano et al (1995), Ölander and Thogersen (2005) also report that external conditions (e.g. recycling infrastructure) are important for moral recycling decisions, thus establishing a link between convenience (economic) and moral motives.

Guagnano et al (1995) conclude that 'science and policy require a socioeconomic theory of behavior that incorporates both external conditions and internal processes', (p.700). During the last decades a number of economists have tried to achieve just that. For instance, Brekke et al (2003), Bruvoll and Nyborg (2004) as well as Nyborg et al (2006) develop neoclassical utility theory by considering moral norms, while, for instance, Holländer (1990), Nyborg and Rege (2003) and Rege (2004) do the same in the case of social norms. However, there exist few empirical economic studies that employ this new strand of research in the waste management field. Survey results from Norway indicate that moral norms and warm-glow effects are important determinants of recycling behaviour in (Bruvoll et al, 2002; Halvorsen, 2008), and Berglund (2006) finds that households' willingness to pay others for sorting the waste is negatively correlated with the existence of moral norms for recycling. The present study adds to this limited empirical research by addressing the role of both economic and norm-based motivation as well as the relationship between these rationales.

A simple economic model of a norm-motivated recycler

In this subsection we present a simple theoretical framework, which can be used to understand household recycling behaviour as well as the welfare impacts of different recycling policies; it builds on a model for a morally motivated green consumer developed by Nyborg et al (2006),[1] and it is in turn heavily influenced by Schwartz's psychological theory for altruistic behaviour (Schwartz, 1970, 1977). According to Schwartz, social norms regarding moral behaviour could be adopted by each of us on a personal level and hence become personal moral norms. When this norm is internalized and activated, no external sanctions are necessary because moral norms are self-enforced. Schwartz (1977) also stresses that it is not enough to have a personal moral norm to undertake a specific action. People could internalize norms, but may not necessarily act in accordance with them. Nyborg et al (2006) provide a good explanation for this:

> *Our model is partial; it considers only one type of green consumer good, while there are a nearly unlimited number of other choices to make in everyday life. However, no-one is capable (cognitively or economically) of contributing to every public good in every possible way; there must be some division of labor in society. Hence, in practice, even individuals with a strong preference for considering themselves to be socially responsible will not feel an obligation to contribute to every good cause.* (p. 354)

Schwartz suggests that in order to influence behaviour a specific norm must be *activated*, and to become activated *problem awareness* and *ascription of respon-sibility* are important. In the case of recycling, individuals must believe that the waste generated by households really harms the environment and that recycling thus will give rise to positive externalities (and affect others' welfare positively). The individual must also feel a personal responsibility to recycle; they should not believe that it is (solely) some other actors' responsibility to solve waste management problems. Following Nyborg et al (2006) we therefore assume that *beliefs about others' recycling effort* will guide people in deciding whether they have a personal responsibility for recycling or not. It seems plausible to assume that individuals who believe that other households take responsibility for recycling will conclude that they also have such a responsibility. Schultz (2002) quotes several studies concluding that there is a positive relationship between recycling and respondents' beliefs about others' recycling efforts.

We assume that each individual allocates his/her leisure time between 'recycling efforts' on the one hand and other activities on the other (labour supply is assumed to be fixed).[2] This implies that if the individual devotes time to recycling activities s/he must give up leisure time (in practice, of course, some may choose to sacrifice work time instead). Thus, recycling incurs an opportunity cost of time but it also generates two types of benefits. *First*, by recycling the individual contributes to an environmental public good and thus confers a non-market benefit both on him-/herself and on the other individuals in society. In the case of household recycling it is reasonable to assume that the personal environmental benefits of the individual's own choice are more or less negligible, but that society as a whole would be better off if everyone chose to recycle. *Second*, we assume that individuals have preferences for a positive self-image as a morally responsible person, defined here as a person who conforms to certain norms of responsible behaviour (Brekke et al, 2003). The analysis builds on the assertion that the 'recycling' alternative is morally superior, and that therefore choosing to recycle will yield a self-image improvement.

For the above reasons it is important to discuss the types of factors that may influence self-image. First, some individuals may be genuinely uncertain about whether they ought to take the responsibility, especially if there does not exist any formal sharing of responsibility through, for instance, laws and regula-tions. Following Schultz (2002), among others, Nyborg et al (2006) therefore suggests that:

> *A natural thing to do, then, is to look around to see who carries this responsibility in practice. If she observes that it is common for people like her to take responsibility (in our case, purchase the green good), it is more likely that she will conclude that she does have some responsibility.* (p. 354).

We assume that beliefs about others' efforts have a positive impact on self-image.[3] Self-image is also assumed to be affected by the positive environmental externalities arising from the individual's choice (and thus affecting other individuals in society). For this reason, the moral – self-image – relevance of household recycling depends positively on the individual's *beliefs* about the total positive *external* effects her recycling efforts give rise to. It should be clear that the strength of these beliefs will largely reflect the individual's perception of her ability to affect the outcome in a positive way; in the literature on environmentally benign consumer behaviour this is often summarized in the concept *perceived consumer effectiveness* (PCE) (e.g. Ellen et al, 1991). For instance, the extent to which the individual perceives that his/her recycling efforts will improve environmental quality (compared to other waste treatment methods) will affect his/her beliefs. Implicit in this is also some valuation of the environmental benefits following the individual's choice; even if individuals believe that their choices imply greater environmental quality various people may perceive the *importance* of this improvement differently.

In the above framework the self-image of being a norm-compliant person represents the major driving force behind households' recycling efforts. For this reason it is useful to elaborate in somewhat more detail on the nature of the norms in question. As was noted above, in the case of recycling many previous studies stress the importance of internalized moral norms among individuals. In such a setting the individual will feel guilt and have a bad conscience if s/he does not contribute. Still, other categories of norms may be equally important. The Swedish producer responsibility ordinance mandates households to recycle (although this is not regularly controlled and violations seldom enforced). This means that in practice legal norms (e.g. explicit expectations from relevant authorities and politicians) may also play a role in influencing self-image and in the end household recycling efforts. In addition, since moral norms typically are activated through social interaction it is also difficult to distinguish between moral and social norms, and it is useful to explicitly test for the impact of social norms, i.e. norms enforced by sanctions from others, on recycling behaviour. Thus, in the empirical investigations we pay attention to both social and legal norms (in addition to moral norms) while still acknowledging the difficulty in empirically distinguishing between moral and social norms.

Finally, it is also useful to bring up the potential relationship between the external conditions influencing the opportunity cost of recycling (e.g. kerbside recycling services) and moral recycling decisions. Guagnano et al (1995) and Ölander and Thogersen (2005) outline the so-called ABC hypothesis. This builds on the notion that not only the absolute size of moral attitudes (A) and external conditions (C) explain norm-based behaviour (B), but so does the relationship between A and C. The hypothesis states that marginal improvements in one of these two variables may not be effective if the other variable weakly or strongly supports recycling. For instance, if the external conditions make it very easy to recycle, almost all will recycle, and moral attitudes toward recycling will not be an important determinant of recycling outcomes. Similarly, if the external conditions make it very hard to recycle, very few will recycle irrespective of moral norms. This implies that marginal improvements in moral attitudes will have more profound impacts on recycling effort when the exter-

nal conditions for recycling are on an intermediate level. In some of the empirical investigations presented below we test these theoretical conjectures.

HOUSEHOLD RECYCLING BEHAVIOUR IN SWEDEN

In this section we summarize and illustrate some central results on household
recycling behaviour from the SHARP research programme. The issue of incentives and constraints behind household recycling was studied using statistical
analyses based on household surveys and data on the actual collection of household waste in Swedish municipalities. One important finding from both types
of studies is that financial incentives and facilitating infrastructure have tangible, positive impacts on recycling efforts. The analyses show, for instance, that
households with access to curbside collection generally report more extensive
recycling of packaging waste, and in municipalities where curbside collection is
prevalent, collection levels for plastic packaging are higher than in municipalities that do not offer this service.[4] The empirical studies also show that
municipalities that have: (a) weight-based waste collection fees; (b) high density
of recycling stations; and (c) provide collection of sorted waste also have higher
collection levels than other municipalities. Taken together, these findings thus
show that policy measures aimed at facilitating household recycling in various
ways have clear impact on the behaviour.

Explicit economic incentives that make it more costly to not recycle seem
also to affect the outcome in various municipalities. However, even though
weight-based fees seems to be an effective method for increasing the collection
of packaging materials, undesirable side-effects of such fees must also be
acknowledged. A weight-based waste fee can give households an incentive for
illegal waste disposal. Empirical research suggests that such negative outcomes
cannot be neglected (Fullerton and Kinnaman, 1996; Dahlén et al, 2007). It is
also important to analyse the administrative costs of introducing such a system
if economic efficiency is to be ensured.

Generally speaking, though, there are few purely economic incentives to
recycle and measures that make the work easier for households are only necessary – but not sufficient – conditions for stimulating increased recycling. Our
research findings confirm that it is also important to activate norms, and the
households studied generally feel a strong personal norm – a moral obligation –
to recycle. However, the strength of the personal norm varies among individuals and this is an important explanation as to why some households recycle more
than others. The social norms are also relatively strong, but differences in the
intensity of these norms explain the variations among household ambitions to
recycle only to a very small extent. These findings should primarily be interpreted as evidence of covariation between social and personal norms. Norms
related to recycling are generally thoroughly internalized and a large percentage
of household members are driven to recycle by 'their inner voice' rather than
direct influence from other people or public agencies.

Figure 9.1 summarizes the results of a household postal survey investigation in the Swedish municipality of Eskilstuna (with a 65 per cent response rate). The investigation (see Berglund et al, 2009, for details) aimed at explaining the self-reported recycling rate at the household level by employing a two-step estimation approach. Specifically, Figure 9.1 shows a number of factors that first of all may activate a personal norm for household recycling and how the prevalence of such a norm – along with other factors – affects households' efforts to sort packaging waste (paper, glass, metal and plastic) for recycling. All solid arrows in the figure indicate a positive (and statistically significant) correlation between the variables. Among the findings are that legal and social norms activate personal norms (thus internalizing the former types of norms), and that older and well-educated people are more likely to feel a personal norm to recycle. The research also shows a strong correlation between household beliefs about the behaviour of other households, and the willingness to acknowledge a personal norm for recycling. One reasonable interpretation is that others' behaviour functions as a moral compass indicating whether the individual should take personal responsibility for a particular issue. It also feels more meaningful and fair to recycle if other people do it too. These results suggest thus that positive news about increases in recycling levels can stimulate households to take even greater personal responsibility for household waste management. In a similar manner the results also show the occurrence of spillover effects between nearby municipalities in the sense that if one municipality has a high collection percentage, the same tends to hold true in nearby municipalities.

The intensity of the personal norm is in turn important to explaining the recycling outcome at the household level, but so are other factors such as access to curbside collection and housing conditions. For instance, households who live in apartments tend to recycle less than other households (e.g. due to less storage space and limited proximity to a car). The dashed arrows in the figure indicate correlations that were empirically tested, but no statistically significant correlations were obtained. The results show, for instance, that the age of household members appears to have no direct effect on recycling behaviour, but instead an indirect impact, in that older individuals are more likely (*ceteris paribus*) to adopt a personal norm to recycle. In other words, that older people in Sweden recycle more than younger people (see also Hage et al, 2009) seems to depend primarily on moral reasons, and is thus not due to a lower opportunity cost of time.

The research summarized in Figure 9.1 also shows that the infrastructural conditions do not affect the intensity of the personal norm, but that the more recycling is facilitated for households, the less significant the personal norm becomes to stimulating the behaviour. Thus in a neighbourhood with extensive curbside collection, activating personal norms through, for example, information campaigns is not as important (although far from negligible). This is consistent with the so-called ABC hypothesis as outlined above.

Other recycling studies within the SHARP programme show that individual problem awareness is important for activating recycling norms as well, and that this can be influenced with information about, for instance, the positive

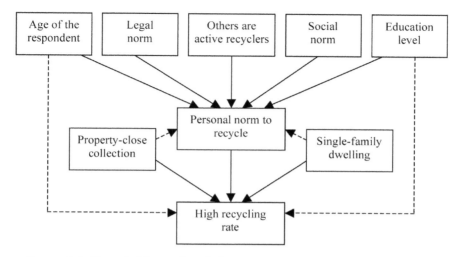

Figure 9.1 *Household recycling behaviour: norm activation and sacrifices*

Source: Based on Berglund et al (2009)

environmental impacts of recycling materials. Another critical factor is that households feel their behaviour is significant to the outcome; for instance, households who do not feel that their recycling efforts will stimulate increased recycling and/or lead to a better environment are also less likely to recycle. The results show that problem awareness and the capacity to make a difference are key factors in understanding recycling of all packaging materials studied in detail (paper, glass, metal and plastic), and they seem especially significant in the case of plastic packaging (Hage et al, 2009).[5]

In sum, overall, the results from the empirical investigations in the SHARP research programme show that household recycling is a matter of both personal sacrifices and morality. Information and infrastructural measures that facilitate recycling in the context of daily life are thus central policy instruments for stimulating recycling (and maintaining the current high level of activity). Information about the positive environmental impact of recycling, the individual's significance to the outcome, and knowledge about others' behaviour are particularly important. Economic incentives – such as weight-based collection fees – also appear to have positive influences on recycling rates.

THE MIXED BLESSING OF RESPONSIBILITY RELIEF

Our research shows that households often spend about 40–50 minutes a week recycling, and that about one third of this time is spend transporting the waste to a recycling station. But a very high percentage (about 50 per cent) of the surveyed households feel that the sacrifices they make are small or even non-existent, while about 20 per cent feel they are great or very great. One explanation for these results is that recycling typically is a well-integrated activity in various 'household projects' (such as meals) and it is generally easy to perform recycling activities in daily life, at least in the presence of a facilitating infrastructure.

However, it is also reasonable to assume households want to spend their time wisely, and the opportunity cost of time is zero only in a hypothetical situation in which there is nothing else to use the time on. Voluntary contributions to other public goods may also be crowded out by recycling. We have shown above that the prevalence of personal norms is an important incentive for households to recycle, and that these norms are generally firmly internalized. A large percentage of households state that they recycle because they want to see themselves as responsible people and many agree with the statement that 'recycling is an activity that makes me feel good'.

According to economic theory, households' opportunity cost of time equals the so-called 'reservation wage', is the lowest amount of money inducing an individual to switch, at the margin, from leisure time to work time. In practice, this sum is often measured as an hourly wage after tax. In Sweden, this is usually presumed to correspond to an hourly cost of about SEK 80 (euro 8). However, our studies show that if one elects to estimate the (net) cost of the time by instead asking households how much (at a maximum) they are willing to pay for the municipality to take over the responsibility, either for all sorting and recycling or for transporting the waste, one arrives at a significantly lower amount of about SEK 4–8 (euro 0.4–0.8) (e.g. Berglund, 2006).

In one SHARP investigation we analysed in more detail Swedish household members' willingness-to-pay (WTP) to avoid having to transport sorted household waste to assigned drop-off stations (see Berglund and Söderholm, 2009). We here paid particular attention to the factors that determine inter-household preferences towards a policy change involving the substitution of curbside household recycling for a recycling scheme in which the responsibility for transporting the waste lies with the household members. Methodologically we acknowledge that to be willing to pay for responsibility relief and deciding upon a specific amount are related issues for the respondents, but they may also be influenced by different factors. For this reason we followed the two-step estimation procedure by Heckman (1979) and analysed these issues jointly in the empirical investigation. This procedure and some central results are illustrated in Figure 9.2.

Starting with the selection model for the yes/no responses, we first note that only about 30 per cent are willing to pay a higher waste collection fee for someone else, such as the municipality, to take over transporting the waste. The probability of rejecting the policy proposal increases with age. This may in part reflect the lower opportunity cost of time for retired people and for older families with grown-up children. Leisure time becomes more valuable as the number of working hours increases. However, as was noted above and as Halvorsen (2008) also suggests: older people may be 'more concerned with the moral obligation of contributing to the community, and [...] younger people are more willing to accept purchasing recycling services' (p. 22). Moreover, the

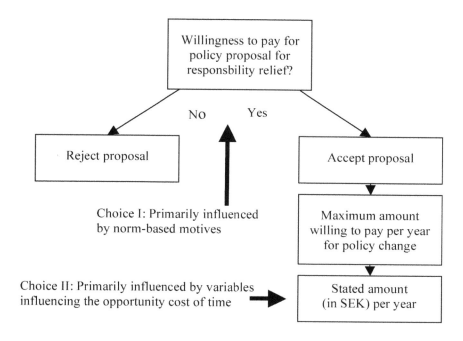

Figure 9.2 *Selection mechanism in willingness-to-pay investigation*

Source: Based on Berglund and Söderholm (2009)

results show that people who feel a strong personal norm are clearly underrepresented in this group. This suggests that even if households' time has a positive (>0) alternative cost, this is balanced against other perceived advantages to recycling (such as enhanced self-image). Interestingly we find that overall a number of variables assumed to influence the household's total time cost – distance to recycling station, transport time use, frequency of sole purpose travels, and income – have very minor impacts on the decision to reject or accept the policy proposal.[6] The above implies that the moral – i.e. norm-based – motives dominate the decision-making process as people are confronted with a general policy proposal.

The conclusion on the importance of norm-based motives gains additional support when analysing the stated reasons provided by respondents for rejecting the WTP offer. In a small follow-up study we approached 200 of the respondents and confronted them with a number of statements relating to different reasons for rejecting this offer. Table 9.1 displays the results from this investigation. We first note that a clear majority of the respondents do not agree with the statement that they rejected the bid because they think that households 'ought to be' responsible for waste transport. Many of the responses indicate the presence of a status quo effect, i.e. individuals have a preference for the present situation over the less known alternative.[7] As much as 57 per cent of the respondents state that one important reason for rejecting the offer

Table 9.1 *Reasons for rejecting the willingness-to-pay offer (percentage shares)*

Reasons	Not at all important		Uncertain		Very important
The waste fee is already too high	2.3	2.2	29.0	28.6	37.9
The existing system is sufficiently good	0.0	1.1	26.7	15.1	57.0
Households should bear the main responsibility for transporting the waste	48.8	17.4	19.8	4.7	·9.3
I do not want to lose the possibility of doing something that I feel pleased to pursue on my own	9.3	1.1	30.0	2.3	57.0

Source: Berglund and Söderholm (2009)

is that they think the existing system is sufficiently good. A large majority express that the existing waste fee is already too high. However, as much as 57 per cent of the respondents also agree entirely with the statement that they do not want to have taken away the possibility to do something that they feel pleased to pursue on their own. Clearly, this result is consistent with our above findings that the presence of norm-based – and even warm-glow – motives lowers the probability that people accept the responsibility relief offer.

When turning next to the stated WTP for those who accepted the policy proposal, we note that WTP decreases with age, but it is generally higher for male respondents, for people who are highly educated and for those who live in apartments. Interestingly we find that overall the time cost variables are statistically significant, and have the expected signs. Income (partly an indicator of the opportunity cost of leisure) has a positive effect on WTP, as do total time spent on transporting waste and the distance to the closest recycling station. These results thus support the notion that once the entire policy package has been accepted, the WTP bid tends to reflect an optimal balance between increased leisure on the one hand and less consumption (i.e. induced by a higher waste fee) on the other. Nevertheless, other issues also appear to be at stake. We find that the more concerned the respondents are about the environmental and health effects of air pollution arising from personal car use, the higher is their WTP. In contrast to the results from the selection mechanism we do not find that the norm compliance motive has any impact on stated WTP.

These findings show that recycling represents an area in which society has succeeded at internalizing norms and creating the conditions for habitual green behaviour in daily life (see also Skill, 2008). From the household's perspective, recycling is in many ways a cost-effective way to take environmental responsibility, which may explain why many households see few advantages to changing the division of responsibility. This is mainly good news, but there may be a downside. Households cannot be expected to take responsibility for all public goods and situations may arise in the future in which technical and/or institutional innovations make it more economically efficient for other actors to take over responsibility for all aspects of household waste management. In such a situation there would be reason for public agencies to activate new norms among households (e.g. riding the bus), but households may perceive the new division of responsibility as a great sacrifice. People would be giving up something they have learnt to like and be expected to do something else instead, which in turn might be more difficult to integrate easily into daily life.

CONCLUDING REMARKS AND IMPLICATIONS

The above studies on household recycling performed within the SHARP programme have led to several key conclusions that may be used as a basis for policy measures in the waste management field. We show in particular that norm-based policy instruments play a key role in engendering household commitment to recycling. For these to be effective, however, it is very important to maintain household confidence that recycling: (a) generally leads to positive environmental outcomes; and (b) that their personal contributions are meaningful in this context. Economic incentives – such as weight-based collection fees – and infrastructure measures that facilitate recycling in daily life have a clearly positive impact on the outcome. Making household recycling of plastic packaging easier by introducing curbside recycling and/or increasing the density of recycling centres would imply higher collection rates. Yet it is imperative to stress the importance of weighing the administrative costs of operating, for instance, curbside recycling against the social benefits of having such schemes in place before supporting widespread adoption of these means (e.g. Kinnaman, 2006).

Given the importance of both economic and moral motivations and the interdependence between these, it is also important that future policy efforts recognize this dual motivation rationale. One important implication of this finding is that policy should preferably be presented in 'packages' emphasizing both the moral obligations of individual recycling efforts as well as the measures introduced to facilitate households' efforts. For instance, with the implementation of weight-based waste collection fees supplementary information should stress the environmental importance of increased material recycling and thus not only direct attention towards the incentive effects of the policy instrument. If this is done successfully the new policy will provide both financial and moral signals, and thus stimulate recycling through both these channels. The importance of norms will also differ depending on the supporting infrastructure in place, and may decrease as highly facilitating property-close collection is introduced. This implies that the effectiveness of information campaigns will decrease if the policy and the external conditions make it much easier for households to recycle.

One key policy lesson is also that positive contributions have spillover effects: if one municipality recycles frequently, neighbouring municipalities tend to do the same, and if households believe that others in the same municipality recycle frequently, they tend to do likewise. This can be utilized in information campaigns that, for instance, showcase neighbourhoods where recycling works particularly well. The analysis also shows, though, that the importance of moral norms decreases as, for instance, property-close collection is introduced. This implies that the effectiveness of information campaigns could decrease if the policy and the external conditions make it much easier for households to recycle.

Recycling represents a good example of how public agencies can activate norms and establish the infrastructure that makes households want to act according to these norms and take active responsibility for the environment in their daily lives. However, we should be careful about drawing too far-reaching parallels to other areas in which the sacrifices are often more extensive. Recycling is generally perceived as easy to integrate in daily life, while other measures (such as reduced car use) impose much greater demands for changes in the way households have chosen to organize their lives. The results show that for a fairly low share of the surveyed population (about one fifth) there appears to be a strictly positive welfare gain from removing the responsibility for transport service, but most people express no willingness-to-pay for this responsibility relief offer. Overall there appears thus to exist a mixed blessing of responsibility relief: on the one hand people are relieved from responsibilities that take time away from leisure activities but they also experience a loss in self-image as the new policy removes from the individual the possibility of providing a public good and do something that s/he feels pleased to pursue on his/her own.

An important policy implication of these findings is that there may exist a 'motivational inertia' making it difficult (or at least costly) for policy-makers to activate new norms in replacement of existing ones. Household effort to promote the provision of public goods without compensation is a limited resource. If efforts are largely devoted to the recycling area, the preparedness to work towards other public goods with potentially greater value to society will be reduced. Still, if recycling of household waste can be handled by central sorting and/or new environmental problems emerge that call for direct household efforts, policy-makers may find it necessary to replace the old norm with a new one. Since people have accumulated a lot of human capital in the recycling field and warm-glow motives are strong, they may perceive the cost of this policy shift as quite burdensome. In economic terms, from the perspective of the household recycling tends to be a cost-effective way of contributing to environmental public goods.

NOTES

1   Their model is in turn a simplified version of a model developed by Brekke et al (2003).
2   See Hage et al (2009) for a simple formalization of this model.
3   This approach is also consistent with what other psychology scholars refer to as normative conformity, i.e. perceiving others' behaviour as a guide to what is morally appropriate (e.g. Moscovici, 1985).

4   The empirical results also show that the cost structure encountered by collection contractors does not affect the outcome in the municipalities, e.g. collection rates are high also in municipalities with low population densities and urbanization rates. One important reason for this is that the remuneration paid to contractors for their work varies among municipalities, and is higher in sparsely populated areas. Accordingly, municipal waste collection is not performed in a cost-effective manner (see also Hage and Söderholm, 2008; Hage et al, 2008).
5   This result could reflect the fact that plastic materials typically are made from non-renewable fossil resources while paper production relies on renewable forest resources that are abundant in Sweden.
6   Indeed a likelihood ratio test indicated that the null hypothesis that these four variables are jointly statistically insignificant could not be rejected. In our case the test statistics equalled 3.95 while the critical value (at the 5 per cent significance level) is 9.48.
7   Evidence of 'status quo' effects is abundant in the economic and social psychology literature. The explanation for this effect is that individuals in general have more knowledge about the present situation and therefore a higher confidence in the present policy compared to potential alternatives (e.g. Heath and Tversky, 1991).

REFERENCES

Andreoni, J. (1988) "Privately Provided Public Goods in a Large Economy: The Limits of Altruism", *Journal of Public Economics*, Vol. 35, No. 1, pp57–73

Barr, S., N. J. Ford and A. Gilg (2003) "Attitudes towards Recycling Household Waste in Exeter, Devon: Quantitative and Qualitative Approaches", *Local Environment*, Vol. 8, No. 4, pp407–421

Berglund, C. (2006) "The Assessment of Households' Recycling Costs: The Role of Personal Motives", *Ecological Economics*, Vol. 56, pp560–569

Berglund, C. and P. Söderholm (2009) "The Mixed Blessing of Responsibility Relief: Assessing Household Preferences for Curbside Recycling", unpublished manuscript, Economics Unit, Luleå University of Technology

Berglund, C., P. Söderholm and O. Hage (2009) "The Economics of Household Recycling Behaviour: The Influence of Norms and Convenience", unpublished manuscript, Economics Unit, Luleå University of Technology

Bergstrom, T., L. Blume and C. T. Clotfelter (1986) "On the Private Provision of Public Goods", *Journal of Public Economics*, Vol. 29, pp25–49

Biel, A. and J. Thogersen (2007) "Activation of Social Norms in Social Dilemmas: A Review of the Evidence and Reflections on the Implications for Environmental Behaviour", *Journal of Economic Psychology*, Vol. 28, pp93–112

Brekke, K. A., S. Kverndokk and K. Nyborg (2003) "An Economic Model of Moral Motivation", *Journal of Public Economics*, Vol. 87, Nos. 9–10, pp1967–1983

Bruvoll, A. and K. Nyborg (2004) "The Cold Shiver of Not Giving Enough: On the Social Cost of Recycling Campaigns", *Land Economics*, Vol. 80, No. 4, pp539–549

Bruvoll, A., B. Halvorsen, and K. Nyborg (2002). "Households' Recycling Efforts", *Resources, Conservation and Recycling*, Vol. 36, No. 4, pp337–354

Chan, K. (1998) "Mass Communication and Pro-Environmental Behaviour: Waste Recycling in Hong Kong", *Journal of Environmental Management*, Vol. 52, No. 4, pp317–325

Dahlén, L., S. Vukicevic, J.-E. Meijer and A. Lagerkvist (2007) "Comparison of Different Collection Systems for Sorted Household Waste in Sweden", *Waste Management*, Vol. 27, pp1298–1305

Derksen, L. and J. Gartrell (1993) "The Social Context of Recycling", *American Sociological Review*, Vol. 58, No. 3, pp434–442

Ellen, P. S., J. L. Wiener and C. Cobb-Walgren (1991) "The Role of Perceived Consumer Effectiveness in Motivating Environmentally Conscious Behaviors", *Journal of Public Policy and Marketing*, Vol. 10, pp102–117

Fullerton, D. and T. C. Kinnaman (1996) "Household Response to Pricing Garbage by the Bag", *The American Economic Review*, Vol. 86, No. 4, pp971–984

Guagnano, G. A., P. C. Stern and T. Dietz (1995) "Influences on Attitude–Behavior Relationships: A Natural Experiment with Curbside Recycling", *Environment and Behavior*, Vol. 27, No. 5, pp699–718

Hage, O. and P. Söderholm (2008) "An Econometric Analysis of Regional Differences in Household Waste Collection: The Case of Plastic Packaging Waste in Sweden", *Waste Management*, Vol. 28, No. 10, pp1720–1731

Hage O., P. Söderholm and C. Berglund (2009) "Norms and Economic Motivation in Household Recycling: Empirical Evidence from Sweden", *Resources, Conservation and Recycling*, Vol. 53. No. 3, pp155–165

Hage, O., K. Sandberg, P. Söderholm and C. Berglund (2008) "Household Plastic Waste Collection in Swedish Municipalities: A Spatial-Econometric Approach", Paper presented at the 16th Annual Conference of the European Association of Environmental and Resource Economists (EAERE), June 25–28, Gothenburg, Sweden

Halvorsen, B. (2008) "Effects of Norms and Opportunity Cost of Time on Household Recycling", *Land Economics*, Vol. 84, No. 3, pp501–516

Heath, C. and A. Tversky (1991) "Preference and Belief: Ambiguity and Competence in Choice under Uncertainty", *Journal of Risk and Uncertainty*, Vol. 28, pp2–28

Heckman, J. J. (1979) "Sample Selection Bias as a Specification Error", *Econometrica*, Vol. 47, pp153–161

Holländer, H. (1990) "A Social-Exchange Approach to Voluntary Cooperation", *The American Economic Review*, Vol. 80, No. 5, pp1157–1167

Hornik, J., J. Cherian, M. Madansky and C. Narayana (1995) "Determinants of Recycling Behavior: A Synthesis of Research Results", *Journal of Socio-Economics*, Vol. 24, No. 1, pp105–127

Kinnaman, T. C. (2006) "Policy Watch: Examining the Justification for Residential Recycling", *Journal of Economic Perspectives*, Vol. 20, No. 4, pp219–232

Moscovici, S. (1985) "Social Influence and Conformity", in Gardner, L. and E. Aronson (eds.), *The Handbook of Social Psychology*, Random House, New York, pp347–412

Nyborg, K. and M. Rege (2003) "Does Public Policy Crowd out Private Contributions to Public Goods", *Public Choice*, Vol. 115, No. 3, pp397–418

Nyborg, K., R. B. Howarth and K. A. Brekke (2006) "Green Consumers and Public Policy: On Socially Contingent Moral Motivation", *Resource and Energy Economics*, Vol. 28, No. 4, pp351–366

Ölander, F and J. Thogersen (2005) "The A-B-C of Recycling", Paper presented at the European Association for Consumer Research Conference, Gothenburg

Rege, M. (2004) "Social Norms and Private Provision of Public Goods", *Journal of Public Economic Theory*. Vol. 6, No. 1, pp65–77

Schultz, P. W. (2002) "Knowledge, Information, and Household Recycling: Examining the Knowledge-Deficit Model of Behavior Change", In Dietz T. and P. C. Stern (eds.) *New Tools for Environmental Protection: Education, Information, and Voluntary Measures*, National Academy Press, Washington DC

Schultz, P. W., S. Oskamp and T. Mainieri (1995) "Who Recycles and When? A Review of Personal and Situational Factors", *Journal of Environmental Psychology*, Vol. 15, No. 2, pp105–121

Schwartz, S. H. (1970) "Moral Decision Making and Behavior", In Macauley J. and L. Berkowitz (eds.) *Altruism and Helping Behavior*, Academic Press, New York

Schwartz, S. H. (1977) "Normative Influence on Altruism", *Advances in Experimental Social Psychology*, Vol. 10, pp221–279

Skill, K. (2008) *(Re)Creating Ecological Action Space. Householders' Activities for Sustainable Development in Sweden*, Linköping Studies in Arts and Science No. 449, Linköping University, Sweden

Swedish Environmental Protection Agency (SEPA) (2006) *Framtida producentansvar för förpackningar och tidningar. Utvärdering av producentansvaret för förpackningar och tidningar samt förslag till åtgärder*, Report 5648, Stockholm

Thogersen, J. (1996) "Recycling and Morality: A Critical Review of the Literature", *Environment and Behavior*, Vol. 28, No. 4, pp536–559

Tonglet, M., P. S. Phillips and A. D. Read (2004) "Using the Theory of Planned Behaviour to Investigate the Determinants of Recycling Behaviour: A Case Study from Brixworth, UK", *Resources, Conservation, and Recycling*, Vol. 41, No. 3, pp191–213

Tucker, P. (1999) "Normative Influences in Household Waste Recycling", *Journal of Environmental Planning and Management*, Vol. 42, No. 1, pp63–82

10

Driving forces and constraints to sustainable household travel behaviour

Louise Eriksson, Annika Nordlund
and Jörgen Garvill

INTRODUCTION

In many Western countries, the car is still the dominant travel mode for everyday travel. In the US there has been a dramatic increase (194 per cent) in vehicle trips and vehicle miles of travel from 1969 to 2001 (NHTS, 2001a). In the year 2001, 86 per cent of the number of trips and 88 per cent of the travelled miles were made by private vehicle (NHTS, 2001b). In Europe today, on average 70 per cent of the travel distance is made by car (Eurostat, 2007). The car is used for trips to work, to the store, to leisure activities, and to give others, such as children, a lift to different locations. Hence, the car is an integrated part of many peoples' lives. However, traffic causes both local and large-scale environmental problems, such as noise, landscape fragmentation and different types of emissions (e.g. carbon dioxide CO_2) (Trocmé et al, 2003; Miedema, 2007; Van Wee, 2007). Given that personal transportation is a significant contributor to environmental problems, the negative environmental effects of car use need to be reduced. Different policy measures may be implemented in order to encourage more sustainable travel behaviour. Three broad strategies are land management strategies, such as planning for more compact cities (Litman, 2008), technological improvements, such as developing cars fuelled by renewable fuel, and reducing the demand for car use through, for example increasing the cost for using cars and decreasing the cost for using alternative travel modes (Gärling et al, 2002). Although all three strategies are needed in order to achieve more sustainable travel behaviour, several researchers advocate that an immediate reduction in the negative environmental effects of transportation demands a change in travel behaviour (see e.g. Hickman and Banister, 2007).

The aim of this chapter is to present empirical evidence for the driving forces and constraints to sustainable household travel behaviour. The review is based on theories within the field of environmental and traffic psychology. The theoretical framework presented by Stern (2000) and elaborated on in Chapter 5 is used as a conceptual framework. According to this framework, four types of factors are important for pro-environmental behaviours: contextual factors, personal capabilities, attitudinal factors and habits. The setting in which travel behaviour is performed consists in Stern's terminology of contextual factors, including the physical and social context. Policy initiatives that may be used to alter the context in different ways are part of this category. Personal capabilities include socio-demographic factors (e.g. gender, age) and personal resources (e.g. income, access to a car) and attitudinal factors, such as environmental beliefs and personal norms, are important for an understanding of the basis for deliberate travel decisions. Furthermore, the repetition of travel behaviour in an everyday context indicates a need to consider habitual aspects. In this chapter, specific emphasis will be given to attitudinal factors relevant for travel behaviour, the travel context and car use habits. Travel behaviour and the possibilities to change travel behaviour are in this chapter viewed from the individual traveller's point of view, through individuals' attitudes, experiences and behaviours.

Results from empirical studies carried out in Sweden within the SHARP programme will be presented and discussed in relation to relevant theories and previous findings. Some of the results have been published in scientific journals (see Eriksson et al, 2006, 2008a, 2008b, 2008d); however, the present chapter provides a more elaborate perspective on these issues and previously published results are integrated with unpublished data and discussed in relation to relevant theories. Examining travel behaviour in a Swedish context provides an opportunity to highlight possibilities as well as barriers for more sustainable travel behaviour, and parallels may be drawn to the situation in other Western countries. In Sweden, more than half of the number of trips and 64 per cent of the travel distance are made by car (SIKA, 2007). Hence, the level of car use in Sweden is comparable to many European countries and somewhat lower compared to the US. Since Sweden is fairly sparsely populated with long travel distances compared to many European countries, the car is an attractive travel option. However, the public transport system is fairly well developed in urban areas, and the opportunities to walk and cycle are, compared to, for example the US, reasonably good, indicating that alternative travel modes may be used at least for certain trips. Hence, just like in other Western countries, there are both facilitating and hindering conditions for sustainable travel behaviour in Sweden.

The chapter consists of seven parts. Following the introduction, the empirical studies of travel behaviour carried out within the SHARP programme is described briefly. Subsequently, factors important for pro-environmental travel behaviour are presented. More specifically, pro-environmental beliefs and norms are highlighted, the travel context is explored from a psychological perspective, and the importance of considering travel habits is reviewed. Based on these factors, the rationale for how travel behaviour may be changed is discussed, and subsequently different transport policy measures are presented. In particular, the acceptability of policy measures, the extent to which car use is reduced in response to policy measures, and how car users prefer to reduce their car use are reviewed. Finally, based on the review, theoretical and practical implications for more sustainable travel behaviour is presented.

EMPIRICAL STUDIES WITHIN THE SHARP PROGRAMME

Within the SHARP programme, four empirical studies examined various aspects important for a change in travel behaviour. More specifically, two questionnaire studies, one field experiment, and one scenario-based experimental study were carried out. In the questionnaire studies, car users' environmental beliefs and evaluations of transport policy measures were examined. The field experiment focused on facilitators and barriers for reducing car use, and more specifically the possibility of interrupting a car use habit and reducing car use was examined. In the scenario-based experimental study, different transport policy measures were evaluated and behavioural adaptations expected to be made in response to policy measures reported.

In the two questionnaire studies, randomly selected independent samples of citizens in four municipalities in Sweden – Piteå, Huddinge, Göteborg and Växjö – were examined in the years 2004 and 2006. Even though the response rate was rather low (around 30 per cent), the samples and the population in the municipalities showed reasonable correspondence concerning background characteristics (see Eriksson et al, 2006, 2008a for more detailed analyses of the attrition). In the present chapter, the main focus is on car users (n = 922 and n = 616, respectively) and the background characteristics of the car users answering the questionnaires are displayed in Table 10.1. In both samples the gender distribution was even and the mean age was close to 50 years. Moreover, the annual driving distance was 10,000 kilometres for the individual car user and 15,000 kilometres in the household.

In the field experiment carried out in the year 2005, car using households in the municipality of Piteå and Huddinge participated. The scenario-based experimental study was implemented in the year 2007 among car owners in the municipality of Växjö. Although the car users were recruited from representative samples in the municipalities, large attrition before and during the studies makes broader generalizations problematic. The main aim of these studies was,

Table 10.1 *Background characteristics for the car users answering the two questionnaire studies within the SHARP programme.*

	SHARP questionnaire 2004	SHARP questionnaire 2006
Sample	General population in Huddinge, Piteå, Göteborg and Växjö	General population in Huddinge, Piteå, Göteborg and Växjö
Sample size	4000	2800
Respondents	31 per cent (N = 1251)	30 per cent (N = 827)
Car users	74 per cent (N = 922)	80 per cent (N = 616)*
Gender (women)	52 per cent	46 per cent
Age	49 years (SD = 14)	50 years (SD = 14)
Education	36 per cent high school, 35 per cent university degree	40 per cent high school, 34 per cent university degree
Household income	Mean 39,700 SEK	Median 35,000 SEK
Children living at home	40 per cent	55 per cent
Households' annual driving distance (median)	15,000 km	15,000 km
Individuals' annual driving distance (median)	10,000 km	10,000 km
Number of cars in household	One car 59 per cent, two or more cars 41 per cent	One car 55 per cent, two or more cars 45 per cent

Note: *only those with a car fuelled by fossil fuel were included in the analyses.

Table 10.2 *Background characteristics for the car users participating in the field experiment and in the scenario-based study carried out within the SHARP programme.*

Sample	Field experiment 2005[a] Car users in Huddinge and Piteå		Scenario-based study 2007[b] Car owners in Växjö		
	Experimental group (n = 27)	Control group (n = 44)	PUB (n = 96)	TAX (n = 92)	TAXPUB (n = 86)
Gender (women)	52 per cent	46 per cent	47 per cent	49 per cent	52 per cent
Age	53 years	53 years	55 years	48 years	49 years
Education	26 per cent high school, 26 per cent university	40 per cent high school, 35 per cent university	25 per cent high school, 59 per cent university	39 per cent high school, 50 per cent university	29 per cent high school, 59 per cent university
Household income (median)	33,600 SEK	40,000 SEK	35,000 SEK	35,000 SEK	35,000 SEK
Individuals' annual driving distance (mean)	10,650 km	10,500 km	12,230 km	12,300 km	12,990 km

Notes: a The importance of car habit strength and personal norm for a car use reduction was examined by comparing a control and an experimental group of car users. The participants in the experimental group were encouraged to deliberately consider a car use reduction and plan for a change if they perceived it to be possible.
b The expected car use reduction was examined in response to individual travel demand management (TDM) measures (raised tax on fossil fuel (TAX), improved public transport (PUB), and the two measures combined into a package (TAXPUB)) in a between-subject design.

however, to examine effects of experimental manipulations, making generalizations of the general car using public less important. In Table 10.2, the background characteristics of the participants in the two studies are described. The gender distribution was even in the different groups and mean age was approximately 50 years. The mean annual driving distance was around 10,500 kilometres in the field experiment and varied between just over 12,000 kilometres and close to 13,000 kilometres in the scenario-based study.

PRO-ENVIRONMENTAL BELIEFS AND NORMS

Attitudinal factors, such as pro-environmental values, beliefs and norms have been given a lot of attention in the field of environmental psychology (see Chapter 5). The value-belief-norm (VBN) theory of environmentalism (Stern et al, 1999; see also Stern, 2000) specifies the value and belief basis for pro-environmental behaviour. According to this model, pro-environmental behaviours, such as using the public transport or bicycling/walking instead of using the car, are perceived as an altruistic behaviour since the behaviour intends to help the environment. In a hierarchical model, altruistic values, general problem awareness assessed by the New Ecological Paradigm (NEP) scale (Dunlap et al, 2000), awareness of the consequences of human behaviour on the environment, and accepting a responsibility to act activate a personal norm. In turn, personal norm, also labelled moral norm, experienced as a perceived moral obligation to act is important for pro-environmental behaviour. Hence, awareness of environmental problems is related to a stronger personal norm and subsequently to a stronger willingness to act pro-environmentally.

Since travel behaviour is performed in a social context, personal norms are not the only norms important to consider. In addition, different social norms may influence the tendency to travel pro-environmentally. According to Schwartz (1977), personal norms are internalized norms while social norms are established and reinforced by the social group. Different types of social norms may be of interest with regard to travel behaviour, for example, descriptive social norms, referring to the use of others' behaviours as indicators of what is normal, and prescriptive social norms, which is the individual's perception of others' expectations on him or her (Cialdini et al, 1990, 1991). Descriptive norms important for travel behaviour are, for example, what travel modes others use for their trips and prescriptive norms concern the travel modes others expect the individual to use. In addition, the expectations coming from the society, for example, whether or not the government or the municipality expect people to travel pro-environmentally, may be regarded as a different type of social norm, that is, a societal norm. In Stern's (2000) framework, social norms are part of contextual factors, although, the individuals' perceptions of social norms (e.g. the perceived pressure to act pro-environmentally) may be considered attitudinal factors.

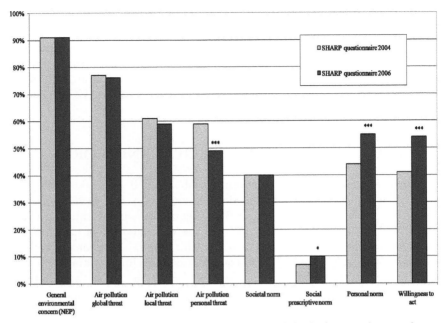

Figure 10.1 *Percentages of respondents with high degree of general environmental concern, high problem awareness, strong pro-environmental norms, and willingness to act measured in the SHARP questionnaires (* p < .05, ***p < .001).*

Note. The items were assessed on a scale from strongly disagree to strongly agree. General environmental concern was assessed on a five-point scale in both questionnaires and the percentage of respondents with a value above 3 is summarized above. The rest of the items were assessed on a five-point scale in the first questionnaire (Q1) and a seven-point scale in the second questionnaire (Q2) and respondents answering 4 and 5 in Q1 and respondents answering 5,6 and 7 in Q2 are summarized above.

Both general environmental beliefs and norms concerning car use reduction were assessed in the questionnaire studies within the SHARP programme. Results are displayed in Figure 10.3. The results showed that the car users displayed a rather high degree of general environmental concern measured by the NEP scale (see Dunlap et al, 2000) and the awareness of problems caused by emissions from personal car use was high. Moreover, 40 per cent of the respondents perceived a pressure from the society to reduce their car use, although the pressure from close others was much weaker. Approximately half of the individuals with car access felt morally obliged to reduce their use of car and a similar share stated that they were willing to reduce the negative environmental threats caused by private car use. In general, the results corroborate previous studies (cf. Bamberg and Schmidt, 2003; Nordlund and Garvill, 2003). The results further showed that between 2004 and 2006 no large changes in any direction were found when it comes to the percentage of respondents having a high level of general environmental concern and problem awareness, although the percentage of respondents with a high awareness regarding the perceived threat posed by air pollution to the person him-/herself decreased slightly. In contrast, the percentage of respondents perceiving a personal moral obligation in relation to a reduced car use and willingness to actually reduce the level of own car use increased between 2004 and 2006.

In general, the results showed that a large share of the individuals with car access were aware of the problems associated with car use, specifically on a global level, even though a smaller share perceived a personal obligation to act. In addition, the perceived pressure from close others to reduce car use was very low. In line with the ideas proposed by the VBN theory (Stern et al, 1999), a lack of normative pressure to reduce the negative effects of own car use may act as a barrier for reducing car use among some car users.

THE TRAVEL CONTEXT

In addition to attitudinal factors, which are internal motivators, contextual or external factors are important for pro-environmental travel behaviour (see Stern, 2000 and Contextual factors in Chapter 5). The physical travel context, such as the distance to various destinations and the range of alternative travel options available (e.g. the possibility of using public transport), as well as the social travel context, such as how others choose to travel, are part of the travel context. To a large extent the external context in Sweden and in many other Western countries supports the use of cars rather than pro-environmental travel behaviour. In general, housing areas in Sweden are separated from the business centres with employment opportunities and as such situated outside the city centres. Moreover, larger shopping malls are often located at external locations outside the housing areas and city centres. This type of urban planning makes travelling long distances necessary and the use of public transport may be complicated by the need to travel to destinations other than the city centre. An historical analysis of how city planning has facilitated car use and created a car dependency is presented in Chapter 7.

Perceived contextual barriers for reducing car use

One way to identify what type of contextual factors makes pro-environmental travel behaviour difficult is to examine car users' perceived barriers. In previous studies, using alternative travel modes, such as public transport, bicycle or walking instead of using the car, have been found to involve additional time and effort (Nordlund, 2002; Shannon et al, 2006). Moreover, having goods to carry, giving others a ride, time constraints, trip length, convenience and needing the car for other trips or work have been identified as common barriers for reducing car use on trips shorter than 8 kilometres (Mackett, 2003). In the field experiment carried out within the SHARP programme, similar barriers were highlighted. When the participants in the experimental group reasoned about not being able to reduce car use, they recurrently mentioned that alternative travel modes, mainly public transport, did not live up to the requirements they had for their trips. For example, alternative travel modes were perceived to be poorer options if the car user had a lot of baggage and the alternatives were also perceived to take too much time and/or be too difficult to use. These perceived barriers may contain both an objective component (e.g. the public transport may be poor) and a subjective component (e.g. the individuals may perceive the quality of public transport to be poor) (cf. Frey, 1988).

Interaction between attitudinal and contextual factors

Since both attitudinal factors (e.g. environmental beliefs and norms) and contextual factors (e.g. the possibility of using public transport and distance to destination) have been found to be important for pro-environmental behaviours, several researchers have been interested in the way these factors interact in order to determine behaviour. The low-cost high-cost hypothesis proposed by Diekmann and Preissendörfer (2003) and the attitude, behaviour, context (ABC) model proposed by Guagnano et al (1995) are two different accounts dealing with the interaction between attitudinal and contextual factors in determining behaviour. In both these accounts the main idea is that the context put boundaries on the attitude–behaviour relation indicating that attitudes and behaviours are only related under certain conditions. According to the low-cost high-cost hypothesis, attitudinal factors are mainly related to behaviour when the context is facilitating, that is, attitudinal factors influence behaviour when it is easy to perform a pro-environmental behaviour. In a slightly different fashion the ABC model stipulates that attitude and behaviour are mainly related when the context is neither facilitating nor inhibiting. Consequently, when the context strongly inhibits pro-environmental travel behaviour and when the context strongly facilitates pro-environmental travel behaviour the relation between attitudinal factors and behaviour is weaker.

However, solid empirical support for either of these propositions is scarce and the studies have only compared facilitating and inhibiting situations leaving out situations where the contextual influence is neither facilitating nor inhibiting. In some studies, attitudinal variables (e.g. personal norm) and behaviours have been found to be related in both facilitating and inhibiting situations, although the correlation tended to be stronger in inhibiting situations (see Hunecke et al, 2001; Wall et al, 2005) while other studies have found no relation between environmental concern and travel behaviour in either facilitating or inhibiting contexts (Diekmann and Preissendörfer, 2003). Based on the SHARP questionnaire study from 2006, however, Eriksson et al (2008c) found partial support for the ABC model. In the analysis, the interaction between distance to different locations and personal norm was examined in relation to car use. Results showed that personal norm and car use was mainly related at an intermediate distance to the public transport stop and to work/studies (i.e. in a neither facilitating nor inhibiting context) and not significantly correlated at a short or a long distance from these locations (i.e. in a facilitating and an inhibiting context). Although, for distance to the shop and the city centre, personal norm and car use was correlated at an intermediate and at a long distance, but not at a short distance. Hence, no support was found for the low-cost high-cost hypothesis, while the ABC model was supported when distance to the public transport stop and to work/studies was used as indicators of facilitating or hindering context. One concern in these studies is how to operationalize facilitating and hindering conditions. Often one dimension, such as travel distance or quality of public transport, are used as indicators although for a comprehensive understanding of how the travel context influence the attitude–behaviour relation different contextual factors need to be considered simultaneously.

Previous studies, and studies within the SHARP programme, generally show that the context is often perceived to hinder pro-environmental travel behaviour. Alternative travel modes are perceived to be inferior compared to the car, making them difficult to use. In future studies, there is a need to identify the main contextual facilitators and barriers with regard to travel behaviour (cf. Stokols, 1987) and to further explore how attitudinal and contextual factors interact in determining behaviour.

Travel habits

According to Stern (2000), habits or routines are important for pro-environmental behaviour. Even though decisions on how to travel and what type of travel mode to use are deliberate decisions at one point in time, travelling the same routes by means of the same travel mode almost everyday may turn the behaviour into a habit. For example, if the car is used repeatedly in a stable context a car use habit may develop if it is perceived to have rewarding consequences. In the literature, habit has been described as an automatic association between a goal (i.e. an intention to act) and behaviour (Verplanken and Aarts, 1999; Aarts and Dijksterhuis, 2000) or as a behavioural script stored in memory (Gärling et al, 2001; Fujii and Gärling, 2003). According to Verplanken and Aarts (1999), habits are characterized by automaticity (e.g. efficiency and lack of awareness), functionality and situational constancy. Habitual behaviours are often useful in an everyday context since they make it possible for the individual to focus on other tasks. However, the habit of frequently using the car without considering other travel options is a barrier for changing travel mode. For example, studies have demonstrated that a strong habit of using a particular travel mode, in contrast to a weak habit, involves less information seeking and a less elaborated travel mode choice (Aarts et al, 1997; Verplanken et al, 1997). Hence, car users with a strong car use habit do not make a deliberate travel mode choice each time they travel.

Interaction between attitudinal and habitual factors

Since habitual behaviour is to some degree automatic and non-deliberate, the importance of attitudinal factors for behaviours developed into habits is interesting. According to Triandis (1980), habits moderate the relation between attitudinal factors and behaviour. The main idea is that attitudinal factors (e.g. attitudes, intention or norms) will have less influence on travel behaviour when the car habit is strong. In contrast, when the habit is weak, that is, when the decision to perform the behaviour is deliberate rather than habitual, different attitudinal factors may to a larger extent influence behaviour. Several studies examining the habitual use of travel mode support this proposition (Verplanken et al, 1994, 1998; Klöckner et al, 2003; Klöckner and Matthies, 2004; Staats et al, 2004). As a consequence, attitudinal factors, such as problem awareness and personal norms may not influence travel behaviour unless the habitual car use is interrupted, indicating that strong car use habits may act as a barrier for pro-environmental travel behaviour.

REMOVING BARRIERS AND FACILITATING PRO-ENVIRONMENTAL TRAVEL BEHAVIOUR

The review of factors important for pro-environmental travel behaviour provides a basis for identifying how travel behaviour may be changed in a pro-environmental direction. The review shows that attitudinal factors, contextual factors and habits are important for pro-environmental travel behaviour and these three types of factors may be targeted in order to remove barriers and facilitate a change.

One way to encourage pro-environmental travel behaviour is to change attitudinal factors (e.g. pro-environmental beliefs and norms) in order to achieve a change in travel behaviour. Attitudinal change has been examined extensively and studies have identified the processes of change, factors important for a change, and under what conditions attitudes may change (for reviews see e.g. Eagly and Chaiken, 1993; Petty and Wegener, 1998; Albarracín et al, 2005). Changing peoples' values, attitudes, norms and other perceptions have also been examined in the field of transportation behaviour. According to Matthies and Blöbaum (2007), it is important to build up, activate and stabilize personal norms in order to facilitate pro-environmental travel behaviour. Moreover, Wen et al (2005) conducted a social and individualized marketing campaign over a period of 12 months, aimed at attitudinal change related to using so-called active transports (i.e. alternatives to personal car use: walking, cycling and public transport). The results showed a significant shift in attitudes, towards more positive attitudes for these active transport modes and, in addition, a decreased use of personal car. Some researchers have, however, presented results showing the difficulty of challenging the current negative attitudes towards travelling by bus, pointing to reasons why public campaigns aimed at changing attitudes may fail (Beale and Bonsall, 2007).

In a different approach the aim is to change the travel context in order to facilitate pro-environmental travel behaviour. Changes of the travel context include for example, increased cost for using the car (e.g. raised tax on fossil fuel, tolls), reduced cost of using public transport, car free zones, improved public transport (e.g. more frequent services, more bus routes), and improved facilities for cyclists and pedestrians. Notably though, contextual changes does not automatically lead to changes in travel behaviour. According to Frey (1988), there is a difference between the objective and the subjective possibilities, so that contextual changes may have certain objective consequences (e.g. a raised cost for using the car) while at the same time the individual may not consider this aspect when deciding how to act. Hence contextual changes may have unpredictable effects. Theoretically this may be explained by the theory of planned behaviour (TPB) (Ajzen, 1988; 1991). According to the TPB, the influence of contextual factors on behaviour is mediated by a sequence of psychological variables so that more distal factors, such as contextual factors, influence beliefs that in turn are important for attitudes, subjective norms and perceived behavioural control. Subsequently, these three factors determine intention to act, and behaviour. In relation to travel mode choice, Bamberg and Schmidt (2001) showed that contextual changes, that is, a price reduction for using public transport, resulted in changes in the perceived behavioural outcome of using public transport and, subsequently, influenced the intention and use of public transport. Hence contextual factors had an effect on travel behaviour, albeit indirect.

Since habitual car use may be a barrier for change, a third approach to encourage pro-environmental travel behaviour is to interrupt travel habits. One way of interrupting habitual car use is to change the context to prevent habitual responses to a particular situation (see Wood et al, 2005). Studies have demonstrated that changing the context through, for example, economic incentives or alterations of the physical environment may influence attitudes, intentions, habits and/or travel behaviour (Bamberg and Schmidt, 1999, 2001; Bamberg, 2003, 2003b; Brown et al, 2003; Fujii and Kitamura, 2003; Matthies et al, 2006). A different way to interrupt habitual car use is to induce a deliberate decision process prior to behaviour (Verplanken et al, 1998). In addition, forming so-called implementation intentions, that is, to plan where, when and how a behaviour will be performed (Gollwitzer, 1993) may further enhance the chances of a behaviour actually being enacted. In the field experiment carried out within the SHARP programme (see Eriksson et al, 2008b), the importance of car habit strength and personal norm for a car use reduction (i.e. a moral motivation) was examined by comparing a control group and an experimental group of car users ($N = 71$). The participants in the experimental group were encouraged to deliberately consider a car use reduction and plan for a change if they perceived it to be possible. Results showed that car users with a strong car use habit reduced their car use if they started to deliberately think about their travel behaviour, made plans for a change, and at the same time had a moral motivation to reduce car use. Hence, after the habit has been interrupted, habitual car users with a moral motivation may reduce their car use.

Overall, targeting these factors, that is, changing attitudes, altering the context and interrupting travel habits in order to change behaviour, have received empirical support. However, studies have also demonstrated the difficulties in changing travel behaviour, and the relations between different factors and behaviours are complex. For example, a contextual change, such as a cheaper public transport, may result in a more positive evaluation of public transport and an increase in the use of public transport among those who sporadically use public transport, while it may have no effect either on attitudes or behaviour among habitual car users. In future studies there is a need to simultaneously examine effects of different types of factors in order to understand how they interact in determining behaviours.

TRANSPORT POLICY MEASURES

Based on the knowledge of factors important for changing travel behaviour, transport policy measures may be designed. In this chapter, the more encompassing term transport policy measures is used for all measures aiming to reduce the negative environmental effects of car use (cf. Rienstra et al, 1999) while the concept travel demand management (TDM) measures is used for measures aiming to change travel behaviour (cf. Loukopoulos, 2005). A range of different measures have been implemented in order to reduce the negative environmental effects of car use, for example different informational measures (e.g. general information campaigns or personalized information), subsidies of alternative travel modes (e.g. public transport, such as bus or train, the facilities used by cyclists and pedestrians), subsidies of more environmentally friendly technology, restrictions of car use (e.g. raised tax of fossil fuel, car free zones, tolls, kilometre charges), and land management tools (e.g. planning for a compact city). Moreover, the measures may target the general public or a specific group, for example people employed by a certain company or people living in a certain area (see Litman, 2003 for a comprehensive overview of different measures). In order to classify the measures, different categorization schemes have been used. For example, a distinction is often made between soft or psychological measures (for example, information and education) targeting attitudinal factors and hard or structural measures (for example, laws and regulations, financial incentives and changes in the physical environment) with the main aim to change the travel context (Vlek, 1996). Furthermore, measures aiming to make the car less attractive are often referred to as push measures, and measures aiming to make alternative travel modes more attractive have been labelled pull measures (Steg and Vlek, 1997).

There is a lot to consider when implementing transport policy measures. For example, there is a need to examine how car users perceive these changes (i.e. soft factors) as well as how car users act in response to these changes (i.e. hard factors) (MOST, 2001). Below, the extent to which car users perceive different policy measures as acceptable, and how car users adapt to different measures will be reviewed.

Acceptability of transport policy measures

If transport policy measures are going to be implemented successfully, the measures' acceptability is important (Vieira et al, 2007; Banister, 2008). The term acceptability refers to the public's degree of positive or negative evaluation of a measure that may be implemented in the future (Schade, 2003) and is comparable to an attitude towards the policy measure (see Bamberg and Rölle, 2003; Schuitema and Steg, 2008). Gärling and Loukopoulos (2007) proposed a model attempting to explain the relation between acceptability and effectiveness. According to the model, the acceptability of measures is important for political feasibility, which in turn is important for the measure's effectiveness. Hence, a low level of acceptability among car users may be a barrier for implementing certain policy measures. Moreover, in accordance with reactance theory (Brehm, 1966), if individual freedom is restricted through, for example, a push measure, the motivation to perform the restricted behaviour, that is, car use, may become even stronger. Consequently, acceptability needs to be considered in order to understand how car users may react toward the measures as well as whether it is feasible to implement various measures.

According to Steg and Schuitema (2007), the attributes of the policy are important for acceptability. For example, a low level of acceptability is generally found for various push measures while pull measures are accepted to a larger extent (see e.g. Jakobsson et al, 2000; Schlag and Schade, 2000; Joireman et al, 2001). Within the SHARP programme, the acceptability of a range of different types of transport policy measures was examined in the questionnaire studies. Two psychological measures, that is, a general information campaign and personalized information about the local public transport, were examined. In addition, different structural measures and combinations of structural measures were analysed. Two push measures, that is, raised tax on fossil fuel and an extended car free centre in the municipality, as well as three structural pull measures, that is, improved public transport, subsidies of renewable fuel, and improved accessibility for cyclists and pedestrians were examined. In Table 10.3 the percentage of car users who found the policy measures acceptable are displayed.

Overall, the results from the questionnaire studies corroborate previous findings in that very few car users found a push measure, such as raised tax on fossil fuel, to be acceptable, while a majority found the structural pull measures to be acceptable (see also Eriksson et al, 2006, 2008a). However, there are exceptions to this clear distinction in acceptability between push and pull measures. With regard to the informational measures, the personalized information about public transport was perceived to be acceptable by almost half of the respondents (45 per cent). In contrast, the general information campaign was only perceived to be acceptable by approximately one quarter of the respondents (27 per cent). The low level of acceptability for the general informational measure in particular, may be explained by the fact that it doesn't actually provide the car user with any new options and the appeal to reduce car

223

use that was part of the measure may have triggered negative reactions among car users. Moreover, the extended car free centre, which is categorized as a push measure, was perceived to be acceptable by around one third of the respondents. Hence, some pull measures are less acceptable even though they don't restrict car use, and some push measures are more acceptable even though they do restrict car use to some extent.

Previous studies have generally found that the acceptability of packages combining push and pull transport policy measures have been rather low (see Bamberg and Rölle, 2003; Schade and Schlag, 2003). However, different combinations of measures may vary to what extent they are perceived to be acceptable. For example, different pricing strategies combined with improved public transport in a study by Thorpe et al (2000) were perceived to be more acceptable compared to a package including zone access control and improved public transport. In the SHARP questionnaire from 2006, the acceptability of two different policy packages was examined (see Table 10.3). In one package a raised tax on fossil fuel was used to improve the public transport and in the other package a raised tax on fossil fuel was used to subsidize renewable fuel. The packages were generally not perceived to be acceptable, although a larger share of car users accepted the packages compared to a raised tax on fossil fuel by itself. Moreover, a larger share of car users supported the package where the tax increase was used to subsidize renewable fuel (34 per cent) compared to when it was used to improve the public transport (23 per cent) (see also Eriksson et al, 2008a).

In addition to considering the attributes of the policy, for example whether the measure is a push or a pull measure, there is a need to examine the individuals' characteristics in order to understand acceptability (see Steg and Schuitema, 2007). Previous studies have demonstrated the importance of background characteristics, such as age, income, level of education and car use, for the acceptability of policy measures (see e.g. Odeck and Bråthen, 1997, 2008). However, different attitudinal factors have often been found to be even more important for acceptability (Rienstra, et al, 1999; Jakobsson et al, 2000; Schade, 2003; Jaensirisak et al, 2005). In the SHARP programme, the importance of different components of the VBN theory combined with different policy specific beliefs in order to explain acceptability were examined. In two studies (Eriksson et al, 2006; 2008a), general environmental beliefs (e.g. problem awareness and personal norm) and policy specific beliefs (e.g. effectiveness and fairness) were found to be important for the acceptability of different policy measures and policy packages. Hence, stronger problem awareness, personal norm to reduce car use and willingness to act were important for a positive evaluation of the measure. In addition, perceiving the measure to be fair and effective was important for acceptability. Moreover, the studies demonstrated that the acceptability of a push measure, such as a raised tax on fossil fuel and packages including a push measure, was higher if the car user had a strong personal norm, while the acceptability of a pull measure, such as an improved public transport, was strengthened by a high level of problem awareness.

Table 10.3 *Percentages in favour of different transport policy measures in the SHARP questionnaires 2004 and 2008*

	SHARP questionnaire 2004	SHARP questionnaire 2006
Psychological pull measures		
General information campaign	27 per cent	–
Personalized information about local public transport	–	45 per cent
Structural pull measures		
Improved facilities for cyclists and pedestrians	–	74 per cent
Improved local public transport	68 per cent	77 per cent
Subsidies of renewable fuel	–	69 per cent
Push measures		
Extended car free centre in municipality	–	34 per cent
Raised tax on fossil fuel	12 per cent	12 per cent
Structural push and pull measures	–	
Raised tax on fossil fuel and improved public transport	–	23 per cent
Raised tax on fossil fuel and subsidies of renewable fuel	–	34 per cent

Note. The items were assessed on a scale from strongly disagree to strongly agree on a five point scale in the first questionnaire (Q1) and a seven point scale in the second questionnaire (Q2), hence only the respondents answering 4 and 5 in Q1 and respondents answering 5,6 and 7 in Q2 are summarized above. Moreover, the levels of price or service changes were only specified for the packages of push and pull measures.

Since the implementation of transport policy measures may be facilitated by a higher level of acceptability among car users, knowledge of how to increase the acceptability of particularly push measures is valuable. Implementing packages of transport policy measures have been suggested to increase the acceptability of measures, in that both push and pull measures can be combined into mutually supporting packages (see e.g. Banister, 2008), and therefore the potential is there for synergies between strategies (Vieira et al, 2007). Based on the results from studies within the SHARP programme, the acceptability of a push measure, such as raised tax on fossil fuel, may increase slightly if it is combined with pull measures, such as improved public transport or subsidies of renewable fuel. Moreover, different attitudinal factors may be targeted in order to increase acceptability. In particular, it may be important to strengthen the personal norm in order to increase the acceptability of push measures. Since effective and fair policy measures are perceived to be more acceptable, it is also important to consider these dimensions both in the design of the policy measures as well as during the implementation process.

Behavioural adaptations in response to TDM measures

In addition to considering the acceptability of transport policy measures, other aspects important from the individual car users' perspective is the behavioural adaptations made in response to different TDM measures, for example car use reduction and/or increased use of alternative travel modes. A range of different studies has examined the behavioural effects of TDM measures, for example experimental studies attempting to provide evidence of a cause and effect relationship between measures and behavioural change, examinations of elasticites revealing the extent to which travel demand is sensitive to price and service changes, and studies of the intention to change travel behaviour in relation to hypothetical measures. The majority of studies have examined economic measures, changes of the physical travel context, or informational measures. Overall, economic incentives and disincentives have been found to lead to a slight reduction in car use, that is, a few percentage changes in car use, or patronage on public transport may be expected as a result of a 10 per cent increase in prices (see e.g. Dargay and Hanly, 2002; Graham and Glaister, 2002; Goodwin et al, 2004; TRL, 2004; Paulley et al, 2006; Dargay, 2007; Holmgren, 2007). The effect of changing the physical context, for example through increased service frequency or new bus routes, is less certain. One review demonstrates that a 10 per cent increase in the service frequency on public transportation resulted in a 5 per cent ridership increase (Evans, 2004). Although, Bamberg and Schmidt (1999) did not find any behavioural effects (i.e. increase in the use of public transport and reduced car use) in a field study as a result of the introduction of a circular bus route. Summarizing results from different studies examining the effect of informational measures (e.g. awareness campaigns and personalized information about alternatives), Möser and Bamberg (2008) found that the measures resulted in a 5 per cent increase in the trips not made by car. Moreover, comparisons of different types of measures indicate that push measures, such as different pricing policies, influence travel demand to a larger extent compared to pull measures, such as different improvements of the public transport system (O'Fallon et al, 2004; Espino et al, 2007). However, these differences have not always been confirmed (see Schuitema et al, 2007).

In addition to examining the effects of individual measures on travel behaviour, studies have also examined transport policy measures combined into packages. In a few studies, packages of transport policy measures have generally been found to influence travel behaviour to a larger extent compared to individual measures (Marshall and Banister, 2000; Wegener, 2004 as cited in May et al, 2006). In the SHARP programme the scenario-based study (see Eriksson et al, 2008) used an experimental between-subject design to examine the effect of one push measure, that is a raised tax on fossil fuel, one pull measure that is, improved public transport, and a combination of the two measures. Three groups of car users evaluated how they would adjust their travel behaviour in response to the TDM measures both in a weekly car diary and on an annual basis. Results showed that the combined measure resulted in a larger expected car use reduction compared to the raised tax and the improved public transport scenarios separately. Hence, the results indicate that the behavioural effect of a policy package including both a push measure and a pull measure is larger than the effect of the two individual policy measures.

Overall, the different types of studies of behavioural effects of TDM measures demonstrate that travel behaviour is to some extent influenced by policy measures, although the changes are generally small and levels of price and service changes are certainly important for the magnitude of the effect. One way to increase the effectiveness of policy measures is to combine measures into packages since this strategy is likely to amplify the behavioural effects to some degree.

Car reducing strategies

In addition to examining how much car use would be reduced as a result of different measures, it is also important to examine how car users would prefer to change their travel behaviour. Several strategies, such as moving closer to the workplace or change to a job closer to home may be adopted in order to travel more pro-environmentally (Cao and Mokhtarian, 2005). Although these strategies are certainly important for pro-environmental travel behaviour, the changes are only viable in a long-term perspective. If changes are going to be made within a shorter time frame, car users may, for example, use the car more efficiently (e.g. trip chaining), car pool with others, switch travel mode to public transport or cycle/walk, choose closer locations, and/or do the activity at home (see e.g. Gärling et al, 2000). Research has demonstrated that various factors influence which type of car reducing strategy is preferred. In several studies, trip purpose, trip length and TDM measure have been found to be important for the chosen car reducing strategy, although two strategies – a more efficient car use and to some extent changing travel mode – are often among the most commonly chosen strategies (see Gärling et al, 2000; Loukopoulos et al, 2006; Schuitema et al, 2007). According to Loukopoulos et al (2006), car users use the least costly adaptation followed by more costly strategies if the reduction goal is not achieved or if the reduction goal increases, that is, in line with the cost-minimization principle.

In the SHARP programme, car reducing strategies were examined both as part of the field experiment and in the scenario-based study of TDM measures. In the field experiment, analyses of how the respondents in the experimental group had reasoned in their attempts to reduce car use showed that mainly the possibility to use alternative travel modes, such as cycle/walk or public transport was considered and not so much other strategies, such as changing destination or cancelling trips. For trips where a change was perceived to be feasible, the car users chose to create trip chains (e.g. to go shopping on the way home from work) and to cycle or walk. Subsequent to the intervention (i.e. where the experimental groupd deliberately considered the possibilities to reduce car use), the respondents in the experimental group and the control group evaluated different car reducing strategies, both to the extent they perceived them to be good or bad and the extent to which they perceived them to be easy or difficult to use. In Table 10.4, the car users' evaluations of different reduction strategies are displayed. Results demonstrate that trip chaining

Table 10.4 *Attitude and difficulty ratings of different car reducing strategies in the SHARP field experiment*

| | Attitude[a] | | Difficulty ratings[b] | |
	Experimental group (n = 27)	Control group (n = 44)	Experimental group (n = 27)	Control group (n = 44)
Trip chaining	1.44 (1.25)	1.37 (1.14)	0.69 (1.44)	0.30 (1.46)
Cycle/walk				
work	0.36 (1.87)	0.60 (1.59)	−0.72 (1.72)	−0.53 (1.50)
shopping	−0.15 (1.64)	−0.13 (1.68)	−0.73 (1.48)	−0.89 (1.48)
other*	0.32 (1.57)	0.04 (1.60)	−0.40 (1.53)	−0.61 (1.51)
Public transport				
work	0.22 (1.80)	0.37 (1.62)	−1.12 (1.51)	−0.67 (1.54)
shopping	−0.73 (1.51)	−0.70 (1.55)	−1.35 (1.06)	−1.52 (0.84)
other*	0.00 (1.67)	0.09 (1.56)	−0.76 (1.39)	−1.06 (1.27)
Car pooling				
work	0.58 (1.53)	0.46 (1.47)	−1.08 (1.11)	−1.05 (1.11)
shopping	−0.07 (1.54)	−0.61 (1.60)	−1.08 (1.13)	−1.48 (0.84)
other*	−0.08 (1.74)	−0.13 (1.71)	−0.88 (1.48)	−1.09 (1.23)
Change destination to make the car trip shorter				
shopping	0.63 (1.55)	0.41 (1.39)	−0.38 (1.58)	−0.04 (1.21)
other*	−0.36 (1.58)	−0.52 (1.49)	−1.08 (1.19)	−1.24 (1.12)
Change destination so that the car is no longer needed				
shopping	0.00 (1.66)	−0.20 (1.47)	−1.04 (1.22)	−0.89 (1.20)
other*	−0.12 (1.45)	−0.33 (1.43)	−0.92 (1.20)	−1.20 (1.13)
Cancel trips				
shopping	−0.04 (1.40)	0.02 (1.45)	−0.27 (1.22)	−0.63 (1.24)
other*	−0.92 (1.32)	−1.22 (1.01)	−0.88 (1.37)	−1.26 (0.95)
Doing the activity at home				
work	0.18 (1.75)	0.33 (1.66)	−0.73 (1.73)	−1.12 (1.37)
other*	−0.17 (1.43)	−0.24 (1.46)	−0.65 (1.65)	−0.74 (1.31)

Note: a Scale -2 to 2 (-2 = bad, 2 = good).
b Scale -2 to 2 (-2 = difficult, 2 = easy).
* all other trip purposes, such as, trips to leisure activities, to visit friends, to drop somebody off or pick somebody up.

was perceived to be the best way to reduce car use. Cycling or walking to work, car pooling to work, and choosing a shop closer to home in order to make the car trip shorter were to some extent perceived to be good car reducing strategies. In contrast, cancelling activities and going shopping by public transport were perceived to be the worse reduction strategies. Moreover, trip chaining was perceived to be the easiest way to reduce car use, while none of the other reduction strategies were perceived to be easy. The most difficult strategy was to use public transport on shopping trips. There were no significant differences between the experimental and the control group either in attitude or in difficulty ratings with regard to the different car reducing strategies.

Moreover, car reducing strategies in response to different TDM measures was examined in the scenario-based study within the SHARP programme (see Eriksson et al, 2008). In line with previous studies, this study demonstrated that a more efficient car use (i.e. trip chaining) and changing travel mode were the most preferred car reducing strategies. However, there were some differences in what kinds of strategy were used in response to the TDM measures. For example, in response to a raised tax on fossil fuel, cycling/walking was mainly chosen on short trips and in response to a combined measure of raised tax and improved public transport, public transport was chosen on both shorter and longer trips.

DISCUSSION

Despite efforts to reduce car use, the level of car use is still high in many European countries and the US. Evidently, changing travel behaviour in a more sustainable direction is associated with several barriers. Attitudinal factors, contextual factors and habits may encourage or discourage the change to more pro-environmental travel behaviour. Among attitudinal factors, the high level of problem awareness among Swedish car users may facilitate a change in travel behaviour although fewer car users display strong personal norms encouraging more pro-environmental travel behaviour. Hence, many car users are aware of the environmental problems associated with car use, particularly on a global scale, while at the same time fewer acknowledge their own responsibility for reducing the problems. Moreover, contextual factors tend to hinder an extensive car use reduction. For example, the physical context, such as the way in which cities are designed with long distances between housing areas and business areas tend to inhibit the use of travel modes other than the car. Hence, even though the public transport system and cycling/walking facilities tend to be well developed, at least in urban areas in Sweden, using the car is still the attractive option. Moreover, car use is perceived to be completely acceptable by others. Since the car is the dominant travel mode (more than 50 per cent of the number of trips, SIKA, 2007), the social descriptive norm for travel mode in Sweden is still to use the car and according to studies within the SHARP programme the pressure from close others to reduce car use, that is a social prescriptive norm, was not particularly strong. Furthermore, using the car for a long time also makes it more difficult to travel in a more pro-environmental way since this choice of behaviour often develops into a habit; hence a strong car use habit serves as a barrier for changing travel behaviour. Overall, a weak motivation to change and a strong car use habit are internal barriers for reducing car use, and inhibiting physical and social travel context are important external barriers. These barriers are evident, not only in a Swedish context, but also in many other European countries and the US.

If we are to achieve more pro-environmental travel behaviour it is necessary to implement strategies removing barriers and facilitating changes in travel behaviour by means of different transport policy measures. Both push and pull measures may be implemented in order to deal with the barriers associated with a reduced car use. In general, structural push and pull measures, such as different economic measures aiming to make public transport more attractive and car use less attractive contributes to a physical travel context encouraging sustainable travel behaviour, and may also interrupt strong car use habits as well as strengthening the car users' motivation to reduce their car use. In addition, psychological measures, such as different informational and educational measures, attempt to influence attitudinal factors targeting for example strong car habits, weak motivation to reduce car use, and car users' perception of the possibilities of using more sustainable travel options. Notably though, there are problems and limitations associated with different policy measures. For example, push measures rather than structural pull measures would most likely be needed in order to interrupt a strong car use habit and individualized psychological measures seem to influence attitudes and behaviours to a larger extent compared to general informational campaigns. In addition, there are several problems associated with implementing certain push measures (e.g. raised tax on fossil fuel) since car users display a low level of acceptability for these measures and the effectiveness of various transport policy measures seem to be limited to only a few percentage reduction in car use. Given that each individual transport policy measure has serious drawbacks, researchers are increasingly recommending a combination of policies to remedy some of these problems (see e.g. May et al, 2006; Vieira et al, 2007; Banister, 2008). According to Vieira et al (2007), there are potential synergies between different policy measures so that simultaneously implementing two policies may lead to a larger effect compared to the two measures implemented separately (i.e. effectiveness), the acceptability of one instrument may be improved by implementing a different measure (i.e. acceptability), and one measure may be used to finance another measure (i.e. financial synergy). In line with the reasoning presented by Vieira et al (2007), and the results demonstrated within the SHARP programme, an economic push measure may be used to finance a pull measure and the package seems to be more effective as well as accepted to a larger extent compared to the measures implemented individually.

In sum, changing travel behaviour to become more sustainable demands both a bottom-up perspective where the focus is on understanding the individual car users' evaluations and behaviours, as well as a top-down perspective where the focus is on finding the most appropriate policy instruments to deal with the environmental problems associated with car use. Effective and acceptable packages of policy measures can be designed by drawing on findings concerning the factors important for a behavioural change, the extent to which different measures influence behaviour and under what conditions behaviour may change. Even though more research is needed in order to identify the type of policy packages car users in different contexts require in order to change their travel behaviour, the findings available today provide some suggestions of what type of measures may be used to influence travel behaviour. For example, focusing on the individual car users' psychological measures such as personalized information campaigns can be used to strengthen individuals' motivation to modify their travel behaviour, for instance by focusing on the local and personal negative consequences of car use while emphasizing the moral motivations for reducing car use. It is also necessary to increase awareness of how travel behaviour can be modified. On a societal and social level, more distinct action from central and local government can strengthen societal norms in favour of reduced car use so that signals from society become more consistent. Social norms in favour of reduced car use should also be enhanced through various local initiatives in neighbourhoods, workplaces and the like. Moreover, since car users feel that alternative modes of transport are unavailable and think poorly of public transport, especially compared to the car, it is necessary to continually improve opportunities to use public transport, ride bicycles and walk. At the same time it is important to constrain car use in different ways, for example through making the use of cars expensive and physically restricting car use. Most importantly, however, there is a need to combine these policies in order to design acceptable and effective policies for sustainable travel.

REFERENCES

Aarts, H. and Dijksterhuis, A. (2000) 'Habits as knowledge structures: Automaticity in goal-directed behaviour', *Journal of Personality and Social Psychology*, vol 78, pp53–63

Aarts, H., Verplanken, B. and van Knippenberg, A. (1997) 'Habit and information use in travel mode choices', *Acta Psychologica*, vol 96, pp1–14

Ajzen, I. (1988) *Attitudes, personality, and behaviour*, Dorsey Press, Chicago

Ajzen, I. (1991) 'The theory of planned behavior', *Organizational Behavior and Human Decision Processes*, vol 50, pp179–211

Albarracín, D., Johnson, B. T. and Zanna, M. P. (eds) (2005) *Handbook of attitudes*, Lawrence Erlbaum Associates, Mahway, NJ

Bamberg, S. and Rölle, D. (2003) 'Determinants of people's acceptability of pricing measures – replication and extension of a causal model', in J. Schade and B. Schlag (eds) *Acceptability of transport pricing strategies*, Elsevier, Oxford

Bamberg, S. and Schmidt, P. (1999) 'Regulating transport: Behavioural changes in the field', *Journal of Consumer Policy*, vol 22, pp479–509

Bamberg, S. and Schmidt, P. (2001) 'Theory-driven subgroup-specific evaluation of an intervention to reduce private car use', *Journal of Applied Social Psychology*, vol 31, pp1300–1329

Bamberg, S. and Schmidt, P. (2003) 'Incentives, morality, or habit? Predicting students' car use for university routes with the models of Ajzen, Schwartz, and Triandis', *Environment and Behavior*, vol 35, pp264–285

Bamberg, S., Ajzen, I. and Schmidt, P. (2003a) 'Choice of travel mode in the theory of planned behavior: The roles of past behavior, habit, and reasoned action', *Basic and Applied Social Psychology*, vol 25, pp175–187

Bamberg, S., Rölle, D. and Weber, C. (2003b) 'Does habitual car use not lead to more resistance to change of travel mode?', *Transportation*, vol 30, pp97–108

Banister, D. (2008) 'The sustainable mobility paradigm', *Transport Policy*, vol 15, pp 73–80

Beale, J. R. and Bonsall, P. W. (2007) 'Marketing in the bus industry: A psychological interpretation of some attitudinal and behavioural outcomes', *Transportation Research Part F: Traffic Psychology and Behaviour*, vol 10, pp271–287

Brehm, J. W. (1966) *A theory of psychological reactance*, Academic Press, NY

Brown, B. B., Werner, C. M. and Kim, N. (2003) 'Personal and contextual factors supporting the switch to transit use: Evaluating a natural transit intervention', *Analyses of Social Issues and Public Policy*, vol 3, pp139–160

Cao, X. and Mokhtarian, P. L. (2005) 'How do individuals adapt their personal travel? Objective and subjective influences on the consideration of travel-related strategies for San Francisco Bay Area commuters', *Transport Policy*, vol 12, pp291–302

Cialdini, R. B., Kallgren, C. A. and Reno, R. R. (1991) 'A focus theory of normative conduct: A theoretical refinement and reevaluation of the role of norms in human behavior', *Advances in Experimental Social Psychology*, vol 24, pp201–234.

Cialdini, R. B., Reno, R. R. and Kallgren, C. A. (1990) 'A focus theory of normative conduct: Recycling the concept of norms to reduce littering in public places', *Journal of Personality and Social Psychology*, vol 58, pp1015–1026

Dargay, J. (2007) 'The effect of prices and income on car travel in the UK', *Transportation Research Part A, Policy and Practice*, vol 41, pp949–960

Dargay, J. M. and Hanly, M. (2002) 'The demand for local bus services in England', *Journal of Transport Economics and Policy*, vol 36, pp73–91

Diekmann, A. and Preisendörfer, P. (2003) 'Green and greenback: The behavioral effects of environmental attitudes in low-cost and high-cost situations', *Rationality and Society*, vol 15, pp441–472

Dunlap, R. E., Van Liere, K. D., Mertig, A. G. and Jones, R. E. (2000) 'Measuring endorsement of the New Ecological Paradigm: A revised NEP Scale', *Journal of Social Issues*, vol 56, pp425–442

Eagly, A. H. and Chaiken, S. (1993) *'The psychology of attitudes'*, Harcourt, Brace, Jovanovich, Fort Worth, TX

Eriksson, L., Garvill, J. and Nordlund, A. M. (2006) 'Acceptability of travel demand management measures: The importance of problem awareness, personal norm, freedom, and fairness', *Journal of Environmental Psychology*, vol 26, pp15–26

Eriksson, L., Garvill, J. and Nordlund, A. M. (2008a) 'Acceptability of single and combined transport policy measures: The importance of environmental and policy specific beliefs', *Transportation Research Part A, Policy and Practice*, vol 42, pp1117–1128

Eriksson, L., Garvill, J. and Nordlund, A. M. (2008b) 'Interrupting habitual car use: The importance of car habit strength and moral motivation for personal car use reduction', *Transportation Research Part F, Traffic Psychology and Behaviour*, vol 11, pp10–23.

Eriksson, L., Garvill, J. and Nordlund, A. M. (2008c) 'Relations between personal norm and car use in facilitating and inhibiting contexts', Poster presented at the 29:e International Congress of Psychology, Berlin, Germany

Eriksson, L., Nordlund, A. M. and Garvill, J. (2008d) *'Expected car use reduction in response to structural travel demand management measures'*, Manuscript submitted for publication

Espino, R., Ortúzar, J. de D. and Román, C. (2007) 'Understanding suburban travel demand: Flexible modelling with revealed and stated choice data', *Transportation Research Part A, Policy and Practice*, vol 41, pp899–912

Eurostat (2007) *'Passenger mobility in Europe. Statistics in focus. 87/2007'* http://epp.eurostat.ec.europa.eu/cache/ITY_OFFPUB/KS-SF-07-087/EN/ KS-SF-07-087-EN.PDF, accessed 18 February 2008

Evans, J. E. (2004) 'Traveler response to transportation system changes. Chap. 9: Transit scheduling and frequency', *TCRP Report* 95. Transportation Research Board, Washington, DC

Frey, B. S. (1988) 'Ipsative and objective limits to human behavior', Journal of *Behavioral Economics*, vol 17, pp229–248

Fujii, S. and Gärling, T. (2003) 'Development of script-based travel mode choice after forced change', *Transportation Research Part F*, vol 6, pp117–124

Fujii, S. and Kitamura, R. (2003) 'What does a one-month free bus ticket do to habitual drivers?', *Transportation*, vol 30, pp81–95

Gärling, T. and Loukopoulos, P. (2007) 'Effectiveness, public acceptability, and political feasibility of coercive measures for reducing car traffic', in T. Gärling and L. Steg (eds) *Threats from car traffic to the quality of urban life: Problems, causes, and solutions* Elsevier, Amsterdam

Gärling, T., Fujii, S. and Boe, O. (2001) 'Empirical tests of a model of determinants of script-based driving choice', *Transportation Research Part F, Traffic Psychology and Behaviour*, vol 4, pp89–102

Gärling, T., Gärling, A. and Johansson, A. (2000) 'Household choices of car-use reduction measures', *Transportation Research Part A, Policy and Practice*, vol 34, pp309–320

Gärling, T., Gärling, A. and Loukopoulos, P. (2002) 'Forecasting psychological consequences of car use reduction: A challenge to an environmental psychology of transportation', *Applied Psychology: An International Review*, vol 51, pp90–106

Gollwitzer, P. M. (1993) 'Goal achievement: The role of intentions', in W. Stroebe and M. Hewstone (eds) *European review of social psychology*, vol 4, Wiley, Chichester, England

Goodwin, P., Dargay, J. and Hanly, M. (2004) 'Elasticities of road traffic and fuel consumption with respect to price and income: A review', *Transport Reviews*, vol 24, pp275–292

Graham, D. J. and Glaister, S. (2002) 'The demand for automobile fuel. A survey of elasticities', *Journal of Transport Economics and Policy*, vol 36, pp1–26

Guagnano, G. A., Stern, P. C. and Dietz, T. (1995) 'Influences on attitude–behavior relationships. A natural experiment with curbside recycling', *Environment and Behavior*, vol 27, pp699–718

Hickman, R. and Banister, D. (2007) 'Looking over the horizon: Transport and reduced CO_2 emissions in the UK by 2030', *Transport Policy*, vol 14, pp377–387

Holmgren, J. (2007) 'Meta-analysis of public transport demand', *Transportation Research Part A, Policy and Practice*, vol 41, pp1021–1035

Hunecke, M., Blöbaum, A., Matthies, E. and Höger, R. (2001) 'Responsibility and environment. Ecological norm orientation and external factors in the domain of travel mode choice behavior', *Environment and Behavior*, vol 33, pp830–852

Jaensirisak, S., Wardman, M. and May, A. D. (2005) 'Explaining variations in public acceptability of road pricing schemes', *Journal of Transport Economics and Policy*, vol 39, pp127–153

Jakobsson, C., Fujii, S. and Gärling, T. (2000) 'Determinants of private car users' acceptance of road pricing', *Transport Policy*, vol 7, pp153–158

Joireman, J. A., Van Lange, P. A. M., Van Vugt, M., Wood, A., Vander Leest, T. and Lambert, C. (2001) 'Structural solutions to social dilemmas: A field study on commuters' willingness to fund improvements in public transit', *Journal of Applied Social Psychology*, vol 31, pp504–526

Klöckner, C. A. and Matthies, E. (2004) 'How habits interfere with norm-directed behaviour: A normative decision-making model for travel mode choice', *Journal of Environmental Psychology*, vol 24, pp319–327

Klöckner, C. A., Matthies, E. and Hunecke, M. (2003) 'Problems of operationalizing habits and integrating habits in normative decision-making models', *Journal of Applied Social Psychology*, vol 33, pp396–417

Litman, T. (2003) 'Issues in sustainable transportation in TDM Encyclopedia', www.vtpi.org

Litman, T. (2008) 'Use impacts on transport. How land use factors affect travel behaviour', Victoria Transport Policy Institute (VTPI), Canada

Loukopoulos, P. (2005) 'Future urban sustainable mobility: Implementing and understanding the impacts of policies designed to reduce private automobile usage', PhD thesis, Göteborg University, Göteborg, Sweden

Loukopoulos, P., Jakobsson, C., Gärling, T., Meland, S. and Fujii, S. (2006) 'Understanding the process of adaptation to car-use reduction goals', *Transportation Research Part F, Traffic Psychology and Behaviour*, vol 9, pp115–127

Mackett, R. L. (2003) 'Why do people use their cars for short trips?', *Transportation*, vol 30, pp329–349

Marshall, S. and Banister, D. (2000) 'Travel reduction strategies: Intentions and outcomes', *Transportation Research Part A, Policy and Practice*, vol 34, pp321–338

Matthies, E. and Blöbaum, A. (2007) 'Ecological norm orientation and private car use', in T. Gärling and L. Steg (eds) *Threats from car traffic to the quality of urban life: Problems, causes, and solutions*, Elsevier, Amsterdam

Matthies, E., Klöckner, C. A. and Preissner, C. L. (2006) 'Applying a modified moral decision making model to change habitual car use: How can commitment be effective?', *Applied Psychology: An International Review*, vol 55, pp91–106

May, A. D., Kelly, C. and Shepherd, S. (2006) 'The principles of integration in urban transport strategies', *Transport Policy*, vol 13, pp319–327

Miedema, H. M. E. (2007) 'Adverse effects of traffic noise', in T. Gärling and L. Steg (eds) *Threats from car traffic to the quality of urban life: Problems, causes, and solutions*, Elsevier: Amsterdam

Möser, G. and Bamberg, S. (2008) 'The effectiveness of soft transport policy measures: A critical assessment and meta-analysis of empirical evidence', *Journal of Environmental Psychology*, vol 28, pp10–26

MOST (Mobility Management Strategies for the next Decades) (2001) '*MOST monitoring and evaluation tool kit (MOST-MET)*', Revised 2003, The MOST consortium, Aachen, Germany

National Household Travel Survey (NHTS) (2001a) 'Our nation's travel: Current issues. U.S.', Department of Transportation, Federal Highway Administration, http://www.trb.org/, accessed 17 June 2009

National Household Travel Survey (NHTS) (2001b) 'Summary of travel trends. 2001 National Household Travel Survey', Department of Transportation, Federal Highway Administration', http://nhts.ornl.gov/2001/pub/STT.pdf, accessed 17 June 2009

Nordlund, A. (2002) 'Environmentally significant behavior: Effects of values, norms, attitudes, and habits', PhD thesis, Umeå University, Umeå, Sweden

Nordlund, A. M. and Garvill, J. (2003) 'Effects of values, problem awareness, and personal norm on willingness to reduce personal car use', *Journal of Environmental Psychology*, vol 23, pp339–347

Odeck, J. and Bråthen, S. (1997) 'On public attitudes toward implementation of toll roads – the case of Oslo toll ring', *Transport Policy*, vol 4, pp73–83

Odeck, J. and Bråthen, S. (2008) 'Travel demand elasticities and users attitudes: A case study of Norwegian toll projects', *Transportation Research Part A*, vol 42, pp77–94

O'Fallon, C., Sullivan, C. and Hensher, D. A. (2004) 'Constraints affecting mode choices by morning car commuters', *Transport Policy*, vol 11, pp17–29

Paulley, N., Balcombe, R., Mackett, R., Titheridge, H., Preston, J., Wardman, M., Shires, J. and White, P. (2006) 'The demand for public transport: The effects of fares, quality of service, income and car ownership', *Transport Policy*, vol 13, pp295–306

Petty, R. E. and Wegener, D. T. (1998) 'Attitude change: Multiple roles for persuasion variables', in D. T. Gilbert, S. T. Fiske and G. Lindzey (eds) *The handbook of social psychology*, vol 1, Oxford University Press, NY

Rienstra, S. A., Rietveld, P. and Verhoef, E. T. (1999) 'The social support for policy measure in passenger transport. A statistical analysis for the Netherlands', *Transportation Research Part D, Transport and Environment*, vol 4, pp181–200

Schade, J. (2003) 'European research results on transport pricing acceptability', in J. Schade and B. Schlag (eds) *Acceptability of transport pricing strategies*, Elsevier, Oxford

Schade, J. and Schlag, B. (2003) 'Acceptability of urban transport pricing strategies', *Transportation Research Part F, Traffic Psychology and Behaviour*, vol 6, pp45–61

Schlag, B. and Schade, J. (2000) 'Public acceptability of traffic demand management in Europe', *Traffic Engineering and Control*, vol 41, pp314–318

Schuitema, G. and Steg, L. (2008) 'The role of revenue use in the acceptability of transport pricing policies', *Transportation Research Part F*, vol 11, pp221–231

Schuitema, G., Steg, L. and Vlek, C. (2007) 'Are pricing policies effective to change car use?', *IATSS Research*, vol 31, pp21–31

Schwartz, S. H. (1977) 'Normative influences on altruism', *Advances in Experimental Social Psychology*, vol 10, pp221–279

Shannon, T., Giles-Corti, B., Pikora, T., Bulsara, M., Shilton, T. and Bull, F. (2006) 'Active commuting in a university setting: Assessing commuting habits and potential for modal change', *Transport Policy*, vol 13, pp240–253

SIKA (Swedish Institute for Transport and Communications Analysis) (2007) *RES 2005–2006. Den nationella resvaneundersökningen* [RES 2005–2006. The national travel survey.] SIKA Statistics 2007:19. SIKA, Stockholm

Staats, H., Harland, P. and Wilke, H. A. M. (2004) 'Effecting durable change. A team approach to improve environmental behavior in the household', *Environment and Behavior*, vol 36, pp341–367

Steg, L. and Schuitema, G. (2007) 'Behavioral responses to transport pricing: A theoretical analysis', in T. Gärling and L. Steg (eds) *Threats from car traffic to the quality of urban life: Problems, causes, and solutions*, Elsevier, Amsterdam

Steg, L. and Vlek, C. (1997) 'The role of problem awareness in willingness-to-change car use and in evaluating relevant policy measures', in T. Rothengatter and E. Carbonell Vaya (eds) *Traffic and transport psychology. Theory and application*, Pergamon, Oxford

Stern, P. C. (2000) 'Toward a coherent theory of environmentally significant behavior', *Journal of Social Issues*, vol 56, pp407–424

Stern, P. C., Dietz, T., Abel, T., Guagnano, G. A. and Kalof, L. (1999) 'A value-belief-norm theory of support for social movements: The case of environmentalism', *Human Ecology Review*, vol 6, pp81–97

Stokols, D. (1987) 'Conceptual strategies of environmental psychology', in D. Stokols and I. Altman (eds) *Handbook of environmental psychology*, Wiley, NY

Thorpe, N., Hills, P. and Jaensirisak, S. (2000) 'Public attitudes to TDM measures: A comparative study', *Transport Policy*, vol 7, pp243–257

Triandis, H. C. (1980) 'Values, attitudes, and interpersonal behavior', in H. E. Howe Jr and M. M. Page (eds) *Nebraska symposium on motivation*, vol 27, University of Nebraska Press, Lincoln, NE

TRL (Transport Research Laboratory) (2004) 'The demand for public transport: a practical guide', *TRL Report 593*

Trocmé, M., Cahill, S., De Vries, J. G., Farall, H., Folkeson, L., Fry, G. L. et al (2003) 'COST 341 – Habitat fragmentation due to transportation infrastructure: The European review', Luxembourg, Office for Official Publications of the European Communities

Van Wee, B. (2007) 'Environmental effects of urban traffic', in T. Gärling and L. Steg (eds) *Threats from car traffic to the quality of urban life: Problems, causes, and solutions*, Elsevier, Amsterdam

Verplanken, B. and Aarts, H. (1999) 'Habit, attitude, and planned behaviour: Is habit an empty construct or an interesting case of goal-directed automaticity?', in W. Stroebe and M. Hewstone (eds) *European review of social psychology*, vol 10, Wiley: Chichester, England

Verplanken, B., Aarts, H., van Knippenberg, A. and van Knippenberg, C. (1994) 'Attitude versus general habit: Antecedents of travel mode choice', *Journal of Applied Social Psychology*, vol 24, pp285–300

Verplanken, B., Aarts, H. and Van Knippenberg, A. (1997) 'Habit, information acquisition, and the proces of making travel mode choices', *European Journal of Social Psychology*, vol 27, pp539–560

Verplanken, B., Aarts, H., van Knippenberg, A. and Moonen, A. (1998) 'Habit versus planned behaviour: A field experiment', *British Journal of Social Psychology*, vol 37, pp111–128

Vieira, J., Moura, F. and Viegas, J. M. (2007) 'Transport policy and environmental impacts: The importance of multi-instrumentality in policy integration', *Transport Policy*, vol 14, pp421–432

Vlek, C. A. J. (1996) 'Collective risk generation and risk management: The unexploited potential of the social dilemma paradigm', in W. B. G. Liebrand and D. M. Messick (eds) *Frontiers in social dilemma research*, Springer, Berlin

Wall, R., Devine-Wright, P. and Mill, G. A. (2005) *Psychological predictors in context: An empirical study of interactions between determinants of car use intentions*, 18th Conference of the IAPES, Vienna, Austria, Designing Social Innovation: Planning, Building, Evaluation, pp117–126

Wen, L. M., Orr, N., Bindon, J. and Rissel, C. (2005) 'Promoting active transport in a workplace setting: Evaluation of a pilot study in Australia', *Health Promotion International*, vol 20, pp123–133

Wood, W., Tam, L. and Guerrero Witt, M. (2005) 'Changing circumstances, disrupting habits', *Journal of Personality and Social Psychology*, vol 88, pp918–933

Part III
Concluding Part

11

Addressing environmental concern at the household level: Concluding remarks

Patrik Söderholm

INTRODUCTION

Households play a key role in environmental policy in the Western world. Consequent upon the ever-increasing focus on individual responsibility for environmental problems as internationally adopted through Agenda 21, environmental policy has an explicit objective to increase and maintain active, individual responsibility for the environment. In this book we have presented some of the core results from a research programme that has studied how environmental policy impinges on the everyday lives of Swedish households and which implications can be derived for the design of future policy instruments. In this final chapter we attempt to provide a synthesis of the most important findings addressed in the different chapters of the book. We highlight the facts that environmental sustainability in daily life is a matter of both moral concerns and personal sacrifices in terms of money, time and other resources, and while policy instruments often (if not for practical reasons) must be more or less uniform across households we must also acknowledge that household behaviour will typically be highly context-dependent.

The remainder of this chapter discusses three central themes that together cover the most important research presented above. The first theme addresses the issue of environmental policy expectations on households and overall policy legitimacy. What are the values and principles that are the basis of Swedish household-oriented environmental policy objectives, expectations and prerequisites, and to what extent are these values accepted by citizens? Moreover, the second theme illustrates how politics enters the domestic sphere and addresses the social and socio-technical contexts in which the daily activities of households take place. Much of this work is based on in-depth studies of individual householders, and it shows the complexity that is involved in the individualization of environmental responsibility, and how the householders manage this in their day-to-day lives. The third theme sheds some light on pro-environmental household behaviour and the impacts and acceptance of policy instruments in three separate areas: waste recycling, consumption of eco-labelled products and transport choice. We discuss general incentives and constraints to sustainable activities, such as personal and social norms, problem awareness and sacrifices, and use these to analyse key differences between, for instance, households' recycling behaviours and transport choice.

SEARCHING FOR THE ECOLOGICAL CITIZEN

Swedish environmental policy has an explicit objective to increase and maintain active, individual responsibility for the environment. The implementation of *effective* policy instruments plays a key role in this policy endeavour. However, the need for collective solutions and thus widespread household participation implies a strong imperative to design policy so that it gains *legitimacy* among the public, meaning that prescribed views on issues like the nature of the problems, possible solutions, allocation of environmental responsibility on a societal level or the design and use of environmental policy instruments are supported or at least accepted by the public. Policy legitimacy is a key prerequisite for the continued development of environmental policy in general and environmental law in particular, in accordance with the democratic principles that call for fundamental popular support for the direction of policy.

The research carried out within the SHARP programme shows that legislation has an impact on households' green behaviour in various ways. The law is often the basis of economic and informative policy instruments. As illustrated by the historical study of households' consumption patterns, mandatory legal requirements aimed at municipalities and other addressees shape social and technical structures and thus largely condition household choices and behaviours. On the other hand, it can be presumed that a mandatory legal requirement aimed at households is meaningful primarily when there is a tangible risk to human health or the environment in the individual case, and not when risks should be ascribed to the collective behaviour of households. The modest application of the law to the lifestyle choices of private households may be seen as an indication that policy-makers prefer to use other types of instruments, rather than legislation that is ascribed to the belief that individuals are relatively concerned about the environment and willing to voluntarily comply with policy directives, as well as rational respondents to economic instruments.

In addition, the reluctance to control directly via legislation may indicate a belief among policy-makers that measures that clearly depart from voluntary compliance lack legitimacy among the public.

Official policy documents at both the national and local levels in Sweden demonstrate clear consensus with the individual focus expressed in most international environmental agreements, particularly Agenda 21. The responsibility for attaining the ecologically sustainable society is described as equally shared among all individuals in Sweden, where all citizens have a duty to actively contribute to favourable social development by how they arrange their lifestyles. The picture of the good citizen thus incorporates active assumption of environmental responsibility in the domestic sphere. While the general policy rhetoric presumes that citizens possess a certain measure of awareness and readiness to assume responsibility for the environmental consequences of their daily actions, it also presumes they are in need of a friendly push in the right direction, in order to clearly see their own best interests and come to understand how this can be achieved in practice. However, the attendant picture of citizens as passive consumers of products and information entails tremendous responsibility for national and local authorities to indirectly guide citizens through information about how this environmental concern should be expressed: guidance as to which values should be defended and how priorities should be set, rather than opening the door to widespread, public deliberations about these matters.

However, our research findings reveal a distinct discrepancy between the image of citizens that emerges in official policy on the one hand and the design of policy instruments and the image reflected by citizens themselves on the other. Firstly, while personal freedom and self-determination are certainly prized by Swedish citizens, environmental protection is also prioritized when people weigh one value against another. This suggests that future environmental policy has good prospects for implementing effective environmental protection measures while remaining legitimate in the eyes of the public. Secondly, the discrepancy becomes apparent in the question of people's motives for behaving in an environmentally friendly way when people explicitly assert that the morally based willingness to do the right thing has greater impact on motivation than financial rewards or punishments. With respect to the future design of policy and policy instruments for the long term, this finding implies that care should be taken to prevent unilateral focus on economic instruments and motives from pushing aside pre-existing moral convictions.

The key implications for environmental policy can thus be summarized in three points. *Firstly*, the opportunities to control households via (direct) legislation are limited. Even though citizens do not always regard personal privacy and freedom as more important than environmental protection, vaguely worded and general environmental requirements have implications for due process and thus also legitimacy. *Secondly*, it is important to focus on infrastructure and physical planning to promote green behaviour at the household level. Environmental awareness is relatively high among households in general, but infrastructures and supporting structures are often lacking. *Thirdly*, policy packages, in which several instruments interact, could be an effective means to respond to morality-based motivations to take personal responsibility for the environment while still providing explicit economic incentives. Attempts to depict the environmental issue only in economic terms are probably not a strategy beneficial in the long term; instead, economic and informative instruments should be clearly complementary. The above suggest there is scope for taking the step in policy away from guidance and information towards more clearly encouraging the development of politically skilled citizens.

THE POLITICS AND COMPLEXITY OF EVERYDAY LIFE

In everyday life citizens must translate any felt moral obligations into day-to-day action, and the SHARP research has illustrated how householders use strategies of compensation and simplification to deal with their environmental responsibilities. The research shows that there are myriad choices that household members must make, and rational to simplify household decision-making and introduce routines and rules of thumb. This can explain why certain activities, such as recycling household waste, are performed to a greater extent than others. Moreover, day-to-day life is not only limited to the specific types of activities that household members perform, but also includes *how* they are performed and by *whom*. Thus, it becomes a matter of reshaping general and abstract objectives and proposals into concrete, everyday practices.

Negotiations within the household concern which members of the household will do what and which activities are relevant and effective. These negotiations, our results show, may be expressed explicitly as well as implicitly and involve factors including gender-based division of labour. This suggests that social and ecological dimensions of sustainable development must be addressed in combination, e.g. environmental policy also involves important gender issues. The empirical findings also show that women are typically more keen on buying organic food (especially with the children's health in mind), while men have more knowledge about energy systems for the home and are able to discuss the consequences of various energy choices based on their environmental impacts.

Sustainable activities are largely characterized by their complexity. It can be difficult to determine what is more sustainable or less so, and this is always judged in relation to something else. Should one choose not to recycle if it requires energy and hot water to rinse recyclable containers, or if recycling stations are so far away that waste must be transported there by car? Is it more sustainable to buy locally produced food that requires no transport, or to buy organically produced food that comes from remote locales and perhaps required more land area? These are all concerns shared by participating household members in the interviews, and it is clear that the complexity sometimes leads them to stick to present habits because they simply cannot decide whether adopting the suggested sustainable activities would be effective or not. But the complexity can also lead household members to adopt a limited number of

Figure 11.1 *A letter to nature*

Source: Skill (2008)

sustainable activities that they believe are 'good', and here recycling is an important example.

Basically, all the studied household members stress the importance of
'environmental awareness'. One way this was expressed is that householders
were aware of a variety of connections between daily activities and the associated environmental impacts. But it also became clear that there was no direct,
linear connection between environmental awareness and green behaviour.
Household members expressed that there is a 'limit' for how far they are willing
to go when it comes to translating their knowledge into daily action. Put bluntly,
sometimes intellectual concern for the environment appears to replace specific
pro-environmental activities (Figure 11.1).

The experiences of the establishment of the first eco-village in Sweden
illustrate how the political debate in the 1970s on alternative paths to development laid the foundation for the emergence of ecologically sustainable forms of
housing. The people who moved to the Tuggelite eco-village made an active
choice to build resource-efficient houses. Heating systems were based on pellet
burners and the houses were also built to utilize 'passive solar energy'. All households sorted and recycled waste and participated in the neighbourhood compost
system. However, life in Tuggelite also faced environmental complexities and
important changes in structures have occurred over time. Latrine systems or
compost systems were installed instead of flush toilets in order to reduce water
consumption and because the inhabitants believed the municipal sewage system
represented an environmentally poor solution. However, after some considerable time had passed, the alternative system was abandoned and today all
households in the estate have conventional flush toilets. Moreover, interviews
with the households who still live in Tuggelite show that a great deal of attention has been given to organic food. The households often bought organic

vegetables from local farmers in the 1980s, but as certified organic foods become more common in the shops, purchases from the retail outlets increased. The households have also actively campaigned for the shops to increase their ranges of organic products and, according to them, they have been successful in these endeavours. Thus acting collectively appeared just as important as making sustainable individual choices.

The establishment of Tuggelite was based extensively on the homogeneous ideological background and composition of the founding group. Taken as a whole, the lessons learnt from Tuggelite include not least that ambition, capacity and knowledge are key characteristics for reshaping daily life and independently translating concern for the environment into habitual behaviours. Moreover, environmental efforts are both an individual and a collective responsibility. The building of Tuggelite was strongly dependent on joint action within the group but also on the support from municipal politicians and civil servants. Even a small group can make significant progress in adapting to a sustainable society, but more far-reaching development towards sustainability will typically require even broader public action.

The historical studies in the SHARP programme provide an additional illustration of how household behaviour is highly contingent on social and technical structures. The Swedish government has, through a number of policy areas and both directly and indirectly, intervened in household consumption patterns since the 1950s, and with significant complications for the environment. The government influence may be regarded as the more or less deliberate construction of systems that impinge on households' daily lives and consumption of specific products and services. The historical investigation has paid particular attention to the socio-technical systems of central importance to household consumption of transport and housing since the 1950s. These are: (a) Swedish post-war housing policy and the associated rationalization of the construction processes; (b) the car adaptation of society; and (c) the post-war rationalization of retail distribution.

The research shows in particular how the Swedish government has in several ways and through a number of different policy areas contributed to the increased consumption of transport, especially car transport. It should be clear that the main objectives of the social housing policy as well as the rationalization of retail distribution was not to contribute to such a marked increase in private use of cars in terms of greater distances between home, work and shopping centres. Still, this illustrates that any policy for sustainable development needs to focus attention on how multiple policy areas affect – directly or indirectly – household consumption patterns. In the case where specific consumption patterns (e.g. car use) essentially are structural requirements, altering norms of behaviour will be difficult. The fact that state intervention historically has had significant impact on the socio-techmnical context in which we consume products and services does, however, open up vital paths for policy aimed at behavioural change, although a fundamental condition is naturally that the government intent on motivating sustainable consumption is cognizant of its own historically determined role in the context.

PRO-ENVIRONMENTAL BEHAVIOUR:
DRIVING FORCES AND POLICY INSTRUMENTS

An important objective of the SHARP programme was to identify and analyse incentives and constraints to sustainable household behaviour, not least with respect to three areas relevant to the environment: waste management, consumption of eco-labelled products (e.g. green electricity) and mode of transportation choices. What distinguishes most demands for personal environmental responsibility is that they require personal sacrifices of some kind in the form of money, time or perhaps less convenience. They benefit the common good in the form of a better environment, but the direct benefit to the individual is often minor. The decision to behave in an environmentally friendly way may be regarded as the outcome of a norm activation process. Norms are informal rules for how people should behave in a given situation ('ride your bicycle to work', 'sort all waste for recycling after meals', etc.). However, the costs (broadly interpreted) related to the behaviour and habits that can facilitate or constrain green behaviour are also highly significant. Still, when comparing across different household activities we find important differences in the strength of internalized norms as well as of the perceived costs of pro-environmental behaviour.

Figure 11.2 illustrates some of the key differences between the three selected household activities. It shows how households in four Swedish municipalities responded to a number of statements pertaining to personal norms ('I feel personal responsibility...'), social norms ('People who are important to me want me to ...'), and their capacity as individuals to influence environmental outcomes. Households' responses were coded on a five-point scale, where '5' indicated 'agree entirely' and '1' indicated 'disagree entirely' (and the figure indicates the average values).

Waste recycling exemplifies an area where Swedish households currently exhibit very high activity. Households manifest a high degree of problem awareness and feel they are playing a meaningful role in achieving sustainable waste management, and these factors are important in explaining inter-household differences in recycling efforts. There are also strong social norms in this area, and a majority of households feel a personal norm – a moral obligation – to recycle. Households that feel other households are taking active personal responsibility for increased recycling tend to do the same. Our studies show that recycling is a well-integrated part of daily life for a majority of households and that many feel the perceived sacrifice is relatively minor. However, the results from the empirical investigations also show that measures that promote recycling (e.g. curbside collection) and make such behaviours more profitable (e.g. weight-based waste collection fees) both contribute to increased recycling rates. Thus, the presence of both moral concerns and personal sacrifices augment our understanding of the relatively high levels of recycling in Swedish households.

Eco-labelled, or green, electricity generally costs more than conventional electricity, but the price premium has been relatively low. Despite this marginal

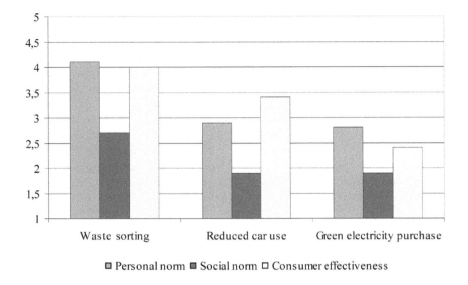

□ Personal norm ▣ Social norm ◻ Consumer effectiveness

Figure 11.2 *Determinants of pro-environmental behaviour*

Source: Söderholm (2008)

sacrifice, only a very small percentage (1–2 per cent) of Swedish households has made an active choice to buy green electricity. Our studies show that the prevalence or absence of norms plays a key role in understanding why certain households express willingness to buy green electricity (and others do not). The stronger the personal norm households express with regard to green purchases on the electricity market, the more likely they are to accept the price premiums offered by electricity suppliers. However, this effect is weakened by the widespread belief that choosing the green alternative makes no positive difference. Although about one third of respondents believed that they at least partially had a personal responsibility for promoting green electricity, most believed the burden of responsibility fell even more heavily on the government and energy companies.

Many also expressed little confidence that these actors are currently meeting their responsibilities. In the light of this, we can understand that there is also uncertainty about the ability to influence electricity generation in a greener direction through individual choices, as long as other groups in society shirk their responsibility. The ability to make a difference proved to be a very important factor in understanding why most households do not choose to buy green electricity. In contrast to the recycling case, information about how other households act in the electricity market had no influence on the willingness to buy green electricity. One possible explanation is that household purchases of electricity are difficult for outsiders to observe, unlike for instance their recycling behaviours.

The car is used for a high percentage of our daily trips and several factors must be considered in order to understand the incentives and constraints to more sustainable travel patterns. Our studies show that the private use of cars is perceived as a serious environmental threat, globally, locally and for individuals personally. People are also aware that their own car use is an environmental problem. On the other hand, few social norms exist, which decree that individuals should reduce their car use and only about half of households with access to cars feel a personal norm to reduce car use. It is also clear that there are costs and sacrifices attached to reducing car use, and alternative transport modes (not least public transport) are perceived too time-consuming or troublesome to use. People have often been using cars for a long time and many have developed a habit of using the car. Unlike recycling, for instance, there are thus several key factors that impede active individual decisions to reduce personal car use.

One should be careful about drawing strong parallels between the relative success of many household recycling programmes and the potential for encouraging active individual responsibility in other areas (such as reduced car use). Recycling typically involves limited personal sacrifices, and can easily be integrated into the current organization of the daily activities of households. Our research even suggests that people are reluctant to accept (and finance) policy proposals (e.g. curbside recycling schemes) that remove some of their current responsibilities in the recycling field. We find instead evidence of the existence of a mixed blessing of responsibility relief: on the one hand people are relieved from responsibilities that take time away from leisure activities, but they also tend to experience a welfare loss as the new policy removes from the individual the possibility of providing a public good that s/he feels pleased to provide on his/her own. An important policy implication of these findings is that there may exist a 'motivational inertia', making it difficult (or at least costly) for policy-makers to activate new norms for environmental activities in replacement of existing ones.

The policy challenges in the eco-labelling and transport behaviour areas appear overall significantly tougher. The potential for using eco-labels on products and services as a means to promote sustainable consumption patterns may be limited. The cognitive demands of individual choices become significant, while the greening of products largely is a collective undertaking involving, not least importantly, producer initiatives. Experiences from the early days of eco-labelling schemes show that campaigns against outright harmful products in many ways effectively complemented individual purchases of environmentally benign products. Peoples' willingness to support market goods with strong public good characteristics is likely to depend on whether participation builds on shared as opposed to individual responsibility. It may often be less complicated to build acceptance for mandatory systems (as long as everyone is expected to contribute) rather than to rely on individual, voluntary choice. Households largely accept that the environmental issue is a matter of collective choice, which to a certain extent constrains the individual latitude for free choice.

Changing travel behaviour to become more sustainable demands both a bottom-up perspective where the focus lies in understanding the individual car users' evaluations and behaviours, as well as a top-down perspective where the focus is on finding the most appropriate policy instruments to deal with the environmental problems associated with car use. The difficulties experienced in bringing about reduced car use among Swedish households depend largely on mixed signals from national and local policy-makers: on the one hand the local policy rhetoric emphasizes reduced car use but the same policy-makers also facilitate car use through new parking spaces and improved road constructions. Stronger societal and social norms are thus needed in this area. Moreover, an effective – and often more accepted – way of reducing habitual use of car transport is to combine push and pull strategies, that is to actively implement policies to discourage car use while facilitating the use of alternative modes of transport. There is also room for activating stronger personal norms for reduced car use. Important strategies could preferably involve targeted information campaigns about, for instance, alternative transport modes, as well as information that raises problem awareness among households, especially of the local environmental impact of car use. Overall, stronger emphasis on the relationship between reduced car use and personal motives – not least among them, better personal health – could prove effective.

FINAL COMMENTS

Social and personal norms play a key role in explaining the prevalence of sustainable activities, but at the same time individual responsibility has its clear limits. Collective measures, such as investment in infrastructure and territorial planning activities, are often needed to promote sustainable activities for which otherwise the personal sacrifices become too burdensome. Typically these measures need also to address the highly context-specific everyday life of most households, thus implying that local solutions and innovations must complement the traditional policy instruments (e.g. fuel taxes, information, etc.). Equally important, however, is to recognize the fact that environmental issues concern both the private and the public sphere of households' lives; the research presented in this volume has illustrated that in many cases there is a clear choice between policy solutions that rely on either shared or individual responsibility. Clarifying the trade-offs between these two policy routes is an important issue for future research. The effectiveness–legitimacy divide should be central here. It also important, though, to recognize the importance of public deliberations on, for instance, the environmental benefits of different household activities as well as to seriously consider one's own personal responsibility to contribute to these benefits. In a democratic society such deliberations are a key to long-run policy acceptance, not least in environmental policy. Environmental issues often have a broad ethical content, and since ethics are a matter for argument, public discourse over what is worth promoting and why is important. As has been noted above, in the Swedish case there is scope for taking the step in environmental policy away from merely guidance and information of consumers towards more clearly encouraging the development of politically competent citizens.

REFERENCES

Skill, K. (2008) *(Re)Creating Ecological Action Space. Householders' Activities for Sustainable Development in Sweden*, Linköping Studies in Arts and Science No. 449, Linköping University, Sweden

Söderholm, P. (ed) (2008) *Hållbara hushåll: Miljöpolitik och ekologisk hållbarhet i vardagen. Slutrapport till Naturvårdsverket från forskningsprogrammet SHARP*, The Swedish Environmental Protection Agency, Report 5899, Stockholm

Index

and income 155–156
and socio-technical structures
157–158, 159
see also car ownership/use; fuel; public
transport
transport policy 7, 211–212, 213,
222–231
acceptability of 223–225
and alternative fuels 35
car reducing strategies 227–229
information campaigns 223–224, 226,
230
legal instruments 32–33
lessons from/future of 230–231, 248
and problem awareness/personal norms
224–225
push-pull measures 222, 223–225,
226, 229–230
range of measures in 222
SHARP studies on 223–225,
226–229, 230
TDM measures 222, 226–227
travel behaviour 2, 5, 7–8, 22, 100,
112–114, 211–231, 240, 245, 246
and attitudes/values 108, 113,
115–116, 212, 215–217, 220, 222,
224, 229
and beliefs/norms 212, 213, 215–217,
220, 224–225, 231
changing 213, 220–222, 248
contextual factors in 102, 113, 212,
217–219, 221, 222, 229
and habit/routine 110, 113, 212, 213,
219–220, 221–222, 229
individualization of 156, 157
interaction of factors in 218–219, 220,
222
and legal instruments 32–33
and personal capabilities 104–105,
212
policy measures for *see* transport policy
problem awareness and 215, 224–225,
229
SHARP studies on 212, 213–217,
218–219, 221–222, 223–225,
226–229
and urban planning 211, 217, 219
see also car ownership/use; public
transport; transport consumption
travel demand management (TDM) 222,

226–227
Trentmann, F. 151
Triandis, H.C. 220
trip chaining 227, 228, 229
trust 60
Tucker, P. 195
Tuggelite eco-village 5–6, 130, 133–146,
243–244
behavioural changes in 144–145
building design in 136
children in 130–131, 141–143, 145
consumption patterns/behaviour in
139–140
energy use/attitudes in 133, 134,
137–138, 142
environmental responsibility in 137,
142, 144, 145–146
heating/hot water in 136, 137, 243
households' behaviour in 137–140
individual motivation in 134–135,
143, 144
inhabitants' profile 6, 133–134, 244
and Karlstad municipality 135, 136,
144
land issues in 135, 136
lessons from 244
origins/development of 133–137, 144
protest group against 135–136
resource use in 133
sanitation in 136, 142, 143, 144, 243
social aspects of 134, 136–137,
141–142
solar power in 135, 136, 243
travel behaviour/attitudes in 138, 140,
142, 145
waste sorting/recycling in 142–143
Turner, B.S. 18, 22

United Nations Conference on
Environment and Development
(UNCED) *see* Agenda 21
United States (US) 142, 151, 159, 163,
211, 212, 229
Ureña, F. 104
Urry, J. 81
utility theory 196

Välsviken eco-village 132–133
value-conflicts 14–17, 37
value-priorities 79–81, 83

For Product Safety Concerns and Information please contact our EU
representative GPSR@taylorandfrancis.com
Taylor & Francis Verlag GmbH, Kaufingerstraße 24, 80331 München, Germany

www.ingramcontent.com/pod-product-compliance
Ingram Content Group UK Ltd.
Pitfield, Milton Keynes, MK11 3LW, UK
UKHW021617240425
457818UK00018B/617